Tech Prep

The Next
Generation

Dan Hull and Julie Hull Grevelle

CORD
COMMUNICATIONS

Permissions Department
CORD Communications, Inc.
P.O. Box 21206
Waco, Texas 76702-1206

ISBN 1-57837-189-9 (soft cover)

Printed in the United States of America

Contents

Foreword   v

Acknowledgment   vii

Contributors   ix

Note to the Reader   xix

Section 1—Taking the Next Step   1

Chapter 1: Raising the Bar   *3*

Chapter 2: Visions of Excellence   *15*

Section 2—A New Curriculum   33

Overview   *34*

Chapter 3: Use of Standards in Curricula   *39*

Chapter 4: Improving the Core Curriculum   *69*

Chapter 5: Designing the New Technical Core   *83*

Chapter 6: Focusing Students   *103*

Chapter 7: Removing the Hourglass Approach to Education   *119*

Chapter 8: Portfolios and Performance   *139*

Chapter 9: Changes for Community Colleges   *151*

Chapter 10: Developing Partnerships   *163*

Section 3—Breaking the Mold in Teaching and Learning   177

Overview   *178*

Chapter 11: Academic Courses Taught in Context   *181*

Chapter 12: Project-Based Learning   *199*

Chapter 13: Telecommunication and Technology   *217*

Chapter 14: Professional Development *239*

Chapter 15: Contextual Learning Practices in Higher Education *257*

Section 4—Employer Support 271

Overview *272*

Chapter 16: Workplace Experiences for Students and Educators *279*

Chapter 17: Ensuring Excellence *293*

Chapter 18: Employers Take a Teaching Role *305*

Chapter 19: An Employer Participation Model *323*

Chapter 20: Business Practices for Partnering *331*

Section 5—Family and Community Involvement 341

Overview *342*

Chapter 21: Helping Students Discover Talents and Career Interests *347*

Chapter 22: Exploring the Workplace in Communities *361*

Chapter 23: The Role of Family and Community *381*

Chapter 24: University Schools of Education As Partners *397*

Section 6—Putting the Vision into Practice 415

The Winning Edge—Tech Prep *417*

Chapter 25: The Next Generation *419*

Index 426

Foreword

Now that the Tech Prep Associate Degree program is celebrating over a decade of service to the students of schools and colleges literally around the world, it is time to chart a course for the future. Tech Prep is now the longest lasting educational improvement initiative among contemporary American education reform efforts. It is possibly the most significant of the reform efforts because it has always kept the improvement of student learning as a clear and driving purpose. It has now become a "movement" with the vision and support of thousands of talented educational leaders across the country.

One of those talented leaders is Dan Hull, who has done more to promote the development of Tech Prep than any other individual in the country. In the writing and editing of this book, Dan and Julie Hull Grevelle have gotten it right in developing a new and reinvigorating vision for this promising exemplary educational program. John Gardner has said,

> A nation is never finished. You can't build it and then leave it standing as the pharaohs did the pyramids. It must be re-created for each generation by believing, caring men and women. If we don't care, nothing can save the nation. If we do believe and care, nothing can stop us.

This book is filled with important thoughts from believing and caring men and women.

Given the changes and challenges of the next century, Tech Prep has the opportunity to act as a leading and unifying force in moving the great American experiment of a universal education system up the road many more miles. To do this will require insightful and visionary educational leaders willing to ask the right questions and take the necessary risks involved in leading change in institutions that resist change.

With the leadership of Dan Hull and his colleagues at the Center for Occupational Research and Development, as well as a host of dedicated educators across the country, Tech Prep has moved from the periphery of education reform to center stage. This volume outlines new directions for the Tech Prep movement. It underscores the fact that this program offers *all* students the opportunity for increased achievement through changes in the traditionally time-structured organization of education and through contextual teaching and learning, which form the pedagogical foundation of Tech Prep.

Educators are urged to use this book to expand the education reform dialogue where it is already in progress and to initiate a dialogue where it has yet to begin.

Dale Parnell, Professor
College of Education
University of South Florida

Acknowledgment

The vision for the next generation of Tech Prep comes from the ideas, diligence, and care for student success that are evident in teachers, administrators, business leaders, and family. This book is an attempt to frame the vision and cite experience and advice from educational researchers and practitioners. Credit goes to all those who have been successful in making lasting change to improve education and preparation of students for careers:

Academic and technology teachers
School and college administrators
Employers
Governmental leaders and policymakers
R & D leaders and
Tech Prep directors

A special thank you to Carolyn Prescott and CORD's editors, Margaret Leary, Kay Liston, and Mark Whitney.

It is a rare opportunity for a father and daughter to share the professional and personal experience of writing and compiling a book. Actually, this is the third book we have worked on together, and finally Julie is getting the credit she has always deserved. We are both grateful for the patience and support provided by our spouses, Rita and David, and for our daughter (granddaughter) Carmen, who arrived two months before this book was completed.

Contributors

Ms. Julie Hull Grevelle has been involved in Tech Prep education since 1990 when she managed the development of *Tech Prep/Associate Degree: A Win/Win Experience*, by Hull and Parnell. Since then, Grevelle has had the privilege of working as a Tech Prep coordinator in Houston, Texas, and has edited and written several publications and conducted workshops on the topic of Tech Prep implementation and evaluation. She directed a national demonstration project of Tech Prep at CORD and, as senior associate, coordinated federal policy for Tech Prep in the National Tech Prep Network.

Mr. Dan Hull has provided leadership, vision, and guidance to Tech Prep concepts and practices since 1982. A registered engineer and engineering manager with fourteen years' experience, Hull founded CORD in 1979 to serve technical and workforce education in the USA and other countries throughout the world. He has written four books, over thirty professional papers, and 1500 pages of educational guides and instructional materials in engineering, optics, lasers, robotics, and electrical power plant operations. He has been keynote speaker in hundreds of educational conferences in the USA and eight foreign countries. In 1997 he was named the G. Harold Silvius Foundation's Outstanding International Leader in Technical Vocational Education and Training; in 1998 he was recognized with the Distinguished Service Award by the National Association of State Directors of Vocational Technical Education.

Dr. Juan R. Baughn is a lecturer at Lehigh University and an international spokesperson for Tech Prep, school-to-career, leadership, and multicultural issues. He has experience in elementary and secondary education, and initiated a districtwide school-to-work program as principal of North Penn High School in Lansdale, Pennsylvania. Since retiring from the public educational system, Baughn has assumed an interim position as principal and superintendent. He is a frequent presenter at national conferences and heads the consulting group, JRB Associates.

Dr. Gene Bottoms is senior vice president of the Southern Regional Education Board (SREB) and has served as director of SREB's *High Schools That Work* initiative since 1987. This is the largest effort in America to improve high schools for career-bound students, involving over 800 high schools in twenty-two states. Bottoms also served as executive director of the American Vocational Association, where he emphasized academics as an integral part of vocational education at the secondary and postsecondary levels, and was director of educational improvement for the Georgia Department of Education for thirteen years.

Dr. Sue Magee Cahill served as English and school-to-work supervisor at North Penn School District in Lansdale, Pennsylvania. As a former assistant principal, she was instrumental in securing over $500,000 in grant monies for the district's School-to-Work/Tech Prep Program. Cahill, who spent twenty years in the classroom, also authored North Penn High School's National School of Excellence document.

Dr. Elaine D. Edgar is the administrator for Tech Prep at the Ohio Board of Regents. For five years, she has worked with the Ohio Department of Education staff to administer the state's Tech Prep initiative to encourage systemic change in secondary education. Edgar represents higher education at the state level, works closely with forty-four colleges and universities implementing Tech Prep programs, and oversees twenty-six Tech Prep consortia. Edgar is one of six members of the National Tech Prep Network Advisory Board. Previously, she worked for ten years at the Ohio State University in administrative positions.

Dr. Walter Edling has been involved in education, teaching, and curriculum development for thirty-seven years, including nine years at CORD. He served as a division director in engineering technology and as academic vice president of a community college. Edling's work has focused extensively on the contextualization of curricula, learning styles, and the integration of academic and technical education. In the last twenty years, he has spoken about educational reform to more than 500 audiences in the United States and worldwide, and has written various materials related to curriculum design. An engineer by profession, Edling worked in manufacturing and atmospheric and space vehicle research prior to his career in education.

Mr. Don Gray began his automotive career in a true hands-on way—at a service station (while he went to technical school) and later at a dealership. He joined General Motors in 1971, and has held a variety of positions with GM and Chevrolet Motor Division. He is GM's general director of service administration and service training, overseeing the training of the company's dealership service technicians nationwide. In 1995, Gray was tapped to spearhead the launch of an innovative strategy for building educational partnerships between dealerships and schools—the effort that has evolved into Automotive Youth Educational Systems.

Ms. Karen R. Holmes, school-to-work coordinator for North Penn School District in Lansdale, Pennsylvania, initiated the business-education Career Development Partnership Program and cochairs its steering committee. She coordinates a districtwide school-to-work program for K-12 and is involved in designing career academies. A frequent presenter at national conferences, Holmes planned and facilitated an eastern regional integration seminar at her school. Having participated in staff development efforts, she was instrumental in developing Career Pathways and a planner used by all secondary students.

Ms. Sharyl Kincaid, school-to-career director at Round Rock Independent School District in Texas, has worked since 1996 with all district campuses to implement career development information. As assistant director of the high school division of the Texas Education Agency, she worked with a mentor school initiative and with *High Schools That Work* campuses. Kincaid served as assistant director for the Capital Area Tech Prep Consortium to help school districts in ten Texas counties implement Tech Prep. She began her educational career as a high school teacher in Leander, Texas.

Ms. Margaret M. Leary is president and chief operating officer of CORD Communications, Inc.. Previously she served as senior associate for editorial development at CORD, vice president of WRS Group, Inc., and editor of *Occupational Health & Safety*, a trade journal. Before entering the publishing field, Leary was a technical translator and a teacher at both the elementary and secondary levels.

Mr. Björn E. Olsson, as president and COO/CEO of Harmon Industries Inc., Blue Springs, Missouri, heads a leading supplier of signal and train control systems to the rail-bound transportation industry in North America and the world. He has gained extensive experience in finance and executive-level management holding managerial positions since 1972 and serving in president and COO/CEO positions for thirteen years. He has had extensive international exposure and has conducted business in all parts of the world.

Dr. Arnold Packer is senior fellow, Institute for Policy Studies, at Johns Hopkins University and chairs the SCANS/2000 Program. He served as executive director of the U.S. Labor Department Secretary's Commission on Achieving Necessary Skills (SCANS). He is coauthor of *Workforce 2000*, which, along with the SCANS reports, has altered the national conversation about human resource education. Packer has had a distinguished career in the federal government, with OMB, the Senate Budget Committee, and the Department of Labor. His most recent books are *College Success* and *Why Numbers Count*.

Dr. Dale Parnell, professor at the University of South Florida in Tampa, has made the subject of teaching and learning his long-time professional and scholarly interest. In his recent book, *Why Do I Have to Learn This?* he outlines some of his recent research into brain-based learning. This research and his long experience in education have convinced Parnell that the commitment of the educational establishment to a time-defined and time-structured organization is one of the major barriers to lasting progress in education reform. He began his professional career as a secondary school teacher, and has served as vice principal, principal, superintendent, college president and chancellor, community college association president, and college professor.

Dr. Roy Peters Jr. has been director for the Oklahoma Department of Vocational and Technical Education since 1986, and before 1986 he served as the department's associate director. For over twenty-five years, the department has promoted the extensive use of competency certificates and a competency assessment system as a forerunner of portfolios to document student achievement. Before moving to the state level, Peters was superintendent at the Canadian Valley Area Vo-Tech School in El Reno, Oklahoma.

Dr. David Pierce has almost four decades of experience with community colleges at local, state, and national levels. He is president of the American Association of Community Colleges, heading the national organization that represents more than 1,100 two-year colleges and their over 11 million students. Pierce has served as a community college instructor, department chair, academic dean, president, chancellor, and director. He interacts regularly with the U.S. Departments of Education and Labor and is active with key higher education organizations. Pierce is a strong proponent of partnerships between education and business, and he serves on the Council on Workforce Excellence of the National Alliance of Business.

Ms. Carolyn Prescott is a senior associate with CORD. Her areas of specialization are curriculum development and technology integration. She was a principal developer of CORD's *Applications in Biology/Chemistry* and has contributed to all of CORD's applied academics materials. Most recently,

Prescott was the project director for the *Math at Work* series, five multimedia games for learning mathematics.

Mr. Fred Rau spent four years in food processing company sales before entering the teaching profession. He taught agriculture, forestry, and science at Centennial High School in Gresham, Oregon, before taking responsibility for cooperative work experience and teaching careers. In 1992, he began his position as business partnership coordinator. He coordinates Experiential School, a mentor program, cooperative work experience, job placement, internships, job shadows, teacher shadows and internships, and other connecting activities with the business community. Rau has been active in school-to-career issues on the local and state levels, and he has served on a number of committees to promote the cause of work-based learning.

Mr. Charles Rouse retired after serving sixteen years as principal of the Leander, Texas, High School. He had spent over thirty years in education, twenty-three of those in administration. Rouse is a past member of the board of directors of the Texas Association of Secondary School Principals. He has participated in Tech Prep-related projects for the past twelve years and was instrumental in developing the first 2+2 program in Texas. The Leander High School model of Career Pathways has been replicated in over 100 schools. Rouse is director of special projects for CORD.

Ms. Sandy Sarvis Brossard displays a characteristic that any good leader needs, that of empowering others. She has spent her career empowering others—particularly teachers, administrators, and parents—to help students. She served most recently as a school district associate superintendent in South Carolina, and has helped teachers, administrators, and parents have the knowledge and skills needed to assist students in making sound career choices that meet the students' individual interests, talents, and abilities. Sarvis Brossard has used her creativity and commonsense approach as she has made numerous workshop and conference presentations nationwide.

Dr. Charles D. Schmitz is dean of the School of Education at the University of Missouri in St. Louis. After a twenty-three year career in roles including professor and associate dean at the University of Missouri-Columbia, he spent a time away from his home state serving as dean of the School of Education at Baylor University in Texas. Schmitz has served in a number of administrative positions, chaired key committees, taught a variety of undergraduate and graduate courses, and advised thousands of undergraduate and graduate students. He has been the driving force for the creation of the Saint Louis Regional Education Park and is increasingly viewed as one of the most significant educational voices of St. Louis as he leads his school in creating the 21st Century School of Education.

Dr. John C. Souders Jr. is vice president for curriculum materials for CORD, where he directs all curriculum development activities. He developed *CORD Algebra* and four new units in the *CORD Applied Mathematics* series that deal with higher-order geometry topics, and he led a project for developing mathematics and science materials for retraining adults in the automotive industry. Souders taught and served as director of research at the U.S. Air Force Academy, where he developed educational research expertise in the area of instructional technology and cooperative education. Souders began his professional career performing research in the area of nuclear engineering with an emphasis on numerical modeling.

Dr. Elaine Sullivan, 1998 NASSP/MetLife Principal of the Year, is principal of Hernando High School in Brooksville, Florida. She began her career as an educator as a social studies teacher, then she became a counselor and later assistant principal. Well-versed in the educational practices and trends of modern schools, Sullivan has transformed Hernando High School into a cutting-edge learning institution, and she plans to use her position as National Principal of the Year to continue to educate the nation on the value of today's students and the importance of a first-rate education.

Ms. Donna Swim serves as school-to-work coordinator for Anita Community Schools in Iowa, where the Anita Community School and its community partnership are recognized as the system leading the way for the youth of the twenty-first century. The learning system is designed to meet the needs of all youth in and out of school and enhances student achievement and centers around the young people's identified learning styles. The Anita Community Schools have been chosen to represent the Iowa School-to-Work Office in the nation's capital, and Swim's coordination of the school-to-work program has contributed to a 50 percent increase in students' attendance in postsecondary training.

Mr. John P. Tobin has served as director of Siemens Applied Technology Training for six years. He supports the Siemens' CEO and Presidents Council in developing youth apprenticeship-type activities, incumbent worker upgrade apprenticeships, and standards for these programs. Tobin has worked with the American Electronics Association and the National Coalition for Advanced Manufacturing in the development of industry-driven standards. His work with the National School to Work Office is related to the development of programs at many of Siemens' manufacturing sites and sales and services locations. Tobin has recently undertaken the executive directorship of the National Employers' Leadership Council. He previously served as a high school principal, administrative superintendent, and as executive assistant to three chancellors of the New York City Public Schools.

Dr. Nancy L. Zimpher assumed the chancellorship of the University of Wisconsin-Milwaukee this fall, after serving as executive dean and professor in the College of Education at The Ohio State University. She is president of the Holmes Partnership, a consortium of seventy-five colleges of education and their local school partners committed to improving the nature of teaching and learning, and she is a member of the policy board of the National Partnership on Excellence and Accountability in Teaching. Zimpher has served as Ohio's co-liaison with the National Commission on Teaching and America's Future and has written extensively on the nature of teacher professional development and instructional improvement. For a decade, she has taught a course on college teaching, and, as she assumes her new position, she will continue to advocate for best practices of contextual teaching and learning.

Note to the Reader

We offer some advice and words of caution before you embark on the task of reading *Tech Prep: The Next Generation*. Designed to be both a reference work and an inspirational book, it is intended to support educational administrators, Tech Prep planners/coordinators, and other consortium members in planning a new vision for Tech Prep. Effective planning involves assessment, reflection, argument, and a review of best practices, a process that each section of this book will carry you through.

For this reason, we suggest you study each chapter, rather than merely reading it. Little will be gained by trying to read the chapters in sequence, from cover to cover. We think it's better to study the introductory and closing chapters and section overviews before looking at individual chapters. Then, after you've read the chapters in one section, go back and reread one or more of them to ensure you've fully understood the concepts and practical advice they contain.

This book reflects the various ideas, beliefs, and experiences of educators, researchers, and employers. Therefore, each contributing author's writing reflects a different perspective and tone. Don't be surprised to find concepts like project-based learning discussed and applied by several authors in slightly different manners; this reflects the diverse applications of Tech Prep across the country. Similarly, you will find school-to-work and its various applications mentioned under different names. We ask that you look beyond differences in usage and open your mind to the possibilities these applications may have in your own consortium, schools, and community.

One of the perplexing things about Tech Prep is its dynamic nature; it changes and improves every year. Consequently, the ideas and practices in this book are not all-inclusive. New initiatives of this reform are being continuously created and tested in schools, colleges, and worksites throughout the country. We sought out some pioneering Tech Prep practitioners to collaborate on this book, and sometimes they look at issues and innovative practices from different perspectives, with different visions.

We hope you will help to create a unique new vision of Tech Prep in your consortium, one that will truly be the next generation of Tech Prep.

Taking the

Next Step

A nation is never finished. You can't build it and then leave it standing as the pharaohs did the pyramids. It must be re-created for each generation by believing, caring men and women. If we don't care, nothing can save the nation. If we do believe and care, nothing can stop us.

Gardner

Chapter 1

Raising the Bar

Dan Hull

We can now reflect on a century almost over and take great pride in some enormous achievements brought about by communities of scientists, public servants, and humanitarians:

- The eradication of diseases such as polio
- Space exploration, including the landing of a man on the moon
- The defense of democracy in the face of threats to human liberty such as Communism and Nazism
- Improvements in human rights
- Environmental cleanup

As we reflect on each of these accomplishments, though, it is only natural to think, "Yes, but we could have done so much more."

- We still have to find cures for cancer and AIDS.

- Human rights are still being violated in communities throughout our country and the rest of the world.

- We may have cleaned up rivers, air, and roadsides, but what have we done about global warming?

These are tough problems, and, if we were to work on them for another century, we would still not be totally satisfied. But we have identified problems, we have made progress, and, most important, we are still trying. This last statement sums up a philosophy commented on recently by a friend who moved to this country as an adult: "The wonderful chemistry in America that makes your country great is your *incurable optimism—* don't ever lose it! You act like you don't know you can be beaten; you'll tackle anything. And, in some measure, you always succeed."

The achievements mentioned above do not address single-element problems; they are complex, multifaceted. Single-element problems lend themselves to solutions by "discoveries," and we've certainly had our share of them:

- The internal combustion engine

- Airplanes

- Transistors (solid-state electronics), the forerunners of modern computers

- Nuclear fusion

- Lasers and fiber optics

These discoveries, however, are generally science- and engineering-based, and do not require changes in human behavior. When the discovery is made, the achievement is "nailed"; what remains to be done consists largely of improvements, expansions, and multitudes of applications.

Achievements related to human behavior are very difficult, if not impossible, to "nail." Most of the time we have to be content with the feeling that we're taking three steps forward and only two backward. Education is one of those human behavior arenas where we all want to see great improvements. But there have been times during this century when many of us have thought that education in this country was taking three steps backward for every two forward.

In 1983 we coalesced our thinking in the report, "A Nation At Risk," which identified national problems in education; and in 1989, the president and state governors set ambitious goals to lead us out of our educational backslide.

During the last sixteen years, several discoveries have been made (or been more clearly understood) that contribute greatly to significant educational improvements, including reaching many of the goals set in 1990.

- *High expectations*—Nearly all people can learn at advanced levels if we match teaching styles with the variety of learning styles in a diverse group of students, and if students can be motivated to learn.

- *Contextual (situational) learning*—We now understand that most people learn best when new information is presented in the context of what they already know and in the way it can be used.

- *SCANS*[1]—We've discovered that the skills employers want most in new workers go beyond technical information, techniques, and the use of specialized equipment. The frustration most employers have with schools is that their graduates don't know how to use information, think critically, solve problems, or work cooperatively with other people on teams. And many are not capable of learning on their own.

---

[1] Secretary's Commission on Achieving Necessary Skills (SCANS), *What Work Requires of Schools: A SCANS Report for America 2000* (Washington, D.C.: Government Printing Office, 1992).

- *Technology*—Computers and the information highway have enormous potential to empower teachers and learners by providing access to information, high-quality educational experiences, and interactivity with others in the learning community—if technology is understood and used properly.

As admirable as these discoveries are, they don't guarantee that education will improve; they must be applied in a change process that involves adoption, advocacy, and practice.

Education Reform

"Education reform" is a lofty term that many people use but few understand. For some, the term means getting school back to the basics, as it was when they were kids. What they don't consider is that the social environment in schools has changed radically over the years. The interests and expectations of kids today are very different from those of one or two generations ago. Also, to be successful in work and in the communities where they live, today's adults must be equipped with a different set of information, abilities, and skills.

In the past twenty-five years, there have been more than twenty educational reform movements, but few have lasted more than four years. Those that did were based on improvements in student learning and in tools and processes that empower teachers to change and improve. Theories alone do not change practice.

The most significant and far-reaching educational improvement process with which I am familiar is Tech Prep Associate Degree (TPAD), or Tech Prep for short. This movement had its roots in secondary/postsecondary articulation in the early 1980s and emerged initially under vocational education reform; it was defined in 1984, strengthened by the applied academics curriculum efforts of the late 1980s and early 1990s, and funded by Congress as a national initiative in 1990.

In high school and college, Tech Prep focuses on, but is not limited to, the "neglected majority." This comprises students with average-to-poor academic achievement, due mainly to the fact that they are contextual learners floundering in an abstract learning environment. Before Tech Prep, many of these students had no plans to attend college and were assimilated into the general track. Many of them dropped out of high school before graduation—not because they lacked intelligence, but because they could not see the connections between the information they were being asked to learn and the ways they might use it in later life.

Since 1991, over 900 Tech Prep consortia (high schools, community colleges, and business partnerships) have been formed, and each year over four million students are enrolled in Tech Prep programs and courses. Is Tech Prep reforming education everywhere? Of course not, but we're doing much better than three steps forward and two steps back. Like most processes in education improvement, Tech Prep is a complex process involving the integration of new discoveries (research) with human dynamics of epic proportions—students, parents, teachers, administrators, community and business leaders, and school boards. The process that has been developed—of getting buy-in from school administrators and business representatives, forming consortia, promoting partnerships, working collaboratively, and keeping parents informed at every step—has been successful and is outlined in other publications. But it is so challenging a task that it deserves mention here.

One of the strengths of our public education system is that it is decentralized; i.e., there are no national curricula or imperatives. The price we pay for this is that it takes years for systemic change to occur and stabilize throughout the country. But, in only a few years, Tech Prep has become a grassroots movement supported by teachers and administrators because it helps students to achieve, to stay in school, to be successful when they leave, and to be able to continue their education whenever the need arises.

Where is Tech Prep working? In lots of places. Here are a few examples.

In a Tech Prep Careers Choice class during her freshman year at Catlin High School in Catlin, Illinois, Stephanie Cord job-shadowed a certified public accountant. During her sophomore year Stephanie applied for an apprenticeship at Devro-Teepak, a Danville, Illinois, company, and was accepted. This meant that she would work for Devro-Teepak for ten weeks each summer. The summer after her junior year, Stephanie began working at Devro-Teepak. After her senior year, Stephanie again worked there, and then entered Danville Area Community College, where she began an associate degree program in business. Stephanie credits Tech Prep with setting her on a career path that offers great opportunities.

Brian Kemp joined a Tech Prep program in his junior year at Batavia High School in Batavia, New York. During the course in fashion buying and merchandising, he interned with a silk-screen printer. Graduating from high school, he continued the course at Genessee Community College. "Tech Prep kept me focused and out of trouble," Brian says. "Most of my school friends went to community college to get a basic degree," he says, "and took four years to do it because they weren't focused. I got my associate degree in one and a half years." After receiving his associate degree, Brian worked at several silk-screening businesses before opening his own, which, after only seven months, is showing a profit.

Ebony Baldwin joined a Tech Prep class as a junior in high school, mainly because she thought that learning a trade would enable her to avoid going to college. However, when she joined the Tech Prep program, she enjoyed the hands-on work and learned that, if she completed the program, she would qualify for a full two-year scholarship at Sinclair Community College in Dayton, Ohio. When she graduated, she was able to transfer fourteen credits from high school to the electronics engineering technology program at

Sinclair, from which she graduated in June 1998. Ebony would like to get a job in computer repair, analysis, or programming. Eventually, she wants to return to college and major in computer programming.

Bill Levad[2] is a senior at Mason City High School, in Mason City, Iowa. Last fall he started a Tech Prep manufacturing technology program. Bill says he now looks forward to going to school; so far, he hasn't missed a day and is making solid Bs. He'll graduate from high school having completed a general machinist program. If he completes an additional year at North Iowa Area Community College, he'll be eligible for a tool and die associate degree.

Are these just isolated stories about kids getting jobs and companies getting better workers? I don't think so.

What Is Tech Prep?

Two questions frequently asked are, "What is Tech Prep?" and "Are most schools involved in Tech Prep?" Unfortunately, the answers are not as simple as the questions.

Tech Prep has a target student population—high school and community college students—but it does not address this group exclusively. Rather, it addresses any students who are contextual learners interested in a career-related education. Tech Prep also reaches into middle schools and encourages students to continue studying at work and in universities, if either or both would be beneficial to them.

Is Tech Prep simply job preparation? No. While Tech Prep is an excellent program for career preparation and workforce development, it is not "job training" in the sense that vocational education was a decade ago. Tech Prep encourages students

---

[2] Information derived from interview courtesy of North Iowa Area Community College, Mason City, Iowa.

while they are in high school to examine careers, select a career major, and enter a plan of study that will lead to that career. But Tech Prep does not "track" students; it allows them to change career majors in high school and, after graduation, to either continue their education immediately or defer it while they enter the job market.

The major improvement in education that Tech Prep offers the neglected majority is increased achievement in useful academics through contextual teaching and learning.

Tech Prep emphasizes that "hand skills" without "head skills" have little or no long-term benefit. It is the blending of these two in integrated curricula that opens up the best of both worlds. But Tech Prep also emphasizes the value of work in the educational experience. Many of the SCANS skills that are so valuable for life and work can be taught best in the context of real worksite learning experiences.

Many high school students and their families are struggling with decisions about how these students can best prepare themselves for adulthood. They want to know more about many careers and how to enter them with the best advantage. Tech Prep offers worksite learning experiences that help students explore their options while there is still time to make choices. This requires employers to share educational roles with teachers through mentoring, job shadowing, and structured, accountable internships or apprenticeships.

This new role for employers in education has powerful potential because, in Tech Prep, it is uniquely American. We have learned much from studying the European apprenticeship system and have adopted some of its principles (such as personal accountability for quality in work), but we apply these to the goals and ideals for education in this country.

Have I defined Tech Prep to your satisfaction? Probably not, if you're looking for a final list of elements or an airtight description of its structure. Tech Prep is a dynamic reform movement, one that is changing and improving each year. It is hard to define or evaluate in traditional ways because it's a "moving target." It is a process and a curriculum structure with a workforce preparation emphasis, into which schools can integrate proven educational improvement elements like contextual learning.

As Tech Prep has become more integrated into school reform, it has shared some of its improvements with other programs such as *High Schools That Work* (SREB), *Breaking Ranks* (NASSP), career academies, and school-to-work. But holistically, Tech Prep is unique: It has been evolving for over a decade; it has large grassroots support; and it deserves the opportunity to continue to lead educational reform in this country.

So what is this book all about? Is it just an opportunity to brag a little and pat ourselves on the back? Absolutely not. With the strong advocacy and support Tech Prep receives at federal, state, and local levels, it is probable that this movement will continue at least five to ten more years, at which time it should pervade most educational systems. Because of this, we need to see the ways Tech Prep should continue to evolve. So this book is about looking at where we've been, where we are, and where we're going; considering new visions of excellence for education in America; and describing some of the progress being made.

Currently, most Tech Prep consortia are practicing the key elements of the movement as they were defined in the early 1990s.

- Seamless articulation between high school and community college curricula is evident in many partnerships.

- Higher expectations of academic achievement are being realized through contextualized teaching and the integration of academic and technical course content.

- More high school students who were not in college prep programs are now setting plans and goals for careers they will pursue after graduation; and they are working these plans, many of which now include higher education.

But Tech Prep is not uniformly successful in all consortia around the country. Some educators have simply repackaged old voc-ed or general education elements and called the package Tech Prep. Seamless articulation has not taken place between some high schools and community colleges. Two-plus-two[3] articulation for some has never moved beyond connecting old voc-ed courses in high schools with old voc-ed courses in community colleges. And the new roles of employers and community colleges are just beginning to become clear as more exemplary practices in businesses, industries, and educational institutions are identified and modeled. Others are moving at a much slower pace than they could.

Like so many change initiatives in our country, the best examples are always tied to strong leadership and vision. I strongly believe that educational leaders in Tech Prep must accomplish two things in the next twelve to eighteen months:

1. We must examine the progress that has been made in each consortium, and, where there are weaknesses or gaps, strengthen or fill them. The benchmarks of good Tech Prep programs are available in numerous publications and from exemplary practitioners. In addition, The Gallup Organization has developed an index for identifying progress and gaps in Tech Prep consortia. It involves surveys of students, employers, and teachers/ administrators to ascertain each group's perception of progress in reaching key elements of educational improvement. Comparing the perceptions of these groups reveals gaps and aids in setting goals for improvements.

---

[3] Two years of high school plus two years of community college.

2.   We must "raise the bar" on educational reform through Tech Prep.

For educational improvement to survive and permeate America's schools and colleges, it must contain a careful, thoughtful blend of the old and the new. There must be continuity alongside effective innovations that have been recently tested and established. Mindless "jumps" from one educational fad to another—and from one administrative leader to another—have left us with an "educational wasteland" of ineffective resources and enthusiasm, waste that we can neither afford nor tolerate.

But it is also imperative that we continue the progress Tech Prep has made to provide a good education for everyone—not just the 20 to 25 percent of the students who relate to and achieve in the established system. Reforming education is like riding a bicycle; if you slow down, you'll probably topple over and crash.

In many ways, Tech Prep consortia are set up with schools in a way similar to Lockheed Aircraft's "Skunk Works," where new ideas and techniques are tried and, when proven successful, passed on to the central part of the organization. Many new, effective elements of education reform have already been tested in Tech Prep consortia; they are ready to be "brought to scale" as we raise the bar and expand this movement.

What Should Tech Prep Be in 2004?

This book is a challenge to every workforce education partnership in the country to create a new vision and a long-range plan. Many of these partnerships are called Tech Prep consortia. Others are called career academies, *High Schools That Work,* or school-to-career programs. Titles aren't very important; common vision and leadership are.

In the following chapter, the rationale and structure for the new visioning will be presented. Sections 2 through 5 contain

twenty-one suggested elements for the new vision, organized
under four broad areas: curriculum, teaching and learning, the
new role of employers, and the role of family and community.
The final section will propose a strategy for each consortium to
consider in establishing its vision for Tech Prep in 2004.

Chapter 2

Visions of
Excellence

Dan Hull

Does public education still fulfill a dream? Or is it a
nightmare?

The great American dream for education is changing. The
old dream, "Work hard in school, go to college, and you'll have
it made after you get your degree," was based on outdated
assumptions:

1. Work hard in school to learn your subjects. Don't ask
    why—you'll be able to use the knowledge somewhere,
    someday.

2. High schools are good places to learn important facts,
    ideas, and ways of thinking and doing.

3. A baccalaureate degree is a guarantee of a good job and
    a prosperous career.

4. Schools are where you should acquire knowledge—not prepare for a career.

5. If you can't go to college, a local business (or plant) will hire you after high school graduation. If you'll just show up on time and do what you're told, you can make a good living.

The reality today is . . .

Most students leave high school with no idea of what career they intend to pursue, much less an education plan that will get them there. More than 75 percent of these students lack the financial means or family assistance necessary to obtain the skills that would enable them to earn higher than minimum wage. The high school diploma that certifies only "seat time" doesn't mean a thing to employers when they consider a job applicant. It says nothing about what a person can do on the job.

Even those students planning to enter college often haven't thought beyond their first semester. Yet many parents are spending a fortune, often going into debt, to give their children some sort of education or training with which to enter a career. High school graduates are entering colleges unprepared in knowledge, discipline, or attitude. The freshman dropout rate at universities exceeds 25 percent. Fifty-six percent of the students entering community colleges have to take at least one remedial mathematics course. Except for certain professional fields of study such as engineering and accounting, a baccalaureate degree does not guarantee that a graduate is qualified for a particular job or career. This is demonstrated by the fact that 25 percent of community college and technical school students enrolled in associate of applied science programs already have undergraduate degrees but have had to return to community college to acquire the knowledge and skills they need to enter the job market.

Today, youth with only a general high school diploma or less are having increasing difficulty in landing jobs that pay more than minimum wage. From 1979 to 1995, males working full time with less than a high school diploma saw their real earnings decline by 25 percent; earnings of males with postgraduate education rose 25 percent.[1] And that's the good news. Females in the workplace continue to receive less recognition, lower compensation, and fewer promotions than their male counterparts.

The profile of educational attainment for Americans 18 years old and older today looks like this:

10.4%	have achieved less than a ninth-grade education;
14.4%	have had some high school but have not graduated;
30.0%	have high school diplomas but no more;
18.7%	have had some college but have not graduated;
6.2%	have earned associate degrees;
13.1%	have earned bachelor degrees; and
7.2%	have earned graduate or professional degrees.[2]

While our country is experiencing one of its longest sustained periods of economic growth, 60 percent of the male workforce is losing real income.[3] This fact illustrates the old adage, "A rising tide does not lift all boats."

But hope is on the way. A new educational system is emerging that could improve the plight of the middle class. This system is built on Tech Prep concepts, structures, and practices. The challenge is to encourage educators across the board to embrace the vision it offers and to put into effect the strategies that will make the vision a reality. This is not something any

---

[1] David Bollier, *Work and Future Society: Where Are the Economy and Technology Taking Us?* (Washington, D.C.: Aspen Institute, 1998), p. 16.
[2] Bollier, p. 38.
[3] Bollier, p. 16.

one sector of the education community can do alone. Everyone involved in helping students learn must take part if there are to be major improvements in teaching and learning.

The great American dream of individual opportunity and prosperity hasn't vanished—but it is changing. Consequently, the way we educate with Tech Prep is also changing. It has started to move toward offering a wide range of effective avenues to productive, rewarding careers for a very diverse population with unique abilities, interests, and value systems.

In their recent book *Prosperity*, Davis and Wessel state, "The next 10 to 20 years will see the flowering of an era of broadly shared prosperity for the American middle class, a contrast to the economic disappointments of the past twenty-five years." [4] Their predictions are based on three forces of future prosperity: technology, education, and globalization. Under the classification "education," they state, "Community colleges, the unheralded aid stations of American education, will help millions move from $7-an-hour jobs to $17-an-hour jobs." [5]

I agree that the 1100+ community and technical colleges in this country have enormous potential to provide educational preparation for high-wage jobs—if they are not predisposed to being the "way station" for underprepared, uncommitted high school graduates or dropouts. These colleges can fulfill Davis and Wessel's prediction only if they receive applicants who know what careers they want to study, have already learned useful mathematics, science, and communication skills, and have successfully completed the basic technical coursework while in high school. Preparing high school students in this manner is a clear, demonstrated purpose of Tech Prep.

---

[4] Bob Davis and David Wessel, *Prosperity: The Coming 20-Year Boom and What It Means to You* (New York: Random House, 1998), p. 3.
[5] Davis and Wessel, pp. 5-6.

In their book *Redesigning Education,*[6] Wilson and Daviss speak of the need to reconstruct the educational process by building a cohesive system around demonstrated learning-improvement strategies and working to perfect the system. They suggest doing this through an iterative process in which new strategies are continuously added and strategies that are neither effective nor compatible are dropped. This is precisely what Tech Prep is all about: continuously improving the preparation of our youth for lifelong careers. To achieve this goal, Tech Prep practitioners must have the foresight and courage to maintain and improve effective practices while recognizing and removing weaknesses.

Broad, effective institutional changes that persist longer than three or four years do not succeed by chance. They are the results of leadership and a clear vision that is compelling enough to inspire commitment and action at the grassroots level; in education, this includes classroom teachers, administrators, employers and other community leaders, and family.

The process of change begins with pioneers who start new initiatives in the pursuit of goals that support their vision. It matures when these successful initiatives are incorporated into a new system, a framework upon which related and supportive initiatives can be proposed, tested, and, when successful, incorporated.

Wilson and Daviss illustrate this process in the quest of human flight:

> For the early few who perfected the airplane, the vision was powered human flight; for the industry they created, the enduring vision has been to carry more people and cargo farther, faster, safer, and more cheaply. . . . [T]hose now

---

[6] Kenneth G. Wilson and Bennett Daviss, *Redesigning Education* (New York: Henry Holt and Co., 1994).

working for quantum changes in our schools occupy the
position in which aircraft builders found themselves before
the Wrights flew at Kitty Hawk; they've seen enticing
glimpses of the future, but no one has yet assembled those
glimpses into a complete and compelling picture. . . . The
Wrights' flight at Kitty Hawk marks the beginning of
powered human flight not because Orville and Wilbur
invented the airplane; they didn't. Others had been aloft
before them; others had developed the internal-combustion
engine, the curved upper surface and flat bottom of the
wing, elevator flaps to control climbs and dives, ailerons
along a wing's trailing edge to aid steering, and the other
parts needed to get a machine into the air. The Wrights'
breakthrough was to integrate these different parts, test
them in a wind tunnel under real-world conditions, and
assemble them into a single, coordinated system that
remained stable in the sky—and thus finally prove that
controlled, sustained human flight was possible. The
brothers' plane was the first to combine several different
innovations into a single, workable system that
demonstrated that the problems that had stymied the vision
of powered human flight could be solved.[7]

The Early Tech Prep Vision

As we examine the early years of Tech Prep, from 1984 to
1996, we see the vision was clearly to **reform vocational
education.** In the minds of parents, counselors, and many
teachers, vocational education in the early 1980s had been
relegated to a track for the educational have-nots. In most
schools and colleges, it was an educational dead-end, with few
options to move laterally or upwardly. With few exceptions,
students entering (or being placed in) vocational education in

---

[7] Wilson and Daviss, chapter 2.

high school or at community colleges had poor academic skills. Vocational education was there to teach hand skills to those who were perceived as not having head skills. This plight was not the fault of many conscientious, hard-working voc-ed faculty members but, rather, the result of an outdated academic system that directed its teaching styles to abstract learners. Thus, students entered vocational education with poor academic knowledge, and they left the same way.

To compound the problem, there was little alignment between vocational studies in high school and the community college. In most cases, students could not progress directly from high school voc-ed to college voc-ed to learn advanced skills. To further complicate the situation, in the late 1970s employers who were reinventing their organizations to stay competitive in a global economy began to ask for new and different skills from vocational students—skills that required both head and hand proficiency.

Tech Prep, as defined by Parnell's *Neglected Majority* in 1985; in federal "Perkins" legislation in 1990; and in subsequent publications by Hull, Parnell, and others, called for four major goals to reform vocational education.

Goal 1—Articulations

Secondary and postsecondary educators within a community (consortium) were to get together and restructure their course offerings so that they were compatible, aligned, and progressive. Seamless articulation agreements were written to eliminate gaps and duplication as students progressed from high school to community college, and advanced standing was given to high school courses with content and expected outcomes comparable to those at community college. Career-oriented high school students were encouraged to continue their studies in advanced programs at community colleges.

This concept of true secondary-postsecondary articulation has come to fruition in many communities throughout our country. Since the passage of the Tech Prep initiative in the Perkins legislation of 1990, over 900 Tech Prep consortia of community college/high school/business partnerships have been formed to cooperate in building this new system.

> An example of such a partnership is the Miami Valley Tech Prep Consortium in Dayton, Ohio, where Sinclair Community College works with 64 high schools and 100 businesses to redesign completely articulated career-based programs in five fields. Every student graduating from a Tech Prep program in a participating high school who is admitted to Sinclair to pursue advanced technical studies is guaranteed a scholarship—from funds provided by local businesses and industries.

Articulation has also occurred between academic and vocational faculties within institutions to close the gap and develop relationships between academic and vocational education. This practice is frequently called "integration," or interdisciplinary learning.

Goal 2—Strengthen academics for all students and use academics as a foundation for technical curricula.

The target high school student population for Tech Prep in the early years was the neglected majority—the middle 50 percent (or 60 percent) of students who, by the ninth grade, had demonstrated poor achievement in academics and had been placed either in voc-ed classes or, even worse, in the general track, a pathway to nowhere. It was painfully obvious that, unless the academic achievement of the neglected majority could be raised in areas such as mathematics, science, and communication (English), other efforts in this reform movement would be only marginally effective. Accordingly, the applied academics initiative began with the understanding that these students were not abstract learners but, rather, applied, or "hands-on," learners.

Beginning in 1984, the state directors of vocational education formed a consortium and commissioned the Center for Occupational Research and Development (CORD) and the Agency for Instructional Technology (AIT) to develop and test curriculum materials in applied mathematics, principles of technology (physics), applied communication, and applications of biology and chemistry. Using Tech Prep funds, vocational leaders in 49 states joined with mathematics and science leaders to train over 30,000 teachers and equip laboratories to implement courses using these materials. Independent evaluations of student achievement in applied academics conducted by Iowa State University, Auburn University, and the University of Georgia[8] showed significant gains in student achievement via applied academics. High expectations of academic achievement for the neglected majority are now the norm in Tech Prep programs. Over five million students have benefited from these courses.

Subsequently, course materials in applied economics (Junior Achievement) and applied humanities (Seattle Community College/Boeing) were developed and tested.

Efforts to change the technical curriculum to build in a stronger academic foundation are not presently as cohesive or widespread as applied academics usage. However, by 1993, the definition of Tech Prep had changed from a 2+2 (high school/postsecondary) program to a 4+2 program. By including all four years of high school in the scope of Tech Prep, time was allocated in the curriculum to raise the academics (grades 9-10) and build the technical curricula on them (grades 11-12).

---

[8] Dan Hull, *Opening Minds, Opening Doors: The Rebirth of American Education* (Waco, Texas: CORD Communications, Inc., 1993), pp. 88-94.

In *Opening Minds, Opening Doors* (1993), Hull laid out a
conceptual framework for the new curriculum, which he
labeled, "build a foundation, build on the foundation."
Curriculum changes that conformed to this model began to be
made, with variations from state to state.

Goal 3—Prepare students for world-class careers.

Findings from several studies and initiatives, independent
of Tech Prep, supported this goal.

- *America's Choice: high skills or low wages!* This study
  (1990) presented evidence that many of the low-skill jobs
  in America were being successfully exported to workers in
  developing countries, where wages were three to ten times
  lower than for similar work in the United States. The
  message delivered was "U.S. workers must develop high
  skills to obtain and keep the higher paying jobs to which
  they are accustomed."[9]

- The National Skill Standards Act of 1994.[10] This joint
  effort by the U.S. Departments of Education, Labor, and
  Commerce attempted to define the requirements for critical
  jobs by forming coalitions of business and industry groups.

- The 1991 Secretary's Commission on Achieving Necessary
  Skills (SCANS) project. This was a successful attempt to

---

[9] National Center on Education and the Economy, *America's Choice: high
skills or low wages!* (Rochester: National Center on Education and the
Economy, 1990).

[10] The National Skill Standards Board is composed of twenty-eight members,
one of whom is the Secretary of Labor, one the Secretary of Education, one
the Secretary of Commerce, and one the chairperson of the National
Education Standards and Improvement Council. An additional eight
members are representatives of business; another eight are representatives of
organized labor; two are neutral human resource professionals; and six are
representatives of educational institutions, community-based organizations,
state and local governments, and nongovernmental organizations.

identify the broad skills employers want from workers in most fields. Two categories of skills other than basic competencies like reading, writing, and arithmetic were identified: personal qualities and thinking skills. The first includes the ability to relate to others in and out of the classroom as well as to develop individual responsibility and self-esteem. The second includes the ability to think and solve problems in an entire system, rather than working on isolated tasks and problems.

- Efforts by Tech Prep practitioners to identify and prepare students for new careers have led schools to build stronger relationships with local employers and to experiment with worksite learning experiences and project-based learning. These provide students with some of the SCANS competencies that are not effectively taught in traditional school environments.

Since 1989, The Boeing Company in Seattle, Washington, has invested over $6 million in Tech Prep programs in Seattle high schools and community colleges. Its purpose is to influence and support educators to provide Tech Prep program graduates who could become Boeing's advanced skilled manufacturing workers of the future. Boeing also provides worksite learning experiences for Tech Prep students and faculty.

In 1996, Boeing hired the first graduates from the 4+2 Tech Prep programs in Seattle. In preemployment interview tests, the Tech Prep graduates scored an average of 96. Scores for non-Tech Prep applicants averaged 65.

Goal 4—Keep educational and career options open.

A hallmark of Tech Prep is its efforts to eliminate tracking in high school. Neither parents, students, nor employers are interested in high school students being narrowly focused into job training for a specific occupation. Granted, some European countries have shown short-term efficiencies in workforce development by their use of a dual-track system in which vocational students are highly specialized through apprenticeships in the early years of secondary education. But, in the United States, we are willing to take a chance on lower efficiency in educational training in order to keep student choices open. The possible near-term shortfall from this practice is more than compensated for by the Tech Prep students who have taken the opportunity to move into higher education and prepare for advanced skill careers.

This does not mean that Tech Prep high school students are not encouraged to explore careers and select broad career fields to study. On the contrary, exploration and selection of broad career majors by high school students not only constitute sound education, but are also effective ways to retain student interest in school. But the curriculum can be restructured in the early secondary grades so that a core of courses common to a variety of occupations within a career major can be taught.

The most important element of Tech Prep in keeping opportunities open is its guarantee of a strong, useful academic foundation in mathematics, science, and communication skills. This type of academic core gives students the ability to learn—to learn more academics, and to learn new and different technical skills that build on the academics. The nature of work in today's rapidly changing environment implies that jobs will constantly require employees to gain new education and training to be successful in their careers. To advance in a career, a person will often need to reenter a higher education institution for additional course work or a degree. The credential most needed to reenter higher education is the demonstration of proficiency in academic fields.

The New Vision

Tech Prep is now a teenager. Although it has not matured uniformly within institutions or among different partnerships (consortia), it has certainly grown in understanding and very strong advocacy; and it has demonstrated that certain of its elements have a significant value—not only for the reform of vocational education, but for all of education. A new, broader vision for Tech Prep is emerging. Several states and local consortia have already begun to formally redefine Tech Prep and have developed plans and strategies to realize this new vision.

Informally, many states and consortia are adding new initiatives. They are discovering ways to broaden and improve Tech Prep—not just to improve vocational education, but to improve the entire educational system. As we look toward the next five to seven years, a new vision of Tech Prep is emerging: *To meet high academic standards, and to provide the best teaching and learning experiences schools can offer to prepare students for life in the real world of work.*

In 1995, we began to identify and document exemplary practices in Tech Prep. In 1997, we looked at the current and future demands on Tech Prep programs. We also discovered other successful initiatives being practiced in Tech Prep consortia. Through the formation of panels of Tech Prep leaders from the National Tech Prep Network (NTPN) Advisory Board, state directors of Tech Prep (NATPL), and others, we compiled a list of issues and narrowed it to twenty-two. These issues have been organized into strategies to support four major goals of the new vision of Tech Prep.

Goal 1—Design the new curriculum structure for workforce education.

1.1   Create a balanced curriculum based on high academic standards and tied to industry standards.

1.2 Develop core curriculum structures around career clusters.

1.3 Enable all students and their families to create career plans.

1.4 Make competence the constant and school time the variable.

1.5 Assess student achievement by performance and portfolio.

1.6 Provide more advanced skills education/training at postsecondary institutions.

1.7 Ensure that pathways to employment and/or higher education are open for high school graduates.

Goal 2—Break the mold in teaching and learning.

2.1 Ensure that academic courses are taught in context and that teachers are comfortable with their new role as facilitators of knowledge acquisition rather than knowledge deliverers.

2.2 Ensure that teachers of all subjects understand the vital role they play in helping implement this education reform.

2.3 Ensure that students are involved in teaching as well as learning.

2.4 Ensure that employers are teaching at the worksite.

2.5 Cultivate contextual teaching practices through professional development.

2.6 Become partners with university schools of education to help them include contextual learning in preservice education.

2.7 Remove the misconceptions about applied academics and contextual learning.

2.8 Use telecommunication and technology in the classroom.

Goal 3—Establish a new role for employers in education.

3.1 Insist on excellence in meeting rigorous academic and technical standards.

3.2 Provide mentors and internships for teachers and learners.

3.3 Support Tech Prep education through public statements of hiring practices.

3.4 Provide data and projections on current and future labor markets.

Goal 4—Encourage family and community support for Tech Prep programs and students.

4.1 Help students discover their talents and career interests.

4.2 Help students explore the workplace in communities.

4.3 Have families help students "learn how to learn" and plan their future.

4.4 Help communities encourage universities to adopt contextual learning practices.

As you review this list of goals and strategies, your reaction may be, "This is not new; we're already working on this." I hope so, but a brief survey conducted in October 1997 showed that most Tech Prep practitioners have not engaged in many of these strategies. At the 1997 NTPN Conference, 776 of the 4700 attendees responded to a poll designed to determine the status of their consortia in regard to strategies pertaining to each of these four proposed goals. The questions they answered were:

- Is this already happening?

- Are you planning or just beginning this?
- Have you not planned to do this yet?

  The results of the poll were as follows:

Goal	Already happening	Planning to do	Not planning to do
1. Create the new Tech Prep curricula	7.6%	45.6%	46.8%
2. Break the mold in teaching/learning	12.4%	46.9%	40.7%
3. New employer roles . . .	16.2%	43.1%	40.7%
4. Family and community involvement	10.0%	39.3%	50.8%

The poll was intended to provide some indication of whether the proposed goals/strategies appropriately address areas that are not already broadly practiced. That was certainly confirmed!

At first glance, the results of this poll might seem discouraging. But, in reality, they are not. Recall that these are new goals, above and beyond the original definition of Tech Prep in the federal legislation. What is clear is that these goals address areas that most Tech Prep consortia have not reached.

But what about the large number (40-50 percent) of respondents who said, "Not planning to do"? The survey did not give respondents an "I don't know" option. So, in the months following the conference (October 1997–May 1998), NTPN members were given an opportunity to complete on the Internet a revised survey that included an "I don't know" response. Only 13 percent of the respondents from the Internet survey chose the "not planning to do" option for any of the goals.

Although this information could not be proven statistically significant, it does indicate that the proposed goals/strategies are not broadly practiced, though they may be either in a planning stage or under consideration.

While all these goals are not dealt with in detail in this book, they are mentioned in the accompanying workbook.

Are these the right goals for a new vision in Tech Prep? I believe they are, and many national and state leaders agree. Are the proposed strategies suitable for all consortia? Probably not all the strategies are suitable for all consortia, but we're not suggesting that they should be. Rather, we propose that each Tech Prep consortium reevaluate its vision and goals using the framework, information, and models set forth in this book, and attempt to answer the question, "What do we want Tech Prep to be in 2004?" I know that a few consortia have recently done this, but I hope that those that haven't would choose some strategies under each goal and begin to make plans to implement and measure them.

The Need for Change and Improvement in Tech Prep

The most profound accomplishments in this world occur when a clear vision is shared by all who are invested in it.

A New

Curriculum

Overview

Everyone agrees that all students deserve a quality education, but there is widespread disagreement about the content and educational methods that serve students best. For the past several years, educators have wrestled with the question of how to educate a student population that is larger and more diverse in terms of race, ethnicity, culture, and language than in the past. In addition, national and international tests indicate that our students are not demonstrating competency in mathematics, science, and communication. To become high-performance achievers in higher education and in the workforce, they must acquire "useful academics" in all three of these areas.

A quality educational system should prepare everyone to be successful in life, in work, and in further education and training. But one educational plan for everyone is not the answer. We should have high standards, goals, and expectations for all students, but we must recognize and provide for diversity in student interests, abilities, learning styles—and learning speeds.

In the early years of Tech Prep, we focused on the "neglected majority" of students because the traditional American educational system did not. It concentrated on the two extremes of achievers—high performing and special needs students—leaving average students to fend for themselves. Whether in vocational education or the general track, these students were neither expected, encouraged, nor prepared to continue their education beyond high school. Tech Prep sought to eliminate tracking of these students by eliminating options that "dumbed down" the curriculum. Through applied methods of teaching, we have proven that nearly all students can learn high levels of math, science, and communication. And we should provide for and expect students to demonstrate this level of performance. High academic achievement is one way to ensure that students are not on a "track" that eliminates them from opportunities in further education and training.

In this "new generation of Tech Prep," we must realize that the new curriculum must be more than just patching in more and better-connected academics. The old voc-ed courses won't work any more; they were designed to support the workforce of a past generation, which did not require strong academic foundations. Today, these courses won't open minds and doors to lifelong careers with multiple options of achievement and responsibility.

The new workplace (which continues to evolve) requires people with advanced skills. Through Tech Prep we have learned that advanced skills are not just "more of the same," but are new skills, built on a solid academic foundation. And the new skills not only are technical but also incorporate the personal, interpersonal, problem-solving, and informational skills needed to survive and be successful in meeting constantly changing and increasing demands of the modern workplace. Thus, the new Tech Prep curriculum should be based on clearly identified and articulated standards: academic, technical (skills), and employability (SCANS) standards. Walter Edling describes how this can be done in chapter 3.

The new curriculum could be described as strong in academics with a career focus, but keeping options open. Can all of this be done without putting students into a narrow track when many are not ready to commit to their life's ambition? Yes, if the curriculum is structured to provide broad career skills in the early years of high school. In addition to an academic core that all students are required to study, the new Tech Prep curriculum will contain a technical core of courses that are common to a cluster of career majors. Most specialization and advanced training for selected occupations will occur after high school (in community colleges, internships, and apprenticeships). For example: Telecommunication technology is an occupational specialization within the electromagnetic career major, which is contained in the engineering and science cluster. Within the high school technical core are typically four courses that could be applied to career majors. This should enable Tech Prep students to be employable after high school, if they choose or have need for full-time employment. The requirements and structure of a technical core curriculum are described in chapters 4 and 5.

The new curriculum assures community colleges that students entering from high school Tech Prep programs possess strong academic and basic technical foundations. This not only allows but requires community colleges to upgrade their offerings to provide advanced skills courses, an opportunity that is infrequently realized today, because most community college leaders do not have this Tech Prep vision and commitment or have not seen a "critical mass" of Tech Prep students at the college to justify the changes. The community college role in Tech Prep is discussed in chapter 9.

All high school students should be encouraged to remain in school at least through graduation, and enter postsecondary education and/or training if possible. Even so, high school students want to know why they are in school and what it will do for them if they persevere. Chapter 6 argues that a high school plan is important for every student—not just for those who are planning to enter universities. It helps them to discover their interests and abilities, and it gives them focus in their educational pursuits. It not only tells them what they must do and why, but it also helps them design and build portfolios to document their accomplishments. A student portfolio, as chapter 8 explains, is more than a transcript of grades in prescribed courses; it is a way for students to demonstrate their abilities and achievements—to other schools, to employers, and to themselves. The new Tech Prep curriculum must identify for counselors, students, and their families the structure upon which to build a career plan and the options that are available.

Related to the new curriculum are the issue of measuring student progress by achievement and mastery instead of seat time (chapter 7) and the pervasive effort to eliminate tracking by keeping options open for student choice (chapter 10).

Creation of the new Tech Prep curriculum is more than the complex task of designing what, when, and where; it must describe how, why, "what if?" and "what's next?" It calls for collaboration among education, business, and labor; among secondary and postsecondary institutions; and among teachers and faculty who have been in either academic or technical "camps." Most importantly, it begs for bold, visionary, and consistent leadership in all sectors and at all levels.

Chapter 3

Use of Standards in Curricula

Walter Edling

One of the most significant factors to affect education reform in recent years is the emergence of nationally published standards that relate directly or indirectly to the education goals for students. These national standards have been followed by similar efforts in most states. In many states, there are also movements to connect assessments of student achievement to standards. By 1995, forty-two states had developed or were developing content standards, and thirty states were moving quickly to adopt performance measures of student mastery. All fifty states were participating in the Goals 2000: Educate America Act, which placed national educational goals into law.[1]

---

[1] John F. Jennings, *Why National Standards and Tests?* (Thousand Oaks, California: Sage Publications), pp. 1-8.

Student promotion and graduation, especially at the secondary level, are increasingly being tied to success in obtaining certain scores on national or state-constructed tests.

National Education Goals

Interest in major education reform emerged during the 1980s. A major focus occurred in 1989 at the first national education summit, which resulted in publication of eight National Education Goals and, eventually, major commitments on the part of the National Governors' Association relating to standards and accountability for student success. At the congressional level, after intense debate spanning several years and a change of administration, the Goals 2000 legislation was passed in 1994. Jennings traces the lengthy political process that led to passage and recounts the issues and concerns that surfaced during the debates, some of which continue today.[2]

In a broad sense, standards are not a new phenomenon but have always existed *implicitly,* and therefore vaguely and inconsistently, among teachers and text writers in a given field. The national focus and legislation produced the new phenomenon of organized efforts to develop and publish written lists or descriptions of standards, which, because they are widely available in written form, are subject to greater visibility and review by many constituencies. In the past, academic subject matter content was largely defined by textbook writers, often at the postsecondary level, who captured the elements of information about the subject that seemed to be commonly accepted. Schools and teachers selected texts and used them as the structural basis for courses. Successful texts were those that sold well, indicating tacit or formal approval of content, organization, and presentation.

---

[2] Jennings, pp. 9-104.

The matter of interpretation of what the benchmarks should be for judging student success was largely left up to individual schools and, to a great extent, to individual teachers. The strongest external influences upon secondary schools were college eligibility requirements, which included completion of specified courses and scores on the Scholastic Aptitude Test (SAT) or American College Test (ACT). The SAT, which was designed to predict student success as a college freshman, accomplishes its intended purpose very well by modeling the intellectual challenges that the student will face in college. It serves as a screening device to identify those students who do not have the desired level of capabilities; however, it is not diagnostic. Translating the expectations of the SAT into specific teaching/learning needs in the classroom is difficult at best. For teachers it is frustrating, since they feel accountable for student success on the SAT but don't know exactly what must be done to maximize success.[3]

The measure of teaching success is often "material covered" rather than the ability of the student to demonstrate a level of competence. Traditional grades are more often a measure of comparison between students than a measure of each student's performance in relation to objective benchmarks.

Other national tests establish de facto standards in specific academic fields. For example, the National Assessment of Educational Progress (NAEP) exams measure core competencies in reading, mathematics, and science. These exams have gained wider use in recent years, partly because the *High Schools That Work* initiative has adopted them as a key component of student assessment within participating schools.[4]

---

[3] Jennings, pp. 1-3.

[4] Gene Bottoms and Deede Sharpe, *Teaching for Understanding Through Integration of Academic and Technical Education* (Atlanta: Southern Regional Education Board, 1997).

Since these exams are content specific, they have the impact of informal standards in selected subject areas.

In the vocational arena, occupational courses and programs have been based on surveys of skill sets that represented job expectations. Processes such as DACUM evolved as systematic approaches to collecting and sorting occupational information. Texts were written based upon the skills and content expectations of the individual occupations. Teachers were selected on the basis of their experience with the skills and information represented in the occupational field.

In vocational courses more than in academic courses, student performance was assessed on the basis of competency lists, with the instructor drawing on personal experience in the field to interpret the required learning. The expected competencies tended to be skill oriented and specifically defined in terms of measurable products or results. As a result, assessment was straightforward and unambiguous. Simple assessment methods sufficed, and different teachers were likely to give similar interpretations of similar levels of performance. For vocational teachers, the emergence of occupational skill standards can be regarded as a logical extension of processes with which they are quite familiar. The big change results from the more complex skills and stronger academic content that are expected within the occupational standards. This evolution has not been adequately met by vocational programs, and criticism of vocational education has been widespread.

Emerging Challenges

With the emergence of the information- and technology-based society, the knowledge, skills, and habits of mind that are needed in work and life are becoming more complex. At the same time the need for well-developed basic skills extends across the workforce.

The education system thus faces two daunting challenges. First, the basic skills in areas such as reading, computation, and communication should be broadly developed in all students to a higher level than ever before. Second, all students need to develop a new set of skills that includes teamwork, observation, leadership, resource management, confidentiality, work ethic, and appreciation of diversity, to name only a few. Analytical thinking and planning are important. Creativity is valued. These complex skills and habits of mind are not well served in traditional education, either academic or vocational.

An examination of current educational practice reveals that there is wide variation in the expectations placed before students, even in regard to basic skills. When the higher-order thinking skills and complex learning issues are examined, they are found to be addressed poorly or not at all. To address these issues, as with any problem solution, it is necessary to identify and clarify the problem. Given the complexity and confusion surrounding educational reform, it is useful to seek a common framework for the issues and to agree upon points of departure that can be used to explore solutions. The development of standards represents part of these efforts.

As might be expected, this search for common ground is not without difficulty and controversy, since it exposes areas of confusion and disagreement and calls for reexamination of habits, traditional practices, and biases. It also intrudes into domains that have been traditionally controlled from within the educational structure with relatively little outside review. Standards provide a common frame of reference around which debate and progress can take place. The development of standards is an iterative process that produces useful results.

Standards

In broad terms, standards fall into three major groups: academic, SCANS, and skill standards.

Academic

First to emerge were academic standards in traditional subject areas such as mathematics, science, and history. Today, there are published national standards for more than a dozen subject areas, and several of those have guided further definition among the many emerging state standards.

SCANS

A second emerging area of standards is best represented by the U.S. Department of Labor's SCANS project, which defined "employability" skills. Employability skills are broader than traditional occupational competencies and represent skills that are useful in most jobs. Also within this category are skills that are important for all students to acquire, namely, those having to do with personal education, career, and life planning. These skills, the best examples of which have been compiled by the National Occupational Information Coordinating Committee,[5] speak not only to counselors but also to curriculum designers and teachers. In a new paradigm, career-planning skills are built into the curriculum as an area of knowledge that is important for students to acquire. With the rapid evolution of technology and work and the changing nature of employer/employee relationships, the ability to plan one's own career directions and development has become critically important.

Skill standards

A third area of standards, often labeled "skill standards," comprises sets of specifications setting forth the knowledge, skills, and habits of mind necessary to perform in given

---

[5] Career Development Training Institute, *National Career Development Guidelines K-Adult Handbook* (Washington, D.C.: National Occupational Information Coordinating Committee, 1996).

occupational settings. Unlike the academic and employability standards, which have no clear antecedent in educational practice, occupational skill standards represent an evolution of traditional vocational competencies.

If the development of standards provides a forum for debate and an opportunity for consensus to emerge from divergent viewpoints, the resulting standards should be a useful source of information to be referenced in educational reform. Resistance to the use of standards arises from early misconceptions that should be corrected. First, it should be noted that standards, academic or otherwise, do not define the totality of content for courses or curricula. Rather, the standards establish a baseline framework representing a consensus concerning important concepts. These concepts must be considered in defining the expectations of the educational process relating to student accomplishment.

Second, standards are in no way intended to define issues of personal or individual choice or infringe on constitutional freedoms that are essential to a democratic society. Standards are appropriate where reasonable consensus exists concerning the universal benefit that will result from their application and where there is a clear understanding that they do not intrude on individual freedoms.

Textbooks, reference materials, teacher expertise, and the hosts of supporting materials used in the educational process are not replaced by standards. The rich variety and myriad details of all the subject fields cannot be captured in standards. Attempts to do so have proven to be cumbersome at best, and the results are not likely to find wide use.

Using Standards to Promote Educational Reform

1. Setting higher expectations

In virtually all published standards, the value of higher-order thinking and more complex expectations for students has been identified. The details of subject content are readily available to teachers in textbooks; the complex concepts and applications usually are not. By defining concepts that transcend basic content, the standards provide a framework for the educational system to incorporate these new goals and expectations and weave them into the subject content.

Reform efforts such as the *High Schools That Work* initiative of the Southern Regional Education Board are working to use these challenging elements of standards to assist teachers in setting more challenging goals and learning activities within existing high school vocational courses.[6]

In a collaborative project involving twenty-seven states, the Center for Occupational Research and Development has developed an organized, computerized structure for listing, searching, and synthesizing national and state standards.[7]

The structure is open-ended in such a way that new or revised standards can be incorporated and processed into curricula as needed. It accommodates and uses academic, occupational, and employability skills in an integrated approach referred to as Integrated Curriculum Standards (ICS). Since it connects academic and occupational standards, it serves as a tool for bridging the traditional gap between these areas of education.

---

[6] Bottoms and Sharpe.

[7] Center for Occupational Research and Development, *Curriculum Integrator: Standards Database* (Waco: CCI, 1997).

State-level student performance tests presently tend to focus on content. As state and national standards continue to develop, it is expected that performance tests will be refined to measure the complex as well as the basic skills. Efforts in several states are under way to compare or "crosswalk" the various standards to ensure that important elements are not omitted. While progress is sometimes slow to the point of frustration, success is being achieved in sorting out the important details in a number of states.

In another initiative, the Mid-continent Regional Educational Laboratory (McREL) has compiled academic standards in an organized structure to help academic teachers and curriculum designers look at these standards in concert.[8] Whether through the use of these tools or through local efforts, most states are aggressively pursuing the application of standards.

These efforts, and others, will continue. The combined effect of further improvement in the standards and in development-facilitating methods for incorporating standards into curricula will enhance the impact of standards in education reform

2. Contextualization of curricula

One of the benefits of standards development processes is that they produce a concise synthesis of important ideas from an area of interest, a discipline, or an occupation. By virtue of the fact that standards are developed from several viewpoints (e.g., academic, occupational, employability, and career development), reference to all can provide a broad and rich perspective for education reform. Teachers, curriculum

---

[8] John S. Kendall and Robert J. Marzano, *Content Knowledge: A Compendium of Standards and Benchmarks for K-12 Education,* comp. Mid-continent Regional Educational Laboratory (Phoenix: Teacher's Pal, 1996).

designers, and developers of educational materials can draw from these ideas and perspectives to form connections among subjects and between academic and technical areas. These connections contribute to a broader context for course content and provide students with perspectives that connect to their personal mental contexts.

Contextual learning, especially when it taps the context residing in the student's mind, is now recognized as a useful tool for student learning. The human brain is highly contextual in its function; that is, it excels at finding meaning and relationships among ideas, and learns much more effectively when presented with new information in ways that lead clearly to connections.[9]

Effective teachers have always intuitively sensed the value of context and have explored ways to develop connections. Team teaching, projects, and thematic strategies are examples of methods that have been used for many years, though on a limited basis. Several major course-material development projects over the last fifteen years have used these ideas to revise the approach to some traditional subjects. Materials relating to communication in context were developed by AIT.[10] Mathematics and science texts based on contextual strategies have been developed by CORD,[11] and a recent project involving The Boeing Company and schools in Seattle, Washington, used similar approaches to courses in other areas such as the

---

[9] Renate Nummela Caine and Geoffrey Caine, *Making Connections: Teaching and the Human Brain* (Alexandria: Association for Supervision and Curriculum Development [ASCD], 1991).

[10] *Communication 2000* (Cincinnati: Agency for Instructional Technology and South-Western Educational Publishing, 1996).

[11] Center for Occupational Research and Development, *CORD Applied Mathematics, Principles of Technology*, and *Applications in Biology/Chemistry* (Waco: CCI).

humanities.[12] An ethics text with a strong contextual focus has been published for community college use.[13]

Each of these projects had to seek out the contextual relationships to be used in the development of text and syllabus materials. As standards are formalized and developed, extension and refinement of these efforts is greatly simplified. In addition, the availability of standards and the compilations and analyses of standards allow educators to access directly a wide range of resources to enhance contextual frameworks in classrooms.

3. Integration of curricula

Although early contextualization efforts focused on individual courses, "integration" can involve many connections across the curriculum and among subjects, and it can include connections vertically from grade to grade and from secondary to postsecondary. The emergence of standards facilitates contextualization on a broader scale, involving the total curriculum. Standards raise cross-disciplinary as well as individual course issues, and provide a structure for looking at the curriculum "forest" as well as the course "trees."

Obviously, the complexity of review and revision of curricula increases considerably as the scope is enlarged. Historically, broad curriculum review has struggled to find a common basis on which conflicting demands can be considered rationally. It is very difficult, for example, to explore the relative merits of math concepts and the elements of a psychology course because, on the most superficial level, the two are, as the saying goes, as different as apples and oranges.

---

[12] South Seattle Community College Advanced Technology Center, Course Materials in Applied Humanities (Seattle: South Seattle Community College Advanced Technology Center, Applied Academics Project).
[13] Michael L. Richardson and Karen K. White, *Ethics Applied* (New York: McGraw-Hill, 1993).

In curriculum building, the typical solution has been a negotiated allocation (usually unsatisfactory to everyone involved) of Carnegie units or credit hours to various subjects. The internal use of the allocated time in each course has then been left to the content specialists.

These debates will not go away totally, regardless of the curriculum development strategies employed. There is one issue, however, that can be addressed by raising the discussion to the level of standards. This issue has to do with the need of the student to develop broader and more complex skills in translating and applying content knowledge. In the apples and oranges debate, these skills have no base of advocacy and do not receive adequate attention in the curriculum. Standards are beginning to provide a common and more neutral language that allows curriculum planners to move to a higher level of collaboration. Standards reveal, among other things, the similarities among disciplines and perspectives that provide common ground for agreement.

This feature of standards forms the fundamental basis for the ICSs developed by CORD.[14] Since any and all relevant standards are represented in the ICSs, academic as well as occupational needs can be considered in concert, and the cross-disciplinary skills become quite evident. Seamless curricula between secondary and postsecondary levels are easier to develop using this framework. One of the unique features of ICSs is that they are not locked into the traditional course structures and the divisions of content between secondary and postsecondary education. They provide a structure for taking a fresh look at joint curriculum development between secondary and postsecondary programs.

---

[14] Center for Occupational Research and Development, *Curriculum Integrator: Implementation Guide* (Waco: CCI, 1997).

An ICS is more complex than a specified element of knowledge or a traditional vocational competency. It represents a multifaceted skill that draws upon academic knowledge, application skills, and workplace perspectives, such as SCANS. Developing and assessing student mastery of an ICS require new approaches to the teaching and learning process.

As an example, an important ICS with the heading "teamwork" establishes the following expectations for student performance:

> **Teamwork**—Participate as an effective member of a team by contributing to the group effort of accomplishing goals. Identify and employ the appropriate role within the group. Use effective communication, interpersonal skills, and learning techniques while working with others of diverse backgrounds. Participate in group decision-making processes incorporating the appropriate role within the group. Evaluate the team's efforts.[15]

It is evident that lecturing to students about such a complex topic and evaluating their mastery with traditional tests will produce, at best, a superficial understanding of the many nuances contained in this ICS. As more creative teaching and learning and assessment strategies are employed, the level of student mastery can be enhanced substantially.

4. Use of project-based learning

Student projects and project-based learning have been used for many years, especially in vocational courses and science laboratories, and typically have focused on course content. The emerging standards provide a basis for the use of broader projects that address the integrated and more complex issues of

---

[15] Center for Occupational Research and Development, *Curriculum Integrator: Digest of Integrated Curriculum Standards* (Waco: CCI, 1997).

the application of knowledge. In fact, project-based learning is considered one of the most useful tools for addressing these issues.

Rather than being designed only to serve course content, projects can also be used to provide learning experiences that incorporate the cross-disciplinary and application skills identified by the standards. Skills such as teamwork, observation, resource management, and ethical habits cannot be taught completely by lecture or reading. To fully develop and understand these skills, students must have opportunities to experience personal applications in real situations with coaching and guidance from a teacher and feedback from peers. These skills are fully developed only in the laboratory of life, and projects provide examples.

A typical project might require a group of five or more students to research the status of recycling efforts in their community and to develop plans for improvements. The students can be left with an open-ended challenge to decide what should be done; how their efforts should be organized; and how their work should be carried out, reported, and evaluated.

Such a project can be used to provide students with experience in developing the teamwork skills expected. At different times, students can be assigned different team roles. The teacher can discuss the challenges of being a team leader, of planning and orchestrating individual efforts, of being a follower with assigned tasks, and of dealing with conflicting ideas and perspectives. The team process can be a topic for discussion before and after the project is carried out, and students can be coached and encouraged to explore strategies to improve team performance, reduce conflict, and improve communication. In short, the process itself becomes part of the learning experience. If such projects are used repeatedly throughout the curriculum and over several years, students gain the experience in working with others that they would otherwise have to develop after leaving school.

The value of such experiences has been long recognized as one of the benefits of student clubs and activities outside the classroom. Unfortunately, these extracurricular activities have not been available uniformly to all students.

5. Use of worksite learning experiences

Worksite learning, if well structured, can represent the ultimate project or life laboratory. To be effective, such experiences should be focused on identified standards. Without focus, the learning that takes place may be vague or, in extreme cases, even counterproductive. Expecting a student to learn about ethics in a work environment where unethical practices occur may be unrealistic, unless the student is guided to interpret and contrast the reality to the ideal. Expecting a student to gain interpersonal skills in a work situation where little or no interaction occurs or where poor communication is practiced may, at best, be a waste of the student's time.

Standards provide a frame of reference to establish parameters for arranging, managing, and assessing the student's worksite experience. In some cases, the specific skill standard that relates to the worksite may be available and can provide highly relevant learning goals for the worksite experience.

The teamwork ICS can serve as one of the learning goals for a worksite experience. Imagine a student invited to participate in a team project under way at the worksite, with the student given responsibility for some facet of the team's efforts. The impact of deadlines, conflicts, communication, and differing roles can be very powerful when the student is placed in a real situation. Many other ICSs lend themselves well to structuring worksite experiences and can be introduced as part of the initial planning between the school and the employer.

6. Use of cooperative learning

Cooperative learning has long been recognized as a useful educational strategy.[16] As the various standards are examined, it becomes evident that cooperative learning may be even more valuable than previously thought. Of the 149 CORD ICSs, which represent over 11,000 elements of nationally published standards, more than 15 percent are complex skills that are exercised in cooperative learning.[17] Skills such as communication, teamwork, leadership, self-expression, appreciation of diversity, and intrapersonal and interpersonal management can be learned and practiced through interaction with others.

For most people, the process of learning is enhanced and made more enjoyable if they have the opportunity to discuss ideas and concepts with others. Cooperative interaction brings to light misconceptions and helps to clarify concepts that are not well understood. It is a process that can directly address ICSs such as teamwork. For example, groups of students can be assigned a task to investigate, discuss, and analyze complex and controversial issues such as global warming or the death penalty, but with the additional challenge of finding the best consensus that can be reached within the group. (On some issues this consensus may not be achieved beyond some definition of points upon which the students all can agree and a statement of points of disagreement.) A follow-up activity can then be for the groups to review their consensus-building techniques with an analysis of what worked and what did not and why.

---

[16] David Johnson and Roger Johnson, "Cooperative Learning: A Theory Base," *If Minds Matter: A Foreword to the Future*, Vol. II (Palatine, Illinois: Skylight Publishing, 1992).

[17] Center for Occupational Research and Development, *Curriculum Integrator: Digest of Integrated Curriculum Standards*, pp. 3-10.

Learning activities of this type go beyond the issue being investigated and begin to teach the process skills that may be even more important for the students to acquire. In this case, the students learn through experience to seek areas of agreement even in regard to issues upon which they may disagree intensely. This skill is one of the cornerstones of teamwork.

Project-based learning connects naturally with cooperative learning. Most projects are effective opportunities to have pairs or groups of students work together. These experiences provide another example of a living laboratory within which a wide range of communication, organization, and interpersonal skills can be developed.

7. Assessment based on standards

As standards have evolved, more attention has been devoted to recommended benchmarks, assessment criteria, and levels of performance that represent satisfactory achievement of the standards. One of the most recent skill standards that has been published lists "performance criteria" for each element, designed to answer the question, "How do we know when the task is performed well?"[18]

Earlier standards did not devote as much attention to assessment criteria; however, the elements of the standards *define* what aspects of student performance should be assessed. Users of the standards find it necessary to develop and validate detailed assessment benchmarks and rubrics. Over time, appropriate assessment criteria will emerge and will provide for measuring student performance in relation to the standards.

---

[18] NorthWest Center for Emerging Technologies, *Building a Foundation for Tomorrow: Skill Standards for Information Technology* (Bellevue, Washington: NorthWest Center for Emerging Technologies, 1997).

The complex skills represented in emerging standards present a challenge to the simple and limited assessment methods that are in wide use. A wider range of techniques such as portfolios, structured observation, scenarios, simulations, and project evaluations will be needed to adequately assess these skills.[19] A number of strategies and tools are listed in the following table.

Table 1. Assessment Design for *Curriculum Integrator*[20]

Assessment Strategies	Description of Assessment Strategies	ICS Ref #	Tools for Assessment
Project	• hands-on demonstration of know-ledge, skills, and attitudes that reveals a student's ability to plan, organize, and create a product or an event • documentation of process of development from initial steps to final presentation		
Portfolio	• collection of pieces of evidence of a student's knowledge, skills, and attitudes • showcase of best work, work in progress • record of student's progress over time • content selection by student in collaboration with the teacher • centerpiece for parent conferences		

---

[19] Walter H. Edling and Ruth M. Loring, *Education and Work: Designing Integrated Curricula: Strategies for Integrating Academic, Occupational, and Employability Standards* (Waco: Center for Occupational Research and Development, 1996), pp. 24-26.

[20] Center for Occupational Research and Development, *Curriculum Integrator: Implementation Guide*, p. 19.

Assessment Strategies	Description of Assessment Strategies	ICS Ref #	Tools for Assessment
On-Demand Demonstrations	• hands-on performance of student, which illustrates levels of knowledge, skills, and attitudes • typically involve a "real-life" problem or situation to solve • focus on the application of knowledge and skills learned in one situation as it relates to a new and different one		
Case Studies/ Scenarios/ Simulations	• analysis of events and individuals in light of established criteria • synthesis of evidence to support generalizations based on individual cases		
Paper/Pencil Tests	• multiple-choice, essay, true-false questions that rely on extended responses to further clarify a student's understanding of the knowledge being assessed • graphic representations that reveal a student's understanding of connections among ideas		
Structured Observation	• observation of events, groups, and individuals that focuses on the salient traits of the skill or attitude being observed		

Tools for Assessment

1 = rubric	2 = structured observation form
3 = checklist	4 = journal
5 = computer programs	6 = annotated notes
7 = graphic organizer	8 = charts for information gathering
9 = cognitive mapping	10 = narrative writing
11 = visuals	12 = videotaping
13 = photography	14 = conferencing
15 = self-report	

Published standards provide a rich source of information for developing assessment rubrics and criteria to assist teachers in determining when students have accomplished desired goals. The teamwork ICS provides a good example.

> **Teamwork**—Participate as an effective member of a team by contributing to the group effort of accomplishing goals. Identify and employ the appropriate role within the group. Use effective communication, interpersonal skills, and learning techniques while working with others of diverse backgrounds. Participate in group decision-making processes incorporating the appropriate role within the group. Evaluate the team's efforts.[21]

By referring to the elements of the various standards that are incorporated into this ICS, it is possible to expand this integrated standard into the following *essential attributes:*[22]

Components	Essential Attributes
Contribute to the group effort of accomplishing goals.	Exhibit concern and encouragement for each team member and team goals. Complete aspects of accepted tasks according to team-established procedures.
Show sensitivity to diverse cultural backgrounds through communication, interpersonal skills, and learning techniques.	Show consideration of cultures and how they differ while working with and for others, while at the same time remaining uncompromising of one's own culture and values. Consideration exhibited through positive, clear, and sensitive communication, appropriate personal contacts, and learning opportunities between parties.

[21] Center for Occupational Research and Development, *Curriculum Integrator: Digest of Integrated Curriculum Standards*, p. 5.
[22] Center for Occupational Research and Development, *Curriculum Integrator: Implementation Guide*, p. 44.

Components	Essential Attributes
Participate in group decision-making processes incorporating the appropriate role within the group.	Cooperate with team members to reach realistic, attainable goals by working toward resolving conflicts, constructing compromises, and building consensus.
Evaluate team's efforts.	Participate in observing team's effort and completing follow-up activities to evaluate team goals.

These attributes form the basis for assessment rubrics that can be keyed to desired levels of performance exemplified by the following sample for the teamwork ICS, which uses a four-level scale:

Sample Rubric for Teamwork ICS[23]

Component: Contribute to the group effort of accomplishing goals.

Level of Attainment	Performance Criteria
World-Class Learner	Consistently exhibits concern and encouragement for each team member and team goals. Completes all aspects of accepted tasks in an exceptional manner according to team-established procedures.
Proficient Learner	Usually exhibits concern and encouragement for team members and team goals. Adequately completes all aspects of accepted tasks according to team-established procedures.
Developing Learner	Occasionally exhibits concern and/or encouragement for team members and team goals. May not complete all aspects of accepted tasks. If completed, tasks may not have been completed according to team-established procedures.

[23] Center for Occupational Research and Development, *Curriculum Integrator: Implementation Guide*, p. 46.

Level of Attainment	Performance Criteria
Emergent Learner	Rarely, if ever, exhibits concern for team members and/or team goals. Does not complete tasks expected of a team member.

Component: Show sensitivity to diverse cultural backgrounds through communication, interpersonal skills, and learning techniques.

Level of Attainment	Performance Criteria
World-Class Learner	Consistently considers all cultures and how they differ when working with and for others, while at the same time remaining uncompromising of own culture and values. High level of consideration is exhibited through positive, clear, and sensitive communication, appropriate personal contacts, and learning opportunities between parties.
Proficient Learner	Usually considers all cultures and how they differ when working with and for others, while at the same time remaining uncompromising of own culture and values. Adequate level of consideration is exhibited through positive, clear, and sensitive communication, appropriate personal contacts, and learning opportunities between parties.
Developing Learner	Occasionally is considerate of most cultures and how they differ while working with and for others while at the same time may or may not remain uncompromising of own culture and values. Very little consideration is present in communication, personal contacts, and/or learning opportunities between parties.
Emergent Learner	Exhibits little if any consideration for other cultures and how they differ while working with and for others and is unaware of own culture and values. No consideration is present in communication, personal contacts, or learning opportunities between parties.

Component: Participate in group decision-making processes incorporating the appropriate role within the group.

Level of Attainment	Performance Criteria
World-Class Learner	Consistently cooperates with team members to reach realistic, attainable goals by skillfully working toward resolving conflict, constructing compromises, and building consensus.
Proficient Learner	Usually cooperates with team members to reach realistic, attainable goals by skillfully working toward resolving conflict, constructing compromises, and building consensus.
Developing Learner	Occasionally cooperates with team members to reach realistic, attainable goals by working toward resolving conflict, constructing compromises, and building consensus.
Emergent Learner	Is not able or is unwilling to cooperate with members to reach realistic, attainable goals. Does not work toward resolving conflict, constructing compromises, or building consensus, and may even weaken the team.

Component: Evaluate team's efforts.

Level of Attainment	Performance Criteria
World-Class Learner	Consistently participates in accurately observing team's efforts and completes follow-up activities to evaluate team goals.
Proficient Learner	Usually participates in accurately observing team's efforts and usually completes follow-up activities to evaluate team goals.
Developing Learner	Occasionally participates in observing team's efforts. May or may not complete follow-up activities to evaluate team goals.
Emergent Learner	Rarely participates in observing team's efforts. Does not complete follow-up activities to evaluate team goals.

The four-level scale used in this example is designed to represent progressive levels of attainment on the part of the student. This approach is more constructive than the traditional approach of separating students by success and failure. The scale definitions are as follows:[24]

World-Class Learner: The learner at this level of the rubric has gone beyond the mastery of the knowledge, skills, and attitudes of the component of the ICS. The world-class learner consistently exhibits high-quality performance.

Proficient Learner: The learner at this level of the rubric has had opportunities to apply the knowledge, skills, and attitudes of the component of the ICS. The proficient learner has mastered the essential attributes, thus proving mastery of the component.

Developing Learner: The learner at this level of the rubric has been exposed to and has had the opportunity to apply the knowledge, skills, and attitudes of the component of the ICS. The developing learner may have only a few essential attributes to master before mastery of the component.

Emergent Learner: The learner at this level of the rubric may or may not have been exposed to the knowledge, skills, and attitudes of the ICS.

With this information available, teachers can use varied methodologies to assess student achievement of complex skills that have not traditionally been well taught or measured. In addition, the assessment is connected directly to the source standards, thereby making it possible to attest to student performance with a level of confidence not otherwise possible. In the absence of standards, attributes, and rubrics, the individual teacher is left with the sole responsibility of

---

[24] Center for Occupational Research and Development, *Curriculum Integrator: Implementation Guide*, p. 42.

interpreting complex expectations with little or no information beyond his or her personal experience.

Standards and the Tech Prep Vision

As the potential benefits of standards are considered in regard to curriculum design and teaching/learning methodology, obvious connections to the new vision of Tech Prep appear. The recognition of new, complex skills that students need to develop has been codified through the standards-development work. The integration and contextualization of curricula and curriculum materials are facilitated by the emergence of areas of consistency and commonality among academic, occupational, and employability skill standards.

Stronger vocational courses built on a solid academic foundation can best be developed if there is clear agreement about the skills students must acquire to respond to the challenges of modern work and society. For collaboration to succeed among education, business, and labor; among secondary and postsecondary institutions; and among teachers and faculty across academic and technical areas, it is necessary to have a common language and frame of reference for meaningful discourse and agreement among these diverse players. Standards provide the language for agreement and collaboration.

The *vision for excellence* must rest on a base representing the strongest and broadest consensus that can be built around the educational reform needs of today's technology- and information-based society. Past efforts at educational reform have tended to be fragmented and representative of only pieces of the education structure. The need for a system view has been identified in emerging standards as part of the skill set that students must acquire; it seems obvious that education must also

function as a system if it is to meet its challenges.[25] Standards
offer a structure for building a solid foundation for a new vision
for the education system.

Steps to Reform Curricula Based on Standards

Standards should represent an essential part of the vision
for reform and provide important contributions to reform goals
and objectives. Considerable preparation may be necessary for
educational institutions, boards, administrators, teachers, and
community leaders to be committed to the use of standards as an
integral part of the reform effort. In their book on the integration
of academic and technical education, Bottoms and Sharpe offer
a ten-step process for curriculum integration; five of the steps
have to do with establishing the climate within which reform
can proceed.[26] Until reform participants share a perception of
the value of standards and an understanding of the multiple
sources of standards that are relevant, it is unlikely that progress
will be made.

When a commitment to the use of standards has been made,
the logical steps to apply standards in curriculum reform include
the following:

Step 1: Assemble all relevant standards.

The extent of this step is determined by the extent of
curriculum reform being contemplated. If only selected courses
are to be reviewed, fewer standards may be relevant than if the
entire curriculum is to be reviewed.

---

[25] Wilson and Daviss, pp. 22-47.
[26] Bottoms and Sharpe, pp. 86-108.

Step 2: Analyze and crosswalk the standards.

As is indicated in this chapter, standards have been developed from many perspectives. There is no assurance that they are completely congruent, and it is essential that the various standards be compared if the curriculum reform is to be responsive to all the expectations set forth. Bottoms and Sharpe, for example, set forth six sources of expectations, some of which are not published and require local collection of information. They include state and national published standards, NAEP core competencies, and SCANS; but they also include perceived expectations of local employers and higher education institutions.[27]

This analysis of standards is not a simple task, and has proven to be a stumbling block in applying standards to curricula. The temptation is to ignore some of the expectations. CORD has addressed this issue by developing an organized structure and carrying out the analysis for a number of standards in selected areas.[28]

Step 3: Align the standards to the curriculum.

After a comprehensive synopsis of standards and expectations has been developed, it must be compared to the goals and objectives of the courses, course sequences, and the total curriculum. The most effective approach is to look at the curriculum in total, across all subject areas and across secondary and postsecondary technical programs. This broad look at curricula accomplishes integration, eliminates duplication, and optimizes the use of student time.

---

[27] Bottoms and Sharpe, pp. 96-97.
[28] Center for Occupational Research and Development, *Curriculum Integrator: Digest of Integrated Curriculum Standards.*

*Step 4: Identify deficiencies in the curriculum
vis-à-vis the standards.*

Accomplishing Step 3 will reveal where deficiencies exist
in the curriculum. In particular, the SCANS skills and the
complex skills represented by ICSs are typically found to be
inadequately addressed.

Step 5: Redesign the curriculum to correct the deficiencies.

When the deficiencies have been identified, the structure
and sequence of the curriculum can be redesigned to address
them.

*Step 6: Design teaching enhancements to support the
standards.*

Both content and teaching/learning strategies can be
modified to address the deficiencies. Some of the techniques
described in this chapter can be brought to bear.

*Step 7: Design assessments that verify attainment of
standards.*

Verification of student success is essential if the curriculum
is to produce student mastery of required skills. The range of
assessment methods and tools must be developed in direct
reference to the standards.

Step 8: Develop an implementation plan.

Curriculum design is only part of the task. Professional
development must be provided to assist teachers in dealing with
the new paradigms, suitable texts and materials must be
provided, laboratories may have to be revised, worksites must
be established, and projects must be designed and implemented.
Plans for all these details should be laid out realistically.

Step 9: Evaluate results.

Considerable effort and cost will go into curriculum reform. The implementation plan should include collection of suitable data to document the effects of the reform on student performance. Not all of the desired changes may be possible in the first effort at reform. The concept of continuous improvement should be adopted with the recognition that reform is an ongoing and never-ending effort.

Chapter 4

Improving the Core Curriculum

Gene Bottoms

Making technical courses demanding is a challenge in most American high schools. Students in technical courses are typically those who plan to go to work, attend community colleges or vocational schools, participate in apprenticeship programs, or enter the military after high school graduation. Although many of these students do not plan to enter four-year colleges or universities, the courses they take in high school should not limit their opportunity to make this choice at a later time.

The Southern Regional Education Board's (SREB) *High Schools That Work* (HSTW), a high school reform program that involves more than 800 high schools in twenty-two states, is working to improve the high school experience and is resulting in achievement for these students. SREB and its state partners seek to raise the academic and technical achievement of these young people by asking schools to eliminate the general track and require students to complete an upgraded academic core[1] and either an academic or a career major[2] of their choosing. This demanding and focused curriculum has the potential to take technical courses out of the elective category, allowing teachers to raise standards since every student must complete a major. It ends the student game of searching for easy credits to meet elective requirements.

Every two years, HSTW schools administer an assessment to seniors who have completed career majors. Questions are taken from the data bank of the highly regarded National Assessment for Educational Progress (NAEP) exam. In 1996, only 20 percent of the 20,000 students who participated in the assessment had completed the HSTW-recommended upgraded academic core and career majors. However, the results show that the average reading, mathematics, and science scores of students who had taken challenging academic and technical courses exceeded the performance standards needed to pass general qualifying exams for employment and to pursue further study. Their scores were as much as twenty-five points higher on various parts of the assessment than those of students who had taken a less intensive curriculum.

Yet many students taking part in the 1996 assessment indicated that expectations and standards in their technical courses were low. Only about one-half of the students reported that technical teachers gave them demanding assignments at least once a week that required them to use mathematics or to read and comprehend technical materials. Well over half the students revealed that they never had homework and had never been given joint assignments involving two or more classes.

---

[1] An upgraded academic core consists of four college-prep English credits and three or more credits in mathematics, science, and social studies, with at least two of each in college-prep courses.

[2] A major is a concentration of four or more courses in a career or academic area and two support courses related to the major.

The opportunity to make class presentations and to participate in class projects that related demanding academic and technical material to real-world problems was equally rare. Experience and achievement results make it unmistakably clear that these are the types of engaging learning activities that improve performance and deepen learning.

Making Course Requirements More Challenging

Making Tech Prep work to increase student achievement is as much about redesigning and refocusing high school technical courses as it is about improving academic studies. The purpose of the technical core in high school is to promote student intellectual and personal development and understanding of essential academic and technical concepts in the context of a good career field, while giving students a realistic picture of the work world. For this goal to be achieved, all students need at least five types of experiences. Together, the experiences represent a new vision of what the technical core curriculum should look like. Let's examine each one.

Learning to solve problems. The days of top-down management are fast disappearing in companies across America. This is not happening to the same degree in classrooms. A technical classroom that is intended to prepare students for the type of work environment they will face in the future should model the management style that is becoming most prevalent. Thus, the teacher should act as a coach, not as a source of all knowledge.

Students are given help in learning how to gather information that will enable them to solve problems. They are also given the freedom to search out new uses for and meanings of the information they gather, to test hypotheses, and to arrive at conclusions based on their research. Through this approach to instruction, students learn how to construct new knowledge and go beyond the obvious to uncover new meanings of and uses for this knowledge. This approach moves students from the simple memorization of facts to the acquisition of relevant knowledge. The insights and skills they gain as a result will allow them to continue to learn and grow in further education or in a career.

Using academic skills to solve technical challenges. Most technical teachers do not expect their students to use academic skills in their technical classes. Only about half the students who participated in the 1996 HSTW assessment said academics were emphasized in technical classes, and even fewer reported that they were required to use academic competencies in completing technical course assignments.

Many schools' answer to the academic problems that technical students face is to require them to do fewer of the things at which they most need practice. A strong technical course addresses that need by offering students regular experience in using academic skills as they deal with technical problems related to their courses of study.

Projects related to real-world problems. Much of the instruction in a technical course can be built around challenging projects that allow students to grapple with and find solutions to problems that are similar to those they might encounter in a career. This type of project-based instruction engages students' interest in a way that no textbook can. Teachers who use projects as a central part of their instruction report that students become enthusiastic, motivated, and challenged to put in their best effort. Students' achievements frequently exceed teachers' expectations, and assessment results prove that students have mastered key concepts central to the course goals.

Learning all aspects of an industry. In a challenging technical course, students are exposed to the planning, management, finances, technical and productions skills, underlying principles of technology, labor issues, and the health and safety aspects of the industry they are studying. Most technical instruction in the past has focused primarily on technical and production skills for a particular family of occupations.

This broader approach to instruction is an excellent way to give students a broad understanding of the opportunities that exist in a given industry. With a wider perspective from which to view an industry, students have their eyes opened to many more options in a field than they would in a more narrowly focused program that prepares them for one level of jobs. They also have an informed view of career ladders that will allow them to advance and grow as they gain knowledge and experience.

Learning to work in teams and independently. An HSTW survey of employers of career-bound graduates confirms what other reports have revealed about what employers feel is important. Being able to work as a team member was given priority by 73 percent of the employers, and the ability to work independently was ranked equally high by 63 percent of the employers.

Technical courses that spoon-feed information to students without allowing them the opportunity to work together to find solutions do not prepare them for workplace challenges. Frequent teamwork experiences mixed with assignments that require students to plan and manage individual work assignments to meet deadlines are essential elements of technical courses, and mirror experiences students will face in the workplace.

Creating a Vision of Excellence

With a firm grasp on the types of experiences that students need in today's technical classes, educators are ready to create a unique vision of excellence for the classes they teach. We will explore four areas of the vision:

- What to teach
- Teaching through authentic projects
- How to teach
- Assessing student performance

What to teach

This may be the easiest or the most challenging of the four areas. A previous chapter provides extensive guidance on developing balanced curriculum content based on standards. Within this broad context of the program of study, each individual course must align in a coherent sequence with other courses.

The content of a technical course must reflect the most critical knowledge and skills needed for success in the technical area to which it pertains. There has been a tendency to focus on narrow subskills (or tasks) associated with an occupation with no concern for how the subskills could be applied to larger "real-work" activities. Sorting out what should be taught involves identifying the most important technical, academic, intellectual, and employability skills required by a range of occupations included in the career major(s) to which the course relates. An advisory committee for the career major, including both instructional staff and representatives from business and industry, can be invaluable in identifying these skills.

Teaching through authentic projects

Projects constitute the major learning activities in the new vision of a technical course. Each project involves a complex series of learning activities that together transmit critical course content. An ideal project allows students to plan, collect, and evaluate information; analyze situations; and develop procedures for solving problems typically encountered in the workplace.

In the process of completing a project, students will learn essential technical skills. They will also be expected to apply academic skills that include writing about their progress, reading technical manuals, using mathematical formulas to arrive at answers, and applying scientific principles. A project may involve designing a product; making parts; assembling, testing, and evaluating a product; developing and/or implementing a plan to meet a community or local business need; or operating a business in the school or community.

Projects require students to become team players and problem solvers. Through the experience, students learn that the ability to solve problems and complete assigned projects on schedule is necessary for success in careers. Most project-based courses require students to complete a series of projects, of varying lengths and complexity.

A final component of any good project is the opportunity for students to report on their work and findings to a panel of outside experts from the career field. Other educators, students, and parents can also be invited to the presentation. This opportunity allows students to showcase their accomplishments and sharpen their communication skills in one culminating activity. The checklist entitled Criteria for Selecting Course Projects, will help teachers evaluate the adequacy of the projects they select to meet course goals.

Criteria for Selecting Course Projects

The project:

- Relates to work that would be done in a real workplace.

- Presents problems and open-ended situations.

- Requires students to organize information, consider alternatives, and use higher-order thinking skills.

- Requires students to apply academic skills needed in the career field.

- Involves both individual effort and teamwork.

- Helps students understand and use the major technology and other authentic tools and materials representative of a career field.

- Allows students to present their projects to an audience of educators, students, and representatives from the career field.

- Has clearly defined quality standards that students can use to evaluate their work and take corrective action.

The mechanical engineering program at Brooklyn Tech in Brooklyn, New York, offers an example of what can happen when a curriculum is redesigned. Enrollment soared after the program adopted a hands-on, problem-solving approach focusing on lab-type activities and projects. Students work on six major problems in the eleventh-grade course; time limits and open-ended design briefs are their only parameters. In the twelfth grade, students work in teams on projects of their own choosing. The open-ended approach sparks student creativity. "We want the students to see that most problems have a wide variety of possible solutions," instructor Edward Goldman explains.

This program's success is repeated in many other technical classes, where course projects have been greeted with enthusiasm by students and have brought them to new levels of achievement. Second-year students in the manufacturing engineering technology program at Libbey High School in Toledo, Ohio, work in self-managed teams to build machine systems for local companies. They apply the skills they've learned during the first year of classes to real problems. The instructor provides technical assistance and teaches additional skills as needed.

At Topeka West High School in Topeka, Kansas, technical and foreign language students worked together to select and do market research on a product for export. Teams of students in an advanced marketing course at McLean High School in McLean, Virginia, devised creative solutions to help a struggling bakery and catering business. The business owner gained some innovative strategies without having to hire a high-priced marketing consultant.

How to teach

A technical classroom committed to the new vision is a busy place that to the casual observer may seem disorganized or even out of control. Students are engaged in a variety of activities. Some may be at computers, searching the Internet for information, preparing CAD drawings, completing desktop publishing projects, or putting the finishing touches on written reports. Teams of students may be debating various options for solving a problem or trying an experiment. Some students may be quietly reading while others are working on models or testing prototypes. The teacher moves from one group to another, asking questions, suggesting options, pointing out problems, or indicating sources of information.

Alternatively, the classroom may be empty because students are visiting other parts of the campus or are out in the community researching problems and working on projects. The teacher keeps students moving forward in their active pursuit of learning. Because students are busily engaged in interesting activities, what you don't see is students slumped in their seats with the bored, glazed-eye look that is so common in traditional classrooms.

Without a strong instructional plan this organized, constructive chaos can become simply chaos. In developing an instructional plan that will work, technical teachers must answer several critical questions. They will need to determine:

- **How to introduce the project** to get student buy-in from the outset. The teacher should help students envision what they are expected to accomplish. One effective strategy is to take students to worksites. Another is to show examples of projects completed by former students.

- **How students will work on the project** to develop both teamwork and independent learning skills. Teachers will need to give students guidelines for effective teamwork, since often this is a new experience for many of them.

- **What students will be expected to do** to complete the project. The teacher should be very specific about how much he or she will lecture and demonstrate, and how much research and independent problem solving by the students is involved.

- **How students will access resources** they will need to complete the project. If students will need to use the Internet and school library to complete research, access must be ensured. If outside experts or other teachers are to be resources, their cooperation must be obtained in advance.

- **How students will be kept on course** as they work on projects. The teacher will need to determine when and how he or she will intervene as students work through projects. Setting students free to construct their own knowledge still requires strong teacher involvement to make sure students do not stray from their goals.

Assessing student performance

When student expectations and instructional strategies change, the purpose and nature of assessment will change too. Assessment becomes a tool for helping students improve—not a way of punishing poor performance. Tests will no longer assess students' ability to memorize unrelated facts. Instead they will be used to assess students' knowledge and understanding of a body of technical and related academic concepts.

Evaluation of what students produce and their ability to explain, analyze, and apply the knowledge they have gained is another important dimension of performance-based assessment.

Strategies should include evaluation of student products, review of portfolios outlining the processes students have followed to complete projects, and written and oral reports about what they have done and what they have learned.

In good technical courses, teachers help students learn how to assess their own performance and take the steps necessary to make improvements. Student assessment can be a valuable tool both to help the student improve and to help the teacher make adjustments in teaching approaches. A teacher at one HSTW site developed a simple questionnaire she asks students to complete each week. Students answer these questions:

1. What did I learn best this week?

2. What do I still need to work on?

3. What can I change that would improve my learning?

4. What could the teacher have done differently to help me improve my skills?

The responses have enabled the teacher to see what she can do differently and where students need help. Even better, as a result of this exercise, the teacher has seen students mature in their views of themselves and become much more responsible.

Creating a Course Syllabus

Imparting a new vision for a technical course to students, parents, and other educators requires the development of a clear and comprehensive syllabus outlining important expectations. There are seven parts to this type of syllabus, each of which we will discuss here.

Part 1—Course Description. This is a three- or four-sentence overview of the course, similar to what might appear in a course catalog. The description should include five vital pieces of information: (1) a one-sentence explanation of the course aim; (2) where the course fits within the program of study; (3) topics that will be covered and expectations for student involvement such as job shadowing, internships, or project-based assignments; (4) the length of the course; and (5) prerequisites.

Part 2—Instructional Philosophy. This section of the syllabus is where the instructor states what will be taught, how it will be taught, course standards, expectations for student performance, and how students will be evaluated.

Part 3—Major Course Goals. The course goals are the major competencies students are expected to acquire. Goals are best limited to eight to ten broad statements that identify the work students will do. The goals are not a recitation of narrow subskills or tasks necessary to complete the course.

Part 4—Major Course Projects. The projects selected to help students acquire the competencies described in the course goals are listed in sequential order in the syllabus.

Part 5—Project Outlines. The syllabus should include an outline for each project in the course. The outlines provide guidelines for what students will be expected to do and under what circumstances, quality standards to be applied, and grading criteria. The outlines include the following information:

- **Situation or Problem**—*A two- or three-sentence description of the problem students will explore*

- **Project Description or Purpose**—*A concise explanation of what the final project outcome is expected to be—a product, a process, a research report, an oral presentation, or a combination of several of these elements*

- **Performance Specifications**—*A list of criteria or quality standards the project must meet*

- **Rules**—*Guidelines for carrying out the project*

- **Assessment**—*An explanation of how student performance will be evaluated*

Part 6—Instructional Delivery Plan. This section of the syllabus outlines the instructional delivery plan the teacher has decided to use. How teams will be organized, what responsibilities each student has, and the requirements for reporting on work are explained here.

Part 7—Assessment. The last part of the syllabus explains how student work will be assessed. Two pieces of information are essential here. The first is a chart showing the evaluation criteria to be used and the weight each will carry. Criteria that might be included are daily participation, projects, performance, tests, and a final examination. The second essential element is a grading scale describing the level of performance expected to earn various letter grades. This portion of the syllabus sets out clearly the relative importance of various criteria and the conditions under which a student's work will be awarded various grades on the scale.

Putting It All Together

Courses rigorous enough to give students the deep understanding of academic and technical content required for continued learning will engage them in a wide range of activities.[3] Students will develop the ability to solve problems both in teams and independently. Course content that is relevant to real-life situations will both motivate students to do their best and prepare them for the reality beyond the high school doors. Using academic skills to solve technical problems will help them see the relevance of all the curriculum. This is the challenge technical teachers face. To offer students less is to shortchange them.

---

[3] Information on designing challenging technical courses can be found in *Designing Challenging Vocational Courses: A Guide to Preparing a Syllabus*, Southern Regional Education Board, 592 10th Street NW, Atlanta, GA 30318.

Chapter 5

Designing the New Technical Core

Walter Edling and Dan Hull

Most descriptions of curricula for Tech Prep programs involve a mixture of "what and when" (content, scope, and sequence) and "how, where, who, and why" (techniques, styles, and environment for teaching/learning). The "how, where, who, and why" are discussed in several other chapters of this book; the following remarks deal primarily with the "what and when."

In the early years of Tech Prep (1986-1992), emphasis was placed on helping "neglected majority" students achieve competency in useful academics, and on articulating technical courses between high schools and community colleges (2+2 programs). "Applied" mathematics, science, and communication courses demonstrated that nearly all students

could learn high levels of useful academics if they were taught
in a manner that matched the students' "contextual" learning
styles.[1] Today, many progressive and successful high schools
and Tech Prep consortia hold their students to high expectations
in academic achievement. Major efforts are under way in many
states to eliminate the high school "general track" because it has
provided a plethora of "dumbed down" academic courses
designed to allow social promotion.

But just incorporating high levels of contextual academics
doesn't change a Tech Prep curriculum. In most 2+2
articulations, the core of the technical curricula remained
unchanged from existing voc-ed courses. These focused on
success in fairly narrow skill areas and, as a consequence, did
not require strong academic foundations.

*Two-plus-two articulated programs have not facilitated—
and never will facilitate—an adequate redesign of Tech Prep
curricula. They are seldom more than patch-ups of existing
voc-ed courses at both the secondary and postsecondary levels.
Redesigned Tech Prep curricula (4+2) must include all four
years of high school to allow an effective, efficient sequencing
of academic and technical courses.*

Why is this? Well, first we need to design—and teach—
courses that truly build on prerequisite courses. We now have
some outstanding contextual courses in mathematics, science,
and communication (English). In most instances, much of the
contextualization has been the result of integrating technical
applications into academic courses. That is, much of the
introductory content of early vocational and technical courses
has been added to the academic courses. Unfortunately, that
content is often repeated in traditional vocational courses.

---

[1] Dan Hull, *Opening Minds, Opening Doors: The Rebirth of American
Education* (Waco, Texas: CORD Communications, Inc., 1993), chapters 3
and 4.

Eliminating such redundancy requires sequential planning of courses and content to ensure student mastery of the content of each course before proceeding to the next. The desired practice has been referred to as "build a foundation; build on the foundation."

Curriculum Redundancy—Example

Principles of Technology, a contextual high school physics course, covers the following electronic concepts and practices: voltage, current, resistance, inductance, capacitance, series and parallel circuits, Ohm's law, power (wattage), sinusoidal motion (alternating current), and laboratory experiences measuring and analyzing electronic quantities and phenomena. The course covers about one-third of the content of a traditional vocational course in DC and AC circuits (the introductory course in electronics). To remove redundancy, the vocational courses should be redesigned within a "scope and sequence" curriculum framework. Concepts introduced in the physics course should be expanded to more complex applications, and the goal of the technical course should be to move student development to a significantly higher level than has been the practice in the past. In most Tech Prep programs to date, this type of redesigned curriculum has not yet been achieved.

Building the foundation will not occur if Tech Prep curricular changes don't begin until the eleventh grade. Many Tech Prep fields of study require strong facility in math and science, and most Tech Prep students will require contextually taught academics to develop this facility. We cannot wait until the students are in the eleventh grade; these courses must be offered at least as early as the ninth grade if they are to be foundational. Hence the need for a 4+2 Tech Prep curriculum.

A cornerstone premise of Tech Prep is that the content of the curriculum should be more fully integrated, not only among courses, but also between secondary and postsecondary programs. This premise has not been fully realized. Integration goes far beyond simple articulation agreements, which often serve only to bridge the gaps between uncoordinated courses. This Band-Aid approach does not address the fundamental problem. A well-designed and coordinated 4+2 sequence of courses can produce a much more efficient and effective program of study. Achieving this level of coordination requires a joint curriculum-planning process that does not exist in most schools, at either the secondary or postsecondary level.

Another curriculum practice that must be eliminated is the lack of a focus on a technical concentration or major. As long as isolated technical courses are elective rather than part of a plan of study, we cannot design or expect students to benefit from a sequence of studies.

Is a "coordinated plan of study" another name for tracking? Absolutely not! It shouldn't and won't be if the curriculum framework is very broad at the base (in the ninth and tenth grades) and at the top (eleventh and twelfth grades) involves technical courses common to many occupations within a cluster. This curriculum approach, combined with high-level academics and the infusion of employability (SCANS) skills, will enable high school Tech Prep graduates to be employable in a cluster of different jobs, without compromising their eligibility to pursue further studies and/or advanced skills.

Expectations for New Tech Prep Curricula

A thorough examination of literature in Tech Prep, vo-tech, school-to-work, and other areas of workforce education reveals many opinions about what should and should not be in a new curriculum—but there is an obvious void of designs and examples of new "what and when" curricula. However, there does appear to be some consensus about the expectations for a New Tech Prep curriculum. We should expect a new Tech Prep curriculum to:

1. Involve students early in high school with the exploration, selection, and development of plans for ongoing education and career preparation. This develops their self-determination skills.

2. Allow students to change career majors or higher education goals at any time in high school without incurring severe penalties. This avoids tracking.

3. Renew student interest in school by connecting content with applications in life and work.

4. Develop critical-thinking and problem-solving skills. This requires students to use information, resources, and technology effectively, and to work both cooperatively and independently.

5. Empower students to learn new information and skills throughout their lives, enabling them to survive and grow in a constantly changing culture and work environment. This helps them learn how to learn.

6. Ensure that students reach local, state, national, and international standards for high academic achievement.

7. Optimize the use of students' time by efficient sequencing of content, smooth transitioning from secondary to postsecondary, and elimination of unnecessary duplication or repetition.

Curriculum/Cluster Definitions and Ground Rules

In the last eight to ten years, reports about standards, workforce education, and educational reform have described occupational sectors and curriculum sectors with a wide variety of terms, sometimes with contradictory or ambiguous definitions. Terms such as "job," "occupation," "career, cluster," "major," and "pathway" have appeared in myriad contexts, often with varied explicit or implicit definitions for the same word. The result is predictable confusion and, in some situations, concern about the implications of terminology.

To provide a common language for discussion, and to ensure clarity for the curriculum descriptions in this chapter, some careful review of terminology is necessary. The structures of workforce curricula are linked directly to the skills, knowledge, and attitudes required in the work environment. Any confusion in the use of terms such as "cluster" or "occupation" will give rise to confusion in curriculum design. It is helpful to consider several commonly used terms in a hierarchy from the most specific to the most general.

Job—The applicable dictionary definition of the term "job" is *a specific duty, role, or function.* It refers to the set duties a person is expected to discharge in a given situation. If the person is given a new set of duties, such as after a promotion, the new situation is in fact a different job. In the early days of vocational education, most programs pertained to jobs that changed little over time. A brick mason performed much the same duties over many years, and an "entry-level job" entailed the same duties as one held by a person with more seniority and experience. Today, entry-level duties do not generally reflect what a person may be required to do in future years. With the rapid evolution of technology and information, even the same job may evolve rapidly, with new duties added.

Originally, vocational-education curricula focused heavily on jobs, since they were stable over time. Today, it is recognized that preparing an individual for a single or entry-level job is not an adequate goal for education.

Career—The term "career" has accumulated a range of interpretations in the last few years, even though the relevant dictionary definition is quite clear: *a field or pursuit of consecutive progressive achievement, especially in public, professional, or business life.* The operative phrase, "progressive achievement," speaks to a series of jobs or activities (usually related to one another) that a person performs throughout a lifetime. The conditional phrase referring to the professions reflects the historical use of the term. Today, the term "career" is increasingly used in relation to many areas of work and is not limited to the professions.

As the workplace has evolved, it has been recognized that a person needs to be prepared for progressive responsibilities, not just those at entry level. This shift has implications for educational programs, because the program content is no longer limited to a specific job, with tasks defined explicitly. New content is required that focuses less on job specifics and more on skills in learning, thinking, adapting, and planning, to name only a few. These so-called "higher-order skills" equip the individual to move from job to job in a career.

Education programs designed to provide the student with these skills have been identified with the term "career." The most common examples have been "career education," "career cluster," "career pathway," and "career major." These terms have variations in meaning; however, they have in common a recognition that the education program focus goes beyond a single job and prepares the student, inasmuch as possible, to progress through a series of jobs. *It is important to note that it is neither possible nor desirable to attempt to prepare the student with all the job-specific skills required throughout a career. The key to successful career preparation is a solid foundation and the ability to learn new information, techniques, and practices as they are encountered.*

Occupation—The relevant dictionary definition of the term "occupation" is: *the principal business of one's life,* and the term "vocation" is given as a synonym. Upon reflection, it can be seen that the term "occupation" is closely related to the term "career," even though there are nuances that distinguish the two. As a practical matter, we will regard "occupation" and "career" as roughly synonymous.

Occupational specialty—This is a category of jobs within a career that is commonly recognized by employers. Sometimes this is called a "technical specialty."

Career pathway—This term identifies a coordinated educational process that is designed to prepare the student for a career or occupation, which means, as discussed above, for a series of progressive, related jobs. The career pathway is designed with a specific entry-level job in mind but incorporates broader and more complex skills. The term "career pathway" has been coined by the Tech Prep community to create a program image that is not limited to the job-specific connotations of traditional vocational programs.

Career major—This term is roughly synonymous with "career pathway" but incorporates both the career concept and the academic major concept that have existed in postsecondary and professional education. At the baccalaureate level, a person studying to become a civil engineer is pursuing a career major, since the jobs in civil engineering include junior engineer, senior engineer, engineering supervisor, engineering manager, engineering consultant, and so forth. At the associate degree level, a person may pursue a career major in electromagnetic technology with an entry job as a photonics technician. But that person is also prepared to work in related jobs even if they are not specifically focused on photonics. People with training who do not choose to complete postsecondary programs may enter employment in a variety of electronics-related jobs, but they will likely require more education and training to progress in a career.

Cluster—A cluster is a group of related careers. "Cluster" is the broadest of the terms we will use; nearly all jobs and careers fall into one of a small number of clusters. The cluster model used in this book incorporates nine clusters; however, by combination or further subdivision, cluster models can be designed that involve as few as six or as many as fifteen. The choice of a cluster model serves as an organizing structure for analyzing jobs and careers and for designing curricula, and is somewhat arbitrary.

The operative mechanism in using clusters is the search for common content among the careers in a cluster to minimize the number of separate courses required to prepare students for those careers. From the viewpoint of the student, clustering of courses provides more flexibility and effectively delays the career choices they need to make. Clusters include careers that require postsecondary education as well as those that do not; consequently, tracking is eliminated. *The option for a student to switch to a different cluster is kept open at all times.*

One grouping of career clusters and career majors is shown in Figure 1.

For example, one specialty within the electromagnetic career major is photonics technology. Photonics technologists design, develop, install, and maintain equipment that uses light, lasers, optics, fiber optics, and electronics. Between 300,000 and 500,000 people work in photonics occupations for over 2000 employers in the United States in fields such as telecommunication, medicine, and automobile manufacturing and repair. Photonics workers include engineers, technicians, assemblers, maintenance people, and sales people.

CAREER CLUSTERS	CAREER MAJORS	
Business, Marketing, and Management Occupations	1. Management 2. Finance 3. Administrative Support	4. Marketing 5. Computer Network Systems
Engineering and Science-Related Occupations	6. Electromagnetic Technology 7. Mechanical Technology	8. Chemical Technology 9. Earth and Atmospheric Technology
Health Occupations	10. Health Diagnostics 11. Health Therapy	12. Health Support
Community and Consumer Service Occupations	13. Legal Services 14. Counseling Services 15. Public Safety 16. Regional Development 17. Grooming Services	18. Family Services 19. Hospitality/Travel 20. Cleaning Services 21. Food Technologies
Arts, Media, and Communications Occupations	22. Creative Arts 23. Applied Arts 24. Liberal Arts	25. Education 26. Information Services 27. Publishing Services
Agriculture, Forestry, and Natural Resources Occupations	28. Agriculture and Conservation	
Construction Occupations	29. Construction Trades	
Service Technician Occupations	30. Light Mechanical Service 31. Heavy Mechanical Service	32. Transportation Service and Repair
Manufacturing and Production Related Occupations	33. Industrial Design, Research and Development 34. Manufacturing and Production Operations	35. Industrial Maintenance 36. Industrial Support 37. Transportation Operations

Figure 1. Career clusters and career majors

Common core curriculum—Courses required of all students to graduate from high school (math, English, social studies, science, technology, physical education, and health).

Cluster core curriculum—Courses that fall outside the common core but that are needed by all careers in a cluster.

Career major core curriculum—Courses, beyond the cluster core, required for a career major.

Technical core curriculum—The technical core represents that content that falls outside the common core and the technical specialty.

Technical specialty curriculum—The knowledge and skills, beyond the common, cluster, and career major cores, required for an occupational specialty. Teaching this content may include using projects and internships as well as technical courses.

Related technical curriculum—Technical material that supports and/or expands the technical specialty content and provides students with options to elect specialized skills on an individual basis. These courses are often referred to as technical electives.

Requirements for the Technical Core

With these definitions in mind, and referring back to the seven expectations for new Tech Prep curricula, we can now state the requirements for the technical core.

1. Provides students with opportunities to explore careers and experience the environment of the workplace.

2. Builds on a challenging academic core of courses in mathematics, science, English, social studies, and technology.

3. Addresses skills identified in academic, technical, and employability standards.

4. Includes courses that are common to many occupations within a cluster and a career major, broadening the high school technical core. Specialization occurs later in high school (or, in some cases, after high school), in either postsecondary studies or internships and apprenticeships.

5. Includes at least four courses in high school that provide a technical concentration for a selected cluster and career major. High school graduates are qualified for employment and higher education in their chosen fields.

6. The high school portion of the core articulates, with potential for advanced standing, to an associate degree

program in the career major at a community or technical college (four to six additional technical courses, leading to a concentration [specialization] at the end of two years).

The proposed new (4+2) Tech Prep curriculum model is shown in Figure 2. Common core courses are shown in the clear (unshaded) boxes. These will vary somewhat with different states and localities, depending on graduation requirements of high schools and community colleges. The lightly shaded courses in high school (grades 9-12) and in the postsecondary (grades 13-14) represent the technical core and technical specialty content. The more darkly shaded courses represent the related technical courses.

This curriculum model focuses on the engineering and science-related cluster in which the career major core extends through high school to cover the extensive technological information required in this cluster. In other clusters, the occupational or technical specialty courses may begin in high school depending on the amount of cluster and career major core preparation that is necessary (Figure 3).

Legend:
- ▒ Technical Core and Technical Specialty
- ▓ Related Technical

Subj./Grade	Language Arts	Math	Science	Social Sciences/Humanities	Health/P.E. and Cluster	Cluster and Career Major
9	English I	Algebra I	Contextual Biology/Chemistry or Biology	U.S. History	Basic Computers	Cluster
10	English II	Geometry	Prin. Tech. I or Physics	World History or Government	Health/P.E.	Cluster
11	English III	Algebra II or Math Models	Prin. Tech. II or Chemistry	Foreign Language, Humanities, or Social Sciences	Health/P.E.	Career Major
12	English IV	Precalculus or Internship	Elective (Fine Arts or Science)	Foreign Language, Humanities, or Social Sciences	Career Major Course (Option) or Elective	Career Major
13.1	English Composition	Precalculus or Math Elective	Lab Science		Related Technical	Technical Specialty
13.2	Technical Writing	Calculus or Elective	Lab Science		Related Technical	Technical Specialty
14.1		Technical Specialty Internship	Computer Science	Psychology	Related Technical	Technical Specialty
14.2	Oral Communication	Technical Specialty Internship		Sociology	Related Technical	Technical Specialty

Figure 2. New Tech Prep curriculum model

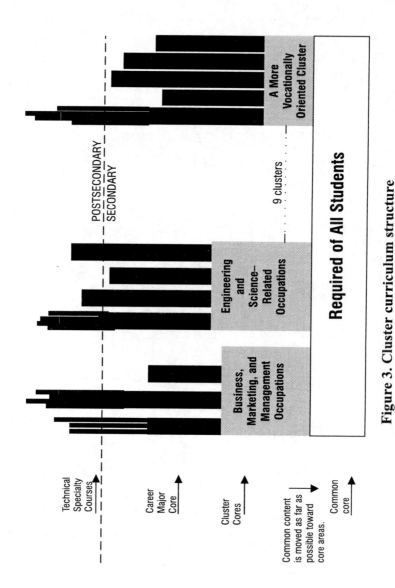

Technical Specialty Courses

Career Major Core

Cluster Cores

Common content is moved as far as possible toward core areas.

Common core

POSTSECONDARY
SECONDARY

A More Vocationally Oriented Cluster

9 clusters

Engineering and Science—Related Occupations

Business, Marketing, and Management Occupations

Required of All Students

Figure 3. Cluster curriculum structure

A First Step in Curriculum Design: Focusing on the Technical Core

The implications of curriculum redesign that responds to all the elements listed are far-reaching. The goals of basing a curriculum on standards and integrating academic and vocational content will affect all areas of the curriculum and may represent an overwhelming task for many schools. Incremental changes will be needed to develop understanding of new curriculum practices in a manageable fashion.

The most obvious difference between the Tech Prep curriculum model in Figure 2 and traditional curricular patterns is the technical core sequence of courses in the secondary program. Designing these courses involves processes that represent a new paradigm for most educators, one that recognizes the shift in vocational/technical programs away from specific jobs and toward careers. The first step in developing this new paradigm is to rethink the curriculum-design process as it applies to the technical core courses. The following points must be considered:

- The "cluster courses" can form the basis for several career majors and a number of technical specialties. Therefore, the design of a cluster course must take into consideration the content of all of the potential career majors and technical specialties. A cluster course designed with only one technical specialty in mind is not a cluster course but only an introductory course to that specialty.

- Similarly, a "career major" course can serve several technical specialties.

- Any content that is common to all technical specialties in a cluster should, if at all possible, be part of a cluster course.

- Any content that is common to all technical specialties in a career major should, if at all possible, be part of a career major course.

In general, these points suggest that the most common content be moved to the earliest possible place in the curriculum. Some exceptions to this practice will be necessary if the common content elements are so advanced—as, for example, in manufacturing—that students are not prepared to deal with them until later in the program. If a significant amount of advanced common material is found, it may be useful to insert a cluster or career major course at the postsecondary level. For the most part, the commonalties reflect basic areas that fit early in the curriculum.

Considering these design parameters, a logical **development process** is as follows:

Step 1: Identify the clusters, career majors, and technical specialties that are needed in the local or regional workforce and for which curricula are to be developed.

Step 2: For each cluster needed, project all the career majors and technical specialties that are likely to be developed in a reasonably foreseeable future.

Step 3: Collect all standards that are relevant to a given cluster. Note that employability standards such as SCANS will also be relevant, as will many of the academic standards. Of course, all occupation-specific standards (skill standards) should be included. If skill standards are not available or are not up to date, groups of employers can be convened to help define the requirements for the technical specialties.

Step 4: Sort the elements of standards into those that are common to all technical specialties, those that are common to all specialties within a career major, and those that are unique to an occupation.

Step 5: The three groupings developed in Step 4 will represent potential content for cluster, career major, and technical specialty courses, respectively.

Step 6: Arrange this content in a trial distribution across the course levels.

Step 7: Develop course goals and objectives and course syllabi. If unreasonable or illogical sequencing of content is evident, adjust as necessary.

The model shown earlier in Figure 2 reflects current experience, which suggests that there is sufficient common content to require two cluster courses and two career major courses in the engineering and science-related occupations cluster. These four courses represent the technical core at the secondary level. In other areas, this allocation of courses may have to be adjusted to reflect the content established from the standards.

In the engineering and science-related example shown, the following two cluster courses are proposed for the ninth and tenth grades:

a. *Technical Practices in Engineering, Science, and Technology—ninth grade*

This course is the introduction to the engineering and science-related career cluster. It provides students with useful learning about and experience in the career major areas and occupations available in this cluster. The information and technology in this course will be applicable to whatever career major a student chooses within the engineering and science-related cluster.

b. *Computer Use in Engineering, Science, and Technology—tenth grade*

This course follows the basic computer course and provides more advanced applications of computers and software that are applicable in engineering, science, and technology. Topics may include computerized data collection, databases, spreadsheets, graphing and drawing software (CAD), basic statistical analysis software, the Internet and other telecommunication links, and the use of programmable calculators, handheld computers, and global position systems.

In the eleventh and twelfth grades are the first two technical courses common to the occupations in the electromagnetic systems career major. These are:

a. *DC and AC Circuits, building on the content learned in the physics* (Principles of Technology) *course*

b. *Digital Electronics and Microprocessors*

If students choose to take another technical course while in high school, it will likely articulate for postsecondary advanced standing at a community college.

Curriculum Integration

Steps 3 through 7 of this process build the framework for integrating and contextualizing these courses and linking the course contents to standards. If academic, employability, and skill standards are analyzed in concert, and if all courses in the proposed sequence are developed simultaneously, integration, contextualization, and linkage to standards become rather straightforward. In traditional curriculum development, courses are developed in isolation, typically by looking only at one set of standards. After course structures are developed in isolation, integration, contextualization, and coordination of content can only be accomplished by retrofitting, which has proven to be cumbersome and ineffective.

The work required to redesign a curriculum to accomplish these goals is substantial, and a challenge for individual schools. Collaboration involving fifteen states is under way to develop detailed syllabi in a dozen or more program areas using the process. The Integrated System for Workforce Education Curricula project[2] has laid the groundwork for carrying out this process; emerging results will soon be available for direct translation to the classroom.

Since standards have been developed in all academic areas, the curriculum-redesign process can be extended to other courses in a curriculum, including those in the common core. The resulting contextualization and broader integration of all aspects of curricula offer a real opportunity to build educational programs that will produce greater achievement and success for all students.

---

[2] Center for Occupational Research and Development, *Curriculum Integrator* (Waco, Texas: CORD Communications, Inc., 1997).

Chapter 6

Focusing Students

Charles Rouse

As American educators prepare for the next century, they should remember the old adage, "Some people go to college; everyone goes to work." They should also remember that "everyone" includes the 70 to 75 percent of American teenagers who will never complete four-year degrees. Pioneers of Tech Prep believe that the fact that so many average high school students are on an educational path to nowhere is the result of neglect on the part of the educational system. Not only should vocational aimlessness be made less common, it should be eliminated. That is, *every* student should have a focus and a plan for entering a career upon graduation.

It is easy for this author, like many other principals and education professionals, to fall into a mind-set that ignores reality. This mind-set holds that (1) the curricula of the general education track, the college-prep track, and the vocational track are sufficient to sort out the needs of each student beyond graduation; and that (2) as long as students meet university entrance requirements and score well on standardized tests, the curricula and teaching methods already in use provide sufficient preparation. That this mind-set is widespread is evidenced by the constant pressure on the part of parent and community organizations to raise standardized test scores and increase enrollments in colleges and universities.

While most educators and parents may believe that higher education is the road to success, the reality is that most teenagers wander through high school and even college with little idea of what comes next. They often flounder in the labor market, wasting a decade or more in intermittent, low-paying jobs. What are schools and businesses doing to give students the appropriate exposure, experience, and education to enter the workforce prepared for shifting economies, improvements in technology, and modern high-performance work organizations? The question should be asked frequently.

Even Tech Prep consortia that have long since adopted sweeping changes in vocational and academic curricula through articulation or applied learning must seriously consider the pathways their students choose as they enter the workforce. Today's students should be prepared to make several career changes during their lifetimes. Tech Prep consortia must look beyond course-by-course workplace connections and vocational skills training and begin to consider the whole of education as preparation for the workplace. They must ensure that, when a Tech Prep student enrolls in a planned sequence of courses, the student has a clear idea of the type of career he or she is preparing for and the nature of the workplace he or she may enter. The student must have a clear understanding of what he or she must do to obtain a job and progress through a career and, more importantly, must have the option of reconsidering and changing from one career to another.

Career Pathways Explained

Like many popular terms in education, the term *career pathways* is used in different contexts to mean different things. For people who want to narrow the focus of secondary education to "job training," career pathways are just another way to track students. This is *not* the purpose of career pathways in Tech Prep programs. The promise of Tech Prep is to open minds and doors, not to close them. Career pathways are intended to help students (with help from their families) to develop career plans to which they can apply their academic and occupational education. The test of whether students are being tracked lies in the curriculum: If it allows students to explore and make career choices without losing options to change their minds or pursue higher education to the limit of their desires and abilities, the students are not being tracked.

Simply put, career pathways are a method of developing and organizing curricula across different strands of careers. The teaching, counseling, and assessment that support career pathways are also designed to focus students toward career goals beyond graduation, the end result being a passport and a portfolio as evidence of work readiness. The objectives of career pathways are to help students:

- understand and consider career options,
- discover workplaces and their relationship to curricula,
- make choices about future education and training,
- understand the expectations for achieving career goals,
- maintain portfolios of progress and achievement, and
- become flexible but focused employees.

If American high schools are going to meet the challenge of educating their students, they must do a better job of preparing those students for the world of work. To accomplish this goal, schools should encourage every student to choose a career

pathway. Every student should have a plan for entering the
workforce or higher education upon graduation.

Career Pathways at Leander High School

Leander (Texas) High School (LHS) has experienced a
significant improvement in student interest and performance as
a result of career pathways. A bedroom community just fifteen
miles north of Austin, Leander is one of a handful of
communities surrounding the Texas capital that have benefited
from high technology. Now a leading center for computer
manufacturing, semiconductor technology, and microelectronics
research, the greater Austin region has seen employment growth
at almost 6 percent annually over the past five to ten years. In
keeping with employment trends, the population in Leander and
similar communities in the Austin area is expected to double in
the next twenty years.

Accommodating the community's steady population growth
has been a tremendous challenge to the education community of
Leander. As in most schools, the process of reform at LHS has
been gradual. Educators were introduced to the concept of
linking education and work when LHS served as a pilot site for
Principles of Technology, an applied physics curriculum that
opened many eyes to the possibilities of students learning
rigorous science and mathematics within the context of work.
Then the process of implementing applied academics and 2+2
got the attention of the business community and the cooperation
of Austin Community College. Tech Prep became a thriving
concept and partnership in Leander and the greater Austin
region. Not only have LHS students benefited from Tech Prep,
businesses such as Dell Computers and IBM have embraced and
enhanced the concept through their active working relationship
with LHS teachers and administrators. By contributing
mentorships, apprenticeships, competency analysis, resources,

and time, the business community has become a driving factor in the continued improvement of Tech Prep.

Positive results of student performance in Tech Prep courses of study proved to the school board, the parents, and the community that the career focus and curriculum relevance were having a strong impact on these students. This success led to the question, "If the career focus for Tech Prep is a strong motivator for some students, what would happen if all students were focused on career paths?" There seemed to be good reason for all LHS students to pursue career pathways.

Thus began LHS' effort to develop a career pathway system that would eventually involve all students and teachers. Cautiously—but eagerly—LHS recruited a business teacher to develop a career pathway in business. The school then developed a second pathway and eventually reached a total of six: business, communication, fine arts, science, service, and technology.

Components of the Leander Career Pathways System

There are five components of the Leander career pathway system: (1) the career pathway portfolio, (2) career education, (3) school/business partnerships, (4) bridge building, and (5) student follow-up and evaluation.

I. The career pathway portfolio

The most important component of the career pathway system is the career pathway portfolio. The portfolio documents the student's successful completion of at least a three-course concentration in one of the six Tech Prep career pathways. Also included in the portfolio are a résumé prepared in the senior year, a letter of introduction from the career pathway director, a letter of recommendation from a teacher, a collection of student work, and a list of accomplishments.

The portfolio, which is developed during the student's four years in high school, provides a cumulative, performance-based assessment of achievements. The portfolio becomes a source of pride for the student and allows the teacher to confirm job readiness and competencies. While putting the portfolio together, the student explores career possibilities and becomes prepared for what lies ahead.

Eventually the student receives a portfolio certificate, or a "passport," indicating which pathway he or she has completed. On the back of the certificate is a list of courses taken along with the teacher's ranking of the student's performance in each course. In addition, each passport outlines the skills and competencies needed to satisfy requirements set by the business partners. The passport then becomes a vital part of the portfolio.

Upon graduation, students can use their portfolios to market their skills and competencies to potential employers. Students will be prepared to compete for more than minimum-wage jobs; a good pathway program can prepare high school graduates to compete for wages starting between nine and ten dollars an hour. Even after a student has finished high school or college, the portfolio can be adjusted to fit new needs or requirements. The portfolio is a flexible tool that is designed to be adaptable to changing career paths.

Today, technology allows students to digitize their portfolios on compact disc. Students can essentially keep computerized chronicles of their high school accomplishments—pathway portfolio information as well as test scores, essays, and even personal anecdotes. With a digital portfolio, employers can learn much of what they need to know about an applicant with the click of a mouse, and the portfolios are easily updated as the student moves beyond high school.

II. Career education

The term "career education" still reminds many educators of the late 1960s movement intended to prepare students for the world of work through the use of revolutionary concepts in curriculum design and teaching. Unfortunately, the foresight and vision of innovators thirty years ago were left behind and dismissed as a fad. In the context of Tech Prep, career education is understood as the process of educating students and preparing teachers and parents and other family members throughout the implementation of the career pathway system.

Career education has three components: (1) curriculum, (2) teaching, and (3) counseling. Each component gives students, faculty, and parents specific goals.

Career Education Goals for Students,
Faculty, and Parents

	Goals
Students	**master the content and understand future options in a chosen career pathway**
Teachers	**balance curriculum requirements while offering unique teaching techniques that focus on each pathway**
Administrators and Counselors	**ensure that all options are available and tailored to address individual student needs during their high school experience and beyond**
Parents and Family	**understand the options available and assist the student in making thoughtful choices about his or her career pathway in school and out of school**

1. A curriculum should balance many driving forces while addressing a common career focus.

When establishing a curriculum for the pathway courses, the school must first examine the curriculum drivers, that is, elements that make up the competencies and skill set. In addition to the usual components—standardized test preparation, university entrance requirements, state requirements, and a district's graduate profile—the curriculum should incorporate components required by businesses at both the national and local levels.

An important first step for LHS was to include skills identified by the Secretary's Commission on Achieving Necessary Skills (SCANS). America has a skills-based economy; it should have skills-based curricula as well. The SCANS skills, validated by Leander's business partners, were the starting point for understanding among teachers of the expectations within and across the curriculum. It has been very important for teachers to understand that their students need to know how to work with resources, information, and systems. Their students must be taught interpersonal skills and must have the foundations of reading, writing, mathematics, and speaking and listening skills. American students need to be able to think in different ways, and they must possess personal qualities such as self-management and integrity.

In addition, teachers should incorporate skills identified by local businesses because that is where most students will begin their careers. This identification can be done through surveys. For example, a high school language arts department could survey local businesses to ascertain the language arts skills needed for entry-level jobs in those businesses. A survey conducted by the language arts department at LHS showed that local business managers identified speaking and listening skills as being of top importance. When the Leander teachers learned this, they incorporated more formal speaking exercises into their curricula.

Besides incorporating appropriate skills into the existing pathway courses, it might be necessary to develop new courses. One successful course could be an introductory course at the freshman level, a career orientation course. In this course, students could be introduced to job trends and the pathways program, and they could be given aptitude tests to help determine their proper pathways. It is important to note that a pathway choice does not "lock" a student into a course of study without the ability to change directions. Students are encouraged to explore within and across pathways to develop more confidence about their future choices.

2. Teaching methods should be in step with changes in the curriculum and reflect the context of each career pathway.

The second vital part of a career education program is the actual teaching. Teachers are an essential part of any career pathway curriculum because they must establish the transition from the classroom to the workplace. Today's curricula are already vastly overcrowded. The only way new skills can be pushed into curricula is through the dedicated, consistent efforts of flexible teachers. Often the process of designing a career pathway curriculum affirms teachers' instincts about outdated teaching material or introduces teachers to new concepts they otherwise would never have found within the school walls.

Teachers at LHS have become fans of the career pathway system because they appreciate the relevance business skills contribute to the learning process. The students have a clear focus. Students who understand their career pathways know that what they are learning in class will be useful to them in the near future. As a result, these students tend to be more motivated to learn and excel. They want more control of their learning and consequently become better students. LHS has found that, through the career pathway system, a small number of dynamic teachers can make a huge difference with the students. If a nucleus of teachers and students believes in career pathways, its enthusiasm can spread to others.

3. *Counseling is the backbone and vital support mechanism for ensuring that each student benefits from the career pathway system.*

Like the teachers, counselors should be educated about the importance of transitioning students beyond school and college and into the world of work. Each counselor at LHS had to develop a full understanding of the process of portfolio development, passports, and courses within each pathway in order to coordinate the efforts of individual students through their pathways. Because counselors provide the most frequent interface with students and parents, success depends on the counselors' choice to make career pathways an effective system for all students. (Hence, counselors are called "gatekeepers.")

Counseling for career pathways is an ongoing process that places counselors in the unique position of being able to see the process from beginning to end. For this reason, LHS involved counselors throughout the development of the system. A counselor's knowledge and experience with parents and students are invaluable in ensuring that all considerations are given attention. As a result of their involvement, the LHS counselors are also better informed and feel more vested in the system when talking with students and parents about its benefits.

Parents and/or family members can become more involved in a student's education than ever before through the career pathway system. Of course, studies only confirm what is understood instinctively by most teachers and educators. Parents and other family members can have the greatest influence in motivating a student to succeed and to develop the confidence needed to master his or her education goals.

Seeking the involvement of family members obviously must begin with their support of the career pathway system. The first question asked by any education professional considering the career pathway system is this: "How do you get family buy-in?" Obviously, many educators have dealt with worried parents and recognize the warning signs of parental discontent with a system such as this one. Experience has shown that the most common objections of parents—that children "shouldn't be forced to lock themselves into a career at such an early age" and that university-bound students do not stand to benefit from the program—are based on misunderstanding. Consequently, as with any new program, conversations and meetings should be held to explain the concept of career pathways and to reassure family members that there are *no barriers to any future destinations.*

The most important point to make with parents is that a career pathway system is designed for all students. When *any* student exits the school system, there is no safety net to support him or her while decisions are being made about the future. Because the training involved in changing career paths *after* school can be expensive and time-consuming, students should become as well informed as they can and choose their career paths wisely. Exposure to a workplace environment and to the skills of a career pathway helps a student make a choice that suits his or her personality and strengths. Isn't it reasonable for all students to have a basic understanding of a career pathway before they begin the career itself?

III. School/business partnerships

The third component of the career pathway system is the school/business partnership. One person should serve as a transition coordinator for the entire pathway process, especially projects involving school/business collaboration. This person should spend time with business representatives one-on-one to fully understand each business's work and required skills. As a conduit of information between businesses and teachers, the coordinator can also promote the partnership and activities within the school.

Some high schools are experimenting with school/business partnerships in which students spend time during the school year at business sites. At LHS, Career Opportunities on Location (often referred to as "COOL week") is a capstone experience that students look forward to year-round. Each spring, groups of juniors spend five consecutive days working at participating businesses. During their week in the workplace, the students are given mock interviews and solve authentic work-related problems. During COOL week, student teams interview employees, research the operations of the company, and learn about corporate culture. At the end of the week, students make presentations to management based on their findings.

In addition to COOL week, LHS conducts a successful mentoring program for students in grades nine through twelve, as well as apprenticeships and internship programs for students who are more focused on their chosen career fields. The personal experience outside the school is even more memorable for students and usually has a strong impact on their performance.

IV. Bridge building

The fourth component of the career pathways system is bridge building. The purpose of bridge building is to give students the tools and techniques to move easily from school to work, military service, or a postsecondary institution. Bridge building is the culmination of four years' work within the career pathways system. By the time a high school student has reached the senior year, counselors and administrators have spent considerable time with the student and his or her parents, reassessing and confirming progress. At this point, each student portfolio contains all the items necessary to document the student's accomplishments over the preceding four years.

During the fall and early spring, a counselor or transition coordinator meets with each senior to discuss the senior's pathway portfolio and plans for the future. A second interview is conducted in late spring, during which more attention is given to the senior's postgraduation plans. At this time, a résumé is developed, the passport certificate, which identifies competencies achieved, is completed, and a recognition ceremony is conducted to present the career passports in the presence of family members. Even after students graduate, the counselors and transition coordinator are available for assistance.

V. Student follow-up and evaluation

Student follow-up is the final component of the career pathways system. By following students after graduation, teachers can better assess what changes and/or improvements are needed. To measure the success of a career pathways system, schools should evaluate increases and decreases in student, family, and business involvement. In addition, annual evaluations should be set in place to review the curriculum and school/business partnership activities. Ultimately, follow-up data and opinion surveys of graduates make it possible for the career pathways system's administrators to analyze the system's long-term impact.

Strategies for Success

Anyone considering the implementation of a career pathways system should take into consideration the lessons learned by LHS. Following are tips for principals on successful implementation.

1. Develop a schoolwide philosophy about preparing students for the world of work.

2. Identify the pathways that best suit your business community and region.

3. Start small—with one or two pathways—so that issues of curriculum design can be worked out and teachers can be brought along slowly.

4. Identify a teacher with leadership qualities to spearhead implementation of the career pathways process. Ensure that he or she has the confidence of other teachers.

5. Survey businesses extensively to determine the skills and competencies they need. Follow up in person to validate curricula and develop channels of communication for a school/business partnership.

6. Give teachers the time and guidance (via professional development) they need to incorporate workplace skills into their curricula.

7. Design passport certificates that appropriately document courses completed and competencies attained. Ensure that these certificates make sense to businesses and that the assessments used validate the level of competence.

8. Select an interest/aptitude inventory that can be used to help students select career pathways. Choices should be made by students and their families, not the school.

9. Provide flexibility in the program and opportunities for students to exercise different pathway options if they become disenchanted with their first choices.

10. Require each student to develop a résumé and provide training on how to do this and to interview for a job.

11. Design a process for developing student portfolios. Include teachers, counselors, and businesses in this process.

12. Recognize students at the completion of their career pathways with a ceremony that involves family.

13. Give all students a chance to experience the workplaces of their career paths. LHS uses the COOL week program. Whatever method is chosen should be named by the students.

14. Build awareness and support among the superintendent and board of trustees before introducing changes.

15. As principal, use every available opportunity, in school and out, to promote the spirit and philosophy of the career pathways system.

Points to Remember When Talking to Parents/Family

1. Career pathways are flexible and allow for students' changes in interests, skills, and choices beyond high school.

2. Students can be involved in more than one pathway. (LHS has had merit scholars complete passports in three or more areas.)

3. Student electives are not a "grab bag," but follow a coherent sequence.

4. Students remain more focused when they have goals in mind.

5. Students learn that seeking employment and pursuing a career involve a systematic process.

6. The passport requirements are rigorous and directly connected to business interests in the real world.

7. The career pathway system is for all students.

The career pathways system is a vehicle through which a school can educate each student to be successful in an ever-changing world. The portfolio is designed to market the skills,

competencies, and attributes that students possess. If students
are counseled about their careers, taught the skills to be
successful in their career areas, and then monitored and assisted
as they enter the workforce, they will have an edge in applying
for jobs and achieving success as adults.

Chapter 7

Removing the Hourglass Approach to Education

Dale Parnell

After spending a lifetime in education (now my forty-eighth year), and after giving close scrutiny to the education reform efforts of the last two decades, I have come to a sobering conclusion. The commitment of the educational establishment, at all levels, to time-defined, time-structured organization is one of the major barriers to lasting progress in education reform. Educational institutions, from kindergarten through graduate school, continue to operate on a system of semesters, grading periods, and hours that largely ignores individual differences in learning speed and learning style. In the vast majority of educational organizations, time is the constant and competence is the variable. The amount of time a learning task should take is predetermined—like sand in an hourglass; everyone has only as much time to complete the task as it takes for the sand to run out.

It is universally recognized by educators that students learn at different speeds. Yet, with rare exceptions, students are still forced to learn whatever they can during a given time period, whether a day, a week, a semester, two years, four years, or twelve years! How many students do you know who are exactly sixteen- or eighteen-week learners? Is it not possible that some students who are now labeled as average or below average learn at different speeds and would do much better if they could go through each learning cycle a few more times? Which is more beneficial to students, to give a final test and a final grade based on what they have learned during a fixed period of time such as a semester, or to test them on what they know and then give them time and an opportunity to learn what they don't?

Probably the greatest obstacle to changing educators' views on the relationship between time and performance is the constant pressure on teachers to cover more and more material in a given period of time. Many teachers fear, with good reason, that contextual teaching and active learning, which are integral to educational reforms like Tech Prep, will not allow time to cover textbook material or follow a required curriculum guide. The need to cover a certain amount of material within a limited amount of time presses teachers and students alike to fall back on the standardized practice of mass production that has remained essentially unchanged for the past one hundred years.

Some History About Time

At the end of the last century, only about 10 percent of the population went to school after the eighth grade. Prior to that time, schools were primarily one-room schoolhouses that served agricultural communities. In fact, some of the agricultural influence remains today. For example, summer vacation grew out of the agricultural need for young people to help in harvesting crops. In Plant City, Florida, a large strawberry-growing center, students at so-called "strawberry schools" help harvest strawberries. The Oregon State University radio station in Corvallis, Oregon, still has the call letters KOAC, which stem from the days when that institution was called Oregon Agricultural College.

The Assembly Line and Mass Production

Then came the industrial age! Fewer people were involved in agriculture and more people stayed in school longer. Questions began to arise about how to meet the educational needs of a diverse and growing school population. The answers were found in the factory model developed by Henry Ford. Educational institutions were organized for assembly-line-style mass production. Scientific management was introduced; teachers, managed by supervisors called principals, deans, or presidents, were thought of as workers whose job was to turn out standardized products in large numbers. Belief in the benefits of standardization became an article of faith in education, but the resulting methods and approaches have become a jail from which schooling at all levels has been unable to escape.

Standardized tests do little to connect subject matter with real-life application or evaluate whether students can solve problems or see things in the mind's eye—both vital competencies for long-term success. We are only now beginning to understand how little standardized multiple-choice tests do to help students become competent at anything—except taking standardized tests. The testing movement, by and large, defies rational observation about how people learn.

IQ tests, which measure primarily verbal and mathematical abilities, are based on the theory that each person possesses a finite, measurable amount of intelligence. As the theory goes, relatively few people have high intelligence, while most have average or below average intelligence—hence the bell-shaped distribution of IQ scores within any given student population. This view of intelligence and ability has led educators to label students with such terms as "able and gifted," "smart," "average," and "special needs" (slow). It is interesting to note that scores on standardized tests such as the ACT (American College Test) or SAT (Scholastic Aptitude Test), both of which are widely used as criteria for college admission, have a bell-shaped distribution almost identical to that of IQ test scores.

Standardized test results often reveal more about upbringing and environment than about ability. Students from time-advantaged homes—homes where the parents talk to their infant children, read to and converse with their young children, and provide their adolescent children with a variety of broadening experiences—tend to do well on standardized tests. This is to be expected, since they have devoted a relatively large amount of time to educational experiences. Students from time-*dis*advantaged homes, on the other hand, many of whom are among the one out of five young people who live below or near the poverty level, are unlikely to have devoted nearly as much time to educational experiences as time-advantaged students. Not surprisingly, they tend to do poorly on standardized tests. This is not to say that they lack ability, rather that they need time and additional educational experiences to catch up. James Coleman observes that variations in family background and the time parents spend with their children make more difference in achievement than do differences in schools.[1]

The most widely used system of standardization of high school credits is still based on the Carnegie unit, the credit that students gain from one yearlong, 180-day high school course.

---

[1] James S. Coleman, "Social Capital, Human Capital, and Schools," *Independent School*, 1988, p. 12.

The Carnegie system, which is based more on seat time than on competence, represents an almost one-hundred-year-old attempt to codify learning. Could the Carnegie unit be transformed into a unit of competence rather than a unit of time? It is unlikely, until the stranglehold of standardized units of *time* can be broken.

Standardized rules and regulations for teacher and administrator licensure and certification relate little to actual performance in the classroom or in administrative offices. Certification in most states is earned primarily by taking a certain number of college- or university-level courses.

Our standardized system of years, semesters, and hours does not take into consideration individual differences in learning speeds and styles. All students are expected to learn whatever schools offer within a given time period. If a student cannot learn what he or she is expected to within that time period, that fact is noted on the student's permanent record in the form of a low or failing grade. Today, assembly-line education, which is an inherited relic of the past, is a significant barrier in the struggle to meet the diverse educational needs of an increasingly diverse population. Any serious attempt at education reform—that is, any attempt that places learning at the heart of the education enterprise—must reverse the traditional relationship between time and competence, treating competence as a constant and time as a variable. Of course, other elements in contemporary educational institutions must be changed as well, but changing education's time-bound structure is critical.

Our current time-bound educational system sorts students on the basis of those who learn within the time allocated and those who do not. To reinforce this sorting process, teachers often grade on the curve and test experts develop norm-based tests.

Extending the School Year

The Boeing Company in Seattle, Washington, has developed an eighteen-week summer Tech Prep internship program (six weeks during each of three consecutive summers) for some 500 high school and community college students. The first summer's session introduces eleventh- and twelfth-grade students to career opportunities in manufacturing and helps them learn basic shop skills that integrate academic and vocational competencies.

The second summer's session is for new high school graduates who are planning to enter community colleges in the fall. Students work on communication skills used in a manufacturing environment and learn teamworking skills.

Finally, the third summer's session, which is for students who are between their first and second years in community colleges, involves mentoring and "job shadowing," where the students work with and learn from Boeing employees on the job.

The internships lengthen the school year for the participating students at little or no cost to the schools. However, the program does require a close working relationship among the high schools, the community colleges, and Boeing. The community colleges recognize this work by granting fifteen quarter hours of college credit toward an associate degree to any student who successfully completes the three summer internships.

Think what this could mean if nearly every employer across the country offered structured summer internships that are closely coordinated with high schools and colleges. Small organizations might be able to take only one or two students, but even that would help. Most high school and college students work during the summer, but that work is not often connected to the students' schooling in any meaningful way. Fortunately, an increasing number of employers are ready to work with schools on programs similar to the one developed by Boeing.

The Standards Movement

Focusing on sorting students is antithetical to helping all students reach higher levels of competence. The goal of politicians and others promoting the standards movement should be to increase student achievement levels. But, before they can reach that laudable goal, these leaders must realize that students learn at different rates and that the very structure of the current educational system works against widespread increases in student achievement.

It is the responsibility of educational leaders at all levels to challenge the current system and to lead in the design of a new system that would give students the time needed to meet the higher standards being instituted across the country. Increasing student achievement does not require lowering the standards but, rather, developing a common understanding that all students will not meet the higher standards within the same time frame.

In most university graduate school programs, teachers give each student an A, a B, or an I (for incomplete). An incomplete remains on a student's record until the student can learn the required material and complete the course. At most graduate schools, the student is given a certain amount of time to complete the course; if he or she fails to complete it within the specified time, the incomplete becomes an F. The more enlightened graduate schools allow the incomplete to remain unchanged on the student record until the course is completed. If the latter practice is good for helping graduate students meet standards, why wouldn't it, or something like it, be good for all students at all levels of education? Because it stresses mastery over time, it encourages the emphasis of the educational process to be on learning rather than on when the sand runs out of one end of the hourglass.

The point is clear: An effective education is one that customizes the education process to match the learning speed and learning style of each student. And so the question becomes obvious: What stands in the way of changing the time-structured organizational patterns of educational institutions? The contemporary demands on educators are mammoth and often unrealistic. Time constraints and community pressures often force teachers to choose between principle and survival. The current national push to increase testing for the purpose of comparing one school to another school, and even one classroom to another classroom, is further entrenching an outmoded mass-production approach to education.

Time for Brain Development

We now know that experiences and environment shape the development of our brains and therefore affect our ability to learn. But active, experience-based learning takes time and cannot usually be achieved in a typical fifty-minute class period. As a consequence, schools continue to take the time-defined approach, providing students with an information-rich but experience-poor education.

The jury is still out as to how, or how much, experience affects the development of the brain. However, an increasing body of research indicates a strong connection between experience and brain development.[2]

It is easy to see how students change both physically and psychologically as they grow and gain experience. Any veteran teacher has observed that, when students are exposed to enriched home environments over time, their ability to learn increases. Since experience affects the structure of physiological organs, it is reasonable to hypothesize that the physical structure

---

[2] See R. Ornstein and F. Thompson, *The Amazing Brain* (Boston: Houghton-Mifflin, 1984); and M. Diamond, *Enriching Heredity: The Impact of Environment on the Anatomy of the Brain* (New York: Macmillan Publishing Company, 1988).

of the brain, which is also a physiological organ, can change if given time to gain appropriate experiences. Allowing sufficient time and experience for brain development is particularly critical in the case of students from impoverished homes, far too many of whom do not complete their high school education. Perhaps more students would do better in school if time were made the variable and competence the constant.

The House Concept and Block Scheduling

The house concept and block scheduling, two promising concepts aimed at giving students time flexibility and a more personalized learning environment, are taking hold in many high schools across the country.

In Providence, Rhode Island, a community high school (grades 9 through 12) called the Metropolitan Center (still under construction) will serve as the hub for a network of twelve smaller schools of some one hundred students each. Each of the smaller schools will focus on community resource activities and lessons. Internships with local employers will also be a core part of the curriculum. The effort is aimed at breaking away from the "cells and bells" approach to school design and scheduling as well as freeing students from the necessity of learning in lockstep with fixed time frames.

Chaska High School in suburban Minneapolis, Minnesota, takes a learner-centered, self-directed approach to education. Operation of this 1600-student school is based on the "house concept." The decentralized schools-within-a-school allow students to have a home base and more personalized attention. The building is designed to support interdisciplinary teaching. Each "house" has its own office and teacher planning areas, where science, mathematics, history, vocational, and English teachers can get together to develop and coordinate lesson plans. Students work at their own pace, often in teams. Students complete some of their work independently using a computer; the computer tracks learning progress and keeps student records.

Reynolds High School in Troutdale, Oregon, a suburb of Portland, also uses the house plan and block scheduling. Reynolds, the largest high school in Oregon, has distinguished itself with many honors. Principal Steve Olczak, a national leader in the Tech Prep and career pathway movement, indicates that block scheduling helps break the time barrier. Students in each house stay with the same group of teachers for a four-hour period each day. Computer stations are available at each house; students often work in teams as well as independently. Removing the time barriers to learning at Reynolds has proven successful; student achievement records at the school continue to climb.

Many more secondary schools across the country are using block scheduling to break the traditional fifty-minute time barrier. Steps must now be taken to ensure, insofar as possible, that students have the time they need to develop required competencies.

Too Much to Cover . . . Not Enough Time!

Textbooks usually determine the content to be covered in a course. Most modern textbook publishers seem to operate on the assumption that more is better. Subject matter is constantly being added to bring books up to date, but very little is deleted. Teachers at all levels of education feel the need to "cover the material," yet they must do so within the constraints of the system of semesters and hours mandated by their institutions. Hence, modern education operates in a state of persistent tension.

How can teachers cover an increasing volume of knowledge (whether students learn it or not) within the fixed amount of time allowed by a time-defined system that has changed little over the last one hundred years? Many teachers fear, with good reason, that encouraging experiential and applied learning in their classrooms will not allow time to cover required textbook and curriculum guide material. As a consequence of the time demands, differences in student learning speed and comprehension are largely ignored.

NYC's Intermediate School 218

Students at New York City's Intermediate School 218 live in a drug-infested area called Washington Heights. By and large, these students come from homes where very little time has been devoted to constructive educational experiences. Concerns of the Children's Aid Society of New York City about the children in this school triggered innovative actions. Late-afternoon and evening programs were initiated to give students additional time to learn. As a way of underscoring the connection between these programs and regular school activities, the programs are referred to as the "extended-day" rather than "after-school" programs.

The Children's Aid Society established an office adjacent to the main school office. A health clinic was established in the school. The clinic is staffed by nurse practitioners and dentists who administer vaccinations, first-aid emergency care, and dental and physical examinations. Healthcare personnel keep in touch with parents on a positive-health basis and encourage parents to visit the school and serve as volunteers.

Adult volunteers help students operate a student store in which students learn about managing, banking, selling, and other business activities. The store gives students an opportunity to engage in active learning in a real-world context. Also, the presence of many adults in and around the school helps to moderate student behavior and provides mentoring services.

Needed: Flexible Time Policies in Education

Most teachers would agree with the premise that how long it takes a student to master a given competency or body of knowledge is not as important as mastery itself. If that premise is true, developing a flexible time policy in educational institutions may be the most important element of any education reform effort, and the implications of such a change are many.

Why shouldn't high schools develop independent study labs that are open after hours and on weekends? Mathematics, reading, and writing labs are standard at most community colleges. Operated on an open-entry basis, these labs are usually supervised by paraprofessionals, teaching assistants, or even volunteers. While the curriculum material used in such labs must be developed by professional teachers, day-to-day operation of the labs can be handled by others.

Why can't the school day be shortened and the school year lengthened? European schools long ago adopted the shorter day-longer year system. In American schools, there is little time for teachers to plan collaborative efforts with colleagues or to work with faculties at other levels to develop continuity in subject matter. Shortening the day and lengthening the year would give teachers the time they need for these activities.

Why can't "work learning" be integrated with "school learning"? The reason this idea has not been widely embraced may be that in the educational arena we tend to think of work outside school as an inferior learning experience. Though the majority of today's high school students work, particularly during the summer, when a student leaves high school before graduating to go to work full time, he or she is written off as a dropout—even though on the job the student may be learning as much as or more than he or she did in school. Of course, no student should be encouraged to drop out of school, but schools should recognize the value of work learning and do more to integrate it with school learning. Much of the discussion in the 1990s about school-to-work transition has centered on helping school officials and employers recognize work learning as a natural extension and enhancement of school learning.

Why can't more textbook publishers package their books with interactive CDs illustrating the difficult concepts in the texts? This would enable students to work on difficult concepts interactively whenever and as often as needed. Computer-assisted instruction offers the same benefits. Educational software, which is becoming more widely available every day, can extend learning time by providing instructional material that supplements classroom work and allows students to repeat the learning cycle as many times as needed for mastery.

The Neighborhood Academic Initiative

The Neighborhood Academic Initiative is a program sponsored by the University of Southern California in Los Angeles. The purpose of the program is to bring students who attend nearby middle schools and high schools to the university campus six days a week to pursue a time-extended course of study. From Monday through Friday, the USC classes start at 7:30 A.M. and run for three or four hours. The students are then bused to their home schools, where they take other courses.

The high school students return to the USC campus for two afternoons a week for one-on-one tutoring. The middle school students are tutored three afternoons a week at their home schools. All students spend Saturday mornings in tutoring sessions at USC; attendance requirements are strictly enforced.

Most of the students in this program come from time-disadvantaged homes. The purpose of the program is to provide the students with experiences similar to those that time-advantaged students might enjoy and to make time the variable in the teaching and learning process.

Many more "why can't" observations could be made, but you get the point. There are ways to make the use of time much more flexible in the schooling process. If we as educators really believe that students learn at different rates, we must restructure school days and school years accordingly. Too often in our educational institutions we have allowed traditional assumptions about how the educational process should work to get in the way of clear thinking about the needs of learners. It is a tricky issue. Educational institutions exist for the purpose of satisfying the needs of students, but they too often meet students on terms that give their own needs higher priority. Habit and precedent are partly to blame. Unless persuaded otherwise, teachers tend to teach the way *they* were taught and organize their schools along familiar, traditional lines.

Ephraim Ben Baruch, a professor at Ben-Gurion University of the Negev in Israel, has studied the impact of various views of time on education in industrialized countries. He postulates that education in modern industrial societies is based on an "hourglass" concept. Every task is allotted a finite amount of time, like sand in one end of an hourglass. Success is achieved by completing each task before the sand runs out.

It is because of this view that the operation of educational institutions is based to such a large extent on fixed units of time—class hours, grading periods, semesters or quarters, and standard-length school years. When student work is assigned and evaluated, time is the constant, competence the variable. Students are told to learn something or master certain competencies within a defined length of time, regardless of individual differences in the ability to acquire, apply, and assimilate knowledge. Students who can accomplish their tasks within the specified time are deemed successful, while students who need more time are not. This paradigm may be applicable to assembly-line production, but it is not applicable to an educational process that recognizes the reality that people learn at different speeds.[3]

Perhaps it is time to revisit Benjamin Bloom's famous concept of "mastery learning," which was first spelled out in

---

[3] Ephraim Ben Baruch, *Conceptions of Time: A Theoretical Framework and Some Implications for Education*, manuscript, 1985, p. 6. Also cited by A. Shapiro, W. Benjamin, J. Hunt, and S. Shapiro in *Curriculum and Schooling: A Practitioner's Guide* (Palm Springs, California: ETC Publications, 1995), p. 217.

1956.[4] In Bloom's model, students are given as much time as they need to learn each lesson and complete each assignment, and the results are assessed in terms of mastery or nonmastery. The teacher works with each student on the way to self-timed mastery, diagnosing problems, assigning rereading and/or restudying where appropriate, and providing special helps such as self-paced technology, tutors, and student coaches (more advanced students who help others). Bloom indicated some forty years ago that one of the worst things we do in education is to deny a student adequate time to master one lesson before moving to the next lesson. Yet, with rare exceptions, that is what is still being done in schools and colleges across America.

There are at least five key factors in learning. Three factors depend on the student and two depend on the teacher. Recognition of these factors sheds fascinating light on the teaching-learning process.

Student-dependent factors are the following:

1. Proficiency in handling time (the amount of time the student needs to master a learning task)

2. Potential for understanding verbal and written instruction

3. Perseverance in the amount of time the learner is willing to spend on a task

Teacher-dependent factors are the following:

1. Quality of instruction (the degree to which a lesson is made real, connected, and understandable for the student)

---

[4] Benjamin S. Bloom, ed., *Taxonomy of Educational Objectives Handbook: Cognitive Domain* (New York: McKay, 1956). See also *All Our Children Learning* (New York: McGraw-Hill), 1981.

2.   Quantity of time allowed for learning (the quantity of
      time allowed for mastery)

The second of the two teacher-dependent factors is our
focus here. Every teacher should examine his or her perspective
on the function of time in the teaching-learning process. Is
flexible time a workable ideal in structuring educational
organizations, or must time remain the constant against which
variations in competence are measured? Unfortunately, because
of education's long-standing tradition of adherence to assembly-
line mass production, it is far too easy to take the latter
approach.

The Search for Synergy

Educational institutions are currently engaged in a "search
for synergy." That is, educators, today more than ever before,
are "practicing what they preach" about how individuals learn.
One hundred years ago, education was part of a society that was
evolving from an agricultural economy into an industrial
economy. Today, education is part of a society that is evolving
from an industrial economy into a technological, information,
and learning economy—and experiencing the same tensions as
occurred one hundred years ago. The evolution taking place
today requires a change in attitudes about the teaching-learning
process, a change in teaching methods, and a change in the way
educational institutions structure the use of time in the learning
process. Change never comes easy! It is the awesome task of
educators to help all of us expand our views about learning and
to ensure, insofar as possible, that all students are given the
same learning opportunities.

True equality of learning opportunity—and the academic
excellence it fosters—will not be achieved unless educational
institutions are willing to adapt what they do to the way students
learn. But they cannot do it alone. The search for synergy will
require the development of new partnerships. The tasks of

developing appropriate educational software, retraining educators, and reorganizing the educational enterprise require broader and more committed cooperation than ever before. No sector of society—education, business, government, or any other—can do it alone. The search for synergy in improving the educational process requires the collaboration of all stakeholders. The fact that this is beginning to happen holds out much hope for the future of education, but, if we are to continue to progress, traditional concepts that are no longer valid—the hourglass concept among them—must be cast aside.

Some Diagnostic Questions

This book sets forth observations about how the Tech Prep movement can continue to evolve and become a major player in education reform efforts. If progress is to be made on that front, it is important that we ask the right questions about our past and current practices in the formal education process. This is just an intelligent way for educators to do some critical thinking about their own institutional practices and move the enterprise up the road a few more miles toward increased student learning. The following questions are offered to give members of local Tech Prep consortia a framework for asking the right questions about the practices of the schools and colleges that make up each consortium.

1. Is time-structured organization the constant, and is individual student competence the variable in your institutions? If so, why?

2. How many students do you know in your institution who could be considered exactly sixteen- or eighteen-week learners? (This is the length of a typical time-structured semester.)

3. Could it be possible that some students who are now labeled "average" or even "below average" (the neglected majority), would learn more and, incidentally, raise

overall school test scores, if they were given the
opportunity to go over the learning cycle a few more
times?

4. When the sand runs out of one end of the hourglass, is
learning over for the students in that class? If they have
not learned what is required in that hourglass time period,
does that mean failing grades that will remain on the
students' records forever? Is that sound educational
practice, or is it malpractice?

5. Which approach will increase student learning: (a) give a
final subject-matter examination and a final grade based
on what has been learned in a fixed period of time such as
a semester, or (b) test on what a student knows and can
do, and then use the test to determine what still needs to
be learned and give some additional time to master that?
Which approach is used in your school or college?

6. Does your institution grade students on the basis of those
who learn within a certain time allocation, or are grades
given upon the basis of subject-matter mastery?

7. Can you identify what stands in the way of changing the
time-structured organizational patterns of the educational
institutions involved in your Tech Prep consortium?

Some Possible Ways to Change the Hourglass Approach to Education

Independent study centers

Every school or college could develop independent study
centers that are open long hours each day and on weekends and
are similar in operation to public libraries. The study materials
should be developed by professional educators, but clerical
people, teaching assistants, or even volunteers could operate the
centers and serve as mentors. Nearly every community college

operates at least one independent study center, and arrangements could be made to place high school materials in these centers and allow high school students to use the centers. The increasing development of the interactive compact disc and computer-assisted instruction materials makes the independent study center an even more likely way to make time the variable and competence the constant in the teaching and learning process. The rapid development of the Internet also holds much promise for the transmission of knowledge through independent study, breaking the time stranglehold that grips much of education.

Simulation

The use of simulation in education is not a futuristic dream. It is already part of the education and training programs of many employers, particularly the military, but it is not widely used in education. With the introduction of the "link trainer" in the late 1950s, the aviation industry took the lead in simulation education and training. Today the dramatic refinements in flight simulation technology have made zero "real plane" time a reality. Simulation duplicates exactly the control-feel dynamics of the airplane during takeoff, cruise, bad weather, wind shears, icy runways, landings, and brake and tire failures. The pilot in training ignores the amount of time it takes to master a given competency. In simulation, time becomes the variable and mastery becomes the constant. Isn't that what we expect of pilots, and isn't that what we should expect of our students? But, is education organized to follow that principle?

Simulation is now being used in foreign language instruction in certain sectors of education. Student work stations are networked to a mainframe computer to track student activity. As an example, a lesson will simulate the student's presence in a Japanese restaurant and ordering from the menu in Japanese. If the student needs help, he or she can call up a glossary showing the English translation of each word. The student can work at his or her own speed until mastery is achieved.

Summer internships

Why not lengthen the school or college year by developing partnerships with employers and establishing structured summer internships that are tied directly to the school curriculum? In this chapter and elsewhere in this book, we have discussed the internship program operated by The Boeing Company. Boeing is a large company, and many will say, "but we don't have a Boeing in our community." However, that should not stop this development. A national Automotive Youth Educational System (AYES) has been developed to encourage auto dealers to offer structured summer internships, not only in the shops but in the front offices, and this program is being implemented across the country. (See chapter 18.) The internship not only offers a way to extend the school year but it offers students practical contextual experience. Any Tech Prep consortium that is not promoting the internship program is missing a grand opportunity to break the 180-day school year stranglehold that grips most of public education.

These are but a few of the many examples of ways to make time the variable and competence the constant in the education process. Leaders of schools and colleges, as well as leaders of Tech Prep consortia across the country, are urged to take on one of the most perplexing issues in education: How can we change the time-structured nature of education to match how individuals learn?

Chapter 8

Portfolios and Performance

Roy Peters Jr.

Mention the word *portfolio* and most people think of artists or models and the portfolios they use to display samples of their best work to prospective employers. Newspaper reporters keep copies of articles they write and publish to illustrate the depth and scope of their writing abilities. A career portfolio is a collection of work that demonstrates the acquisition of important knowledge and skills. It is an effective means of communicating professional growth and achievement.

Experience with portfolios may come early in life. Many first-graders are encouraged to keep examples of their best work—writing assignments, lists of books read, good grades received, and, of course, their works of art. As students progress through school, these collections of work samples become more sophisticated and more reflective of the students' skills and abilities. An artist applying for a position in an art show might carry a large folio of work to an interview. Performing artists might include videos of their performances in their portfolios. To help prospective employers evaluate the skills mastered during their occupational education programs, Tech Prep students would include items such as competency certificates, examples of projects, photographs, and letters from their instructors.

Portfolios Should Serve All Students

The process of keeping portfolios allows students to document their accomplishments and goals. Tech Prep students should develop individualized career portfolios that, by highlighting their best work, trace their progress from each phase of their education and training to the next. A complete portfolio might include grade reports, awards and honors, journal entries, competency profiles, examples of school assignments, and a summary of work experience (both paid and unpaid). The career portfolio is a student-developed tool the student can use to document the acquisition of competencies that are necessary for success in the classroom and/or on the job.

Tech Prep students can use portfolios to document competencies acquired in academic and technical classes as well as through worksite experiences. Portfolios can then serve as useful tools in evaluating candidates for scholarships, internships, and apprenticeships. Depending on the articulation agreements in place, portfolios can also serve as a basis for, or at least provide documents pertaining to, evaluating students for advanced standing or academic credit at postsecondary institutions.

The Purpose of the Portfolio

The debate over portfolios usually centers around whether they should be taken into consideration in high-stakes assessment (e.g., assessment of a student's qualifications for admission to a highly selective college) or should be used simply as a means of showcasing student abilities to potential employers. The problem with using portfolios in high-stakes assessment is that they are not standardized and are therefore difficult to grade and defend. Because grading portfolios is more subjective than grading multiple-choice tests, studies of the validity of portfolios are difficult to conduct. While portfolios *can* be proven as reliable measures through an interrater reliability process (i.e., using multiple raters who achieve similar scores), most educators would agree that the portfolio should be *part of* the assessment process rather than a *replacement for* more traditional assessments such as standardized tests.

In *Frames of Mind: A Theory of Multiple Intelligences*, Howard Gardner argues that some students possess a "test-smarts" intelligence that enables them to perform well on standardized tests such as those used to award scholarships and grant college admission. At the same time, he points out, many students who fail to perform well on the same tests have other abilities that are valuable both inside and outside school. Consequently, standardized test scores may not be accurate predictors of how students will perform in the workplace.

If Gardner is correct, and many employers would probably agree that he is, employers need some means other than standardized test scores for evaluating the skill levels of graduates of secondary and postsecondary institutions, particularly graduates of occupational training programs. Employers need to see a variety of specific indicators of student achievement—diplomas, transcripts, teacher evaluations, and the like. Too often educators receive complaints about graduates *after* they are hired. If the employers had investigated the students' school work, they could have predicted gaps in work skills.

A portfolio is an ideal mechanism for communicating these work skills clearly to potential employers. For example, employability skills—dependability, teamwork, initiative, follow-through, and interpersonal skills—cannot be assessed on objective tests. They *can* be assessed, however, from entries in a student's career portfolio, which may include letters of recommendation from teachers and employers, videos of the student making a presentation or facilitating a meeting, photographs of completed projects, and other items.

There is definitely a place for both objective assessments (e.g., multiple-choice tests) and subjective assessments (e.g., portfolios) in education. When both types of assessment are used, the teacher or potential employer gets a realistic picture of the student's abilities—including not only what the student *has* accomplished but also what the student *can* accomplish.

The Benefits of the Portfolio

As students develop their portfolios, they learn the importance of monitoring their educational progress and career-planning activities. The portfolio-development process teaches students how to highlight their best technical skills. This proves to be a valuable skill in itself in the students' future job searches. Students benefit from the process of developing and maintaining portfolios by

- learning to take responsibility for compiling portfolio materials that best demonstrate their strengths and skills,

- increasing their awareness of the relationship between their growth and achievement and the attainment of their career goals,

- learning to select the accomplishments that will best sell them to employers and address marketplace needs,

- learning more about careers in their fields of interest as well as the courses and skills necessary for effectively pursuing those careers, and

- improving writing, research, and other skills related to portfolio development.

Developing a portfolio is an ongoing process because the portfolio must be edited and expanded as the student adds to his or her accomplishments and acquires new skills or improves existing skills. The benefits of continuously updating the portfolio are that it ensures the relevancy and quality of the portfolio and, even more importantly, that it keeps students focused on their goals. Students are required to collect, select, and reflect. This self-evaluation motivates them to formulate their own criteria for good work, exercise higher-order thinking skills, and engage in problem solving. The career portfolio system gets students actively involved in their own education by requiring them to evaluate their work and plan for future improvements.

Studies have shown that teachers working with students on portfolios are motivated to reevaluate, reorganize, and rework their own teaching methods. Families, too, feel more involved in their students' education when they look at the portfolio. It serves as a forum for discussion of their students' interests, abilities, and aspirations.

Challenges to Consider

Inherent in the advantages of the career portfolio system are several challenges and concerns that must be addressed by both students and teachers. Students must commit the time required to "collect, select, and reflect" in sufficient quantity and quality to make the career portfolio truly indicative of their skills and abilities. Teachers must allow additional time for planning and meeting with students individually to review and comment on their work. The logistics of paying for and storing the portfolio binders or notebooks must also be worked out.

There are concerns that portfolios may overrate students, since students often seek help from their peers, parents, and teachers in revising or rewriting their portfolio entries. This practice raises several questions. Do portfolios accurately reflect the abilities of students? When students have different levels of assistance, can an evaluator, such as a potential employer, trust the portfolio as an accurate indicator of the individual's abilities? How can teamwork efforts be judged accurately? When low-achieving students, for example, have higher scores on group work than on individual work, as is often the case, how much weight should be given to the team scores?

To deal effectively with these challenges and concerns, teachers need in-service training to learn the best techniques for helping students compile effective portfolios. This training should include suggestions on what items should be included in the portfolios, ideas on how these items should be collected and organized, and portfolio-assessment strategies. Because the career portfolio system calls for new training for teachers, it is also essential that administrators support the philosophy of portfolios as part of the instructional process. The career portfolio system is much more successful if it is enthusiastically endorsed by the school's administration, teachers, and student services staff. These key people must provide encouragement, guidance, and support for the process of portfolio development.

Components of a Portfolio

There are no required portfolio components. Portfolio content will vary from one student to the next, depending on each student's educational goals and experiences in school. The career portfolio is truly a student-managed record of experiences and projects. The following model lists elements that should be considered for inclusion in the career portfolio.

Career portfolio model: Possible components

1. Documentation of educational skills

    - technical skills acquired

    - academic skills acquired

    - transcripts

- photographs, videos, and artwork from class projects
- test scores from courses taken, ACT score, or SAT score
- documents stemming from writing or research projects

2. Documentation of job-related skills

- documents pertaining to internships or shadowing experiences
- skills demonstrated on the job
- documents stemming from class projects
- competency certificates
- photographs or videos of work projects
- instructor or mentor evaluations
- progress reports

3. Documentation of employability skills

- teamwork and interpersonal skills
- good attendance and punctuality
- dependability and the willingness to take initiative
- written and verbal communication skills
- critical thinking and problem-solving skills

4. Career development plan

- résumé
- letters of application
- letters of reference
- career assessments

- aptitude, interest, ability inventories
- descriptions of career and educational goals
- four- or six-year plans of study, or locally developed student plans

5. Documentation of activities, awards, and community service

- leadership activities
- participation in sports, clubs, hobbies, and extracurricular activities
- awards
- community service

Building a Portfolio

Most Tech Prep students begin their portfolios in traditional paper and folder format. The students must realize from the start that a career portfolio represents performance over a period of time and that it will change accordingly. Just as the students' parents periodically update the news clippings, snapshots, report cards, and artwork displayed on their refrigerators to spotlight their children's most recent accomplishments, students will revise and edit their portfolios to represent their most current competencies and achievements.

The sophistication of a student's portfolio will evolve over time as well. For example, the portfolio of an eleventh-grade health occupations student applying for an after-school job might be a three-ring binder or a folder containing letters of reference from teachers, vocational student contest results, photographs of a health fair project, and comparable items. By the time this student has advanced through Tech Prep to the postsecondary level, he or she may have produced videos demonstrating various tasks and interactions with patients during an internship at a local hospital.

The foundation of career portfolio development is management. Students just beginning the process should discuss with their teachers various items that could be included in the portfolios and on what basis they should be selected. Below are four steps that students should follow as they work through the portfolio development process.

- *Collecting.* Begin the process of portfolio development by collecting items for a working portfolio. Include samples of favorite projects or work. As the number of work samples increases, evaluate and select favorite pieces to display in the career portfolio.

- *Organizing.* Organize the portfolio in a three-ring notebook, in a folder, or on diskette. Include a letter of introduction, table of contents, and statement of purpose. These will assist the reader in reviewing the portfolio.

- *Reviewing.* List all items in the portfolio. Edit the list and expand the portfolio as you add to your accomplishments and acquire new skills or improve existing skills. This ongoing review process will ensure the relevance and quality of the portfolio's content.

- *Updating.* Review the portfolio often and update the content so that it represents your best work. Continue to add materials such as awards, certificates, and samples of work. Keep duplicate copies of the components in case the portfolio is lost.

The Portfolio As a Performance Assessment

Most assessment in school is short-term—a chapter quiz, a semester test, or a test of a specific skill competency. Ironically, when students leave school to go to work, they enter a world of long-term projects—projects that demand the ability to manage and evaluate oneself, to learn from trial and error, to monitor and revise processes, to work effectively as part of a team, and to make subjective judgments. Portfolios offer a way to assess learning and performance by a means other than assessing a student's ability to memorize facts. Portfolios help students connect what they are learning in the classroom to jobs they will perform after they are out of school.

Portfolios give students the opportunity to evaluate themselves and grow from their own evaluations, but a portfolio is ultimately a shared responsibility. Whereas, in traditional assessments, students are graded by their teachers—often on their first draft or on a small portion of their actual knowledge of a subject—portfolio assessment involves students, teachers, parents, and even employers from the community. This is not to suggest that portfolio assessment should replace traditional forms of assessment but, rather, that a student's portfolio is a valid source of information and should be taken into consideration as part of the overall assessment process. Portfolios allow teachers and schools to focus on student outcomes. Additionally, they provide prospective employers with evidence of student achievement and give them opportunity to interact with students. For example, employers in the community might visit the school to review student portfolios and provide feedback to students. These employers could indicate whether the students would qualify for jobs in their respective companies. They might also suggest ways in which the students could improve their employability skills and give the students tips for documenting their strengths in their portfolios.

The important thing to remember is that portfolios are not intended to sift out students but, rather, to serve as information tools. They are not meant to replace objective assessments but can be used along with objective measures to provide more information about students. In *Portfolio Assessment,* Allan De Fina says standardized tests show only the product; they provide no clues as to how students produced the product. Portfolios, on the other hand, reveal their process of production.[1] Portfolios motivate students to participate in learning, self-evaluation, and goal setting. Both types of assessment are valuable in preparing students to be effective employees.

---

[1] Allan A. De Fina, *Portfolio Assessment: Getting Started* (New York: Scholastic Professional Books, 1996).

Chapter 9

Changes for Community Colleges

David Pierce and Dan Hull

From 1990 to 1998, most community colleges were not significantly affected by Tech Prep. Articulation agreements were built around the colleges' existing curricula, which required little change except for DACUM activities and new courses requested by employers. New Tech Prep students for this community college/high school partnership began at the beginning—in the high school.

Big changes took place in high school, with the teaching of applied academics and the curricular adjustments in vocational courses required for them to fit into the articulation agreements. In some consortia, many Tech Prep students have transitioned from high school to community colleges, and many of these colleges have responded by making systemic adjustments to

151

curricula and teaching styles. But most community colleges are only now beginning to see the critical mass of Tech Prep students required to trigger these adjustments.

Nearly half a million Tech Prep students graduate from high school each year, and many want to make a smooth transition to community or technical colleges. These students have above-average academic achievement, know what they want to study and eventually work at, and can use computers proficiently. In addition, many of them have completed the first several courses in their technical core curricula. The challenge for community colleges is to ensure that these students feel that the college is prepared to serve their unique needs and abilities and enable them to advance in their career preparation.

Tech Prep has evolved into one of the most important and revolutionary educational reform efforts of the twentieth century. Properly constructed as a cooperative effort among high schools, community colleges, and employers, Tech Prep can raise the proficiency of the workforce, increase the number of students enrolling in community colleges, and reduce the dropout rate in high schools. Tech Prep provides a structure for involving all parties who have an interest in producing technically skilled workers. If implemented properly, Tech Prep will produce much improved teaching and learning, stronger incentives for students to pursue their goals, and a much higher-quality workforce. It is a win-win program, but, for it to be completely effective, community college leaders must develop an informed commitment to Tech Prep and sustain this commitment over time.

This commitment will involve the decision to make sweeping changes. These include redesigning and upgrading curricula for technical courses so they provide advanced knowledge and develop significant skills in students, requiring the use of contextual teaching methods, and becoming lifetime credentialing agents for Tech Prep students.

Internal changes are also required in the way faculty members teach to the diverse learning styles of students. External changes are required to enable the college to become something of an extension of the high school campus. This presents an opportunity to allow high school students to share in technical courses and to use laboratories on the college campus, thus building cooperation between education providers and exposing secondary students to the postsecondary environment.

Providing Advanced Skills—New Curricula

It is quite possible that nothing is as important to the teaching/learning process as curriculum design. Poor design— that is, design that lacks clear goals—is difficult if not impossible to overcome.

In general, curriculum design should focus on a six-year (4+2) span of time. By thinking in terms of six years, curriculum designers should have ample time to develop a sequence of learning modules that leads to attainment of the highest skills required by the associate degree. In effect, the end point for skill requirement becomes the starting point for curriculum design. It then becomes a matter of designing back from that point toward the entry point for students, which typically occurs at the beginning of the freshman year in high school. Each course must build on the one preceding and lead logically to the one that follows. In this way, students are challenged, time is used efficiently, and the end result is a useful, marketable product.

Advanced-skills programs

A question frequently asked is whether all programs should be "advanced-skills" programs. The answer is a guarded "yes." Certainly all programs properly designed and supported by a Tech Prep consortium should be considered advanced skills, unless they are designed for adult students who are not coming directly from high school. Even then, if a proper bridge program exists, the technical program should be at the advanced-skills level.

For over two decades, typical new students at community and technical colleges have entered with deficient achievement levels in mathematics, science, and communication (English) skills.[1] Most AAS programs in community colleges were designed for those typical students. It has been difficult, if not impossible, to design a two-year advanced-skills curriculum for students requiring remediation. Yet, some advanced-skills curricula have been designed at community colleges for Tech Prep students. But in many instances, there has not been a critical mass of these students to justify the effort and expense. As larger numbers of high school Tech Prep graduates enter community colleges, this situation is changing. With this change in the student body, there should be a change in postsecondary curricula.

Programs that do not teach advanced levels of academics and skills, even if they are well-designed programs, probably should not be considered associate degree programs but, rather, candidates for certificate program status. It should be remembered that an associate degree signifies the completion of an organized course of study that includes a general education core. An associate degree program should cover the knowledge required for a person to be a competent, responsible citizen, as well as the knowledge that allows a student to acquire an organized set of technical skills. These skills should satisfy the requirements of the current job market as well as lay the groundwork for future job requirements.

---

[1] In 1995, 56 percent of students entering community college were placed in remedial mathematics before algebra I. See the AMATYC study entitled *Crossroads in Mathematics: Standards for Introductory Mathematics Before Calculus* (Memphis, Tennessee: Prentice-Hall, 1995), ix.

The emerging availability and use of occupational skill standards also influence curriculum design. In large part, these standards are being developed and, in effect, certified by the industries involved. Skill standards are fast becoming benchmarks for use in curriculum building and will increasingly serve to determine when advanced skills have been attained.

Advanced-skills programs could also address cross training. In cross training, a student pursues competence in one specialization in high school and competence in a different but usually related specialization at a postsecondary school. For example, the initial specialization may be in construction, the second in business management.

Incentives for change

The best incentive for community colleges to change is that growing numbers of better-prepared students are graduating from better high school programs as a result of solid Tech Prep planning and thinking. This provides an unprecedented opportunity for colleges to create programs that produce well-trained graduates with advanced technical skills.

A growing percentage of Tech Prep graduates will apply to community or technical colleges, and they will expect the best in content and teaching methodology. Unless improvements are made, they may be disappointed. Many community colleges have not changed their programs to accommodate Tech Prep graduates. This was commented on recently by the principal of a high school near a highly regarded community college. The principal voiced disappointment over how inadequately the college had adjusted its curricula and teaching strategies to accommodate graduates of her school. She felt that the students were being short-changed and were becoming disillusioned by the community college's apparent lack of responsiveness to positive change at the high school.

Community colleges must recognize when change is occurring and adapt their practices accordingly. Even without curriculum redesign, students can be assessed for and assigned advanced placement. Though this isn't a total solution, it is a start, and may prevent disillusionment while curriculum redesign proceeds.

Requiring Contextual Teaching in Community Colleges

Most high school Tech Prep students are applied, or "contextual," learners. That is, they learn best, are most interested, and reach higher levels of achievement when academic subjects such as mathematics, science, English, and social studies are taught in the context of how they are used in life and work. Contextual learning is enhanced by the use of teaching methods that involve discovery, application, problem solving, cooperative learning, and project-based learning.

Contextual learning is a complex and multifaceted process. It acknowledges that the mind seeks meaning in context and searches for relationships that make sense and appear useful. This is quite different from educational constructs that divide knowledge into separate, largely unrelated "subjects." Contextual learning helps students discover the links between what they know and what they are learning, whether it be in a classroom, in a laboratory, or at a worksite. Educators using a contextual learning approach choose and design learning environments that incorporate as many forms of experience as possible. For instance, a physics class studying thermal conductivity might be given the task of measuring how the quality and amount of insulation material in the school affect the amount of energy needed to heat or cool the building. Students in a geometry class might apply the Pythagorean theorem as they lay out the foundation of a rectangular deck with string and tape measures. Such hands-on activities allow students to *experience* what they are learning.

As Tech Prep students who have benefited from contextual teaching practices leave high school and enter postsecondary studies, their learning styles will pose a challenge for teachers. Community colleges can serve these students best if they incorporate contextual teaching practices. Significant progress has already been made in a few community colleges, including Cuyahoga Community College (CCC) in Cleveland, Ohio, and Firelands College, a campus of Bowling Green State University in Huron, Ohio. Firelands is host to all classes in the eleventh- and twelfth-grade industrial technician Tech Prep program. At CCC, special mathematics courses developed around specific Tech Prep fields of study are taught contextually. A team-taught course combining science and mathematics has also been developed so that students can receive mathematics and science credits for one course. While these courses were originally developed for Tech Prep students, they have been so successful that they are now open to the entire student body. (See chapter 10.)

The Tech Prep programs at CCC and Firelands represent significant but, unfortunately, isolated progress. Most community college faculties have not yet given serious consideration to contextual learning or articulation. Moreover, the CCC and Firelands programs call for a fundamental change in the teaching role—from deliverer of information to learning facilitator—that few instructors have been willing or able to make. By and large, the "sage on the stage" has yet to give way to the "guide on the side."

Faculty resistance to this type of teaching change at the postsecondary level is predictably high—just as it was in high school Tech Prep programs from 1990 through 1995. In the next five to seven years, resources must be provided that will enable community colleges to undertake major efforts to (1) provide information on contextual teaching and learning, (2) offer professional development in contextual teaching and learning, and (3) conduct research on the effects of contextual teaching on Tech Prep student achievement in community colleges. Two national efforts in this area are already under way.

In 1995, the American Association of Community Colleges identified "teaching and learning" as one of its five programmatic themes. This has resulted in an emphasis on their conference agenda and topics for the *Community College Journal,* such as "The Coming Challenge."[2]

In 1995, funded by an NSF grant, the American Mathematical Association of Two-Year Colleges (AMATYC) developed new math standards for community colleges. The standards call for math concepts to be illustrated with real-world examples. AMATYC and CORD have since developed model curriculum elements that integrate the strategies of mathematical modeling, contextual learning, and laboratory exploration. The elements could be used in courses designed to address the needs of contextual learners through hands-on activities, collaborative exercises, and computer simulations. Course materials proposed under the CORD/AMATYC project would include nine algebra modules, each containing workplace scenarios and problem-solving applications; a laboratory equipment list for classroom setup; applications that provide both practical and theoretical grounding in mathematical concepts; a professional development program to prepare teachers in the use of the new materials; and a report on student performance and classroom effectiveness. Development of the materials is awaiting funding.

Project-based learning programs are also being tested at community colleges as a vehicle for introducing contextual teaching practices. For more information, see chapter 12.

---

[2] Dan Hull and John C. Souders Jr., "The Coming Challenge," *Community College Journal,* Vol. 67, No. 2, October/November 1996.

Providing Technical Courses and Laboratories for High School Students

Over 950 Tech Prep articulation agreements have been enacted since 1990. This represents a large, unprecedented interaction among high school mathematics, science, and vocational teachers; community college academic and technical faculties; and representatives of business and industry. Usually, an articulation agreement signifies consensus among these parties about what should be taught, what sequence the technical content should follow, and what constitutes student mastery of course goals and objectives.

With the development of skill, academic, and employability (SCANS) standards and the development of new Tech Prep curricula such as those described in chapters 3, 4, and 5, new mathematics, science, and technical courses must be offered for Tech Prep students in high schools. Many of these courses require new laboratories and teachers with knowledge, skills, and experience that go beyond those of the current high school teaching staff. In some cases, there might not be enough students in a high school Tech Prep program to justify the expense of new labs and teachers. Thus, it makes sense for secondary and postsecondary schools to share their facilities and teaching staffs.

In many cases, agreements have been made for eleventh- and twelfth-grade Tech Prep students to take coursework at their local community colleges. In some consortia, two years of the Tech Prep program are taught at a community or technical college. In others, one year is taught there. For instance, the Trident Area Consortium for the Technologies in Moncks Corner, South Carolina, offers a program that culminates in an accelerated associate degree/youth apprenticeship. In their senior year, high school students receive course instruction at Trident Technical College in coordination with the Robert Bosch Corporation, the company that sponsors the apprenticeship. Upon completion of the program, students receive high school diplomas, associate degrees, and journeyman certification, all within thirteen years.

The advantages of such an arrangement go beyond the cost-effectiveness of eliminating duplication of services; high school students are more highly motivated and develop greater maturity when they study, even part time, at "the college." It is also an excellent opportunity for community colleges to recruit focused, well-prepared students from local high schools. The financial issues related to dual enrollment and reimbursement are not entirely different from those frequently encountered and solved in other articulation agreements.

Other cooperative enrollment agreements have been made. For example, Oklahoma City Community College students can enroll for postsecondary credit in technical courses offered at Francis Tuttle Technology Center (an area vocational technical center), where they can benefit from access to that institution's advanced laboratories and highly skilled faculty.

Lifetime Credentials for Tech Prep Students and Graduates (Alumni)[3]

The expanded vision of Tech Prep includes the reality that most workers will undergo a lifetime of "on again, off again" education and training as they progress in their careers through many changes in jobs and workforce environments.

More than ever before, people need a single entity to evaluate their credentials and maintain a continuous record of them to provide to schools and potential employers. Community colleges are the logical organizations to assume this

---

[3] Private conversations with Dr. Arnold Packer, Johns Hopkins University.

responsibility, and Tech Prep is the ideal program in which to begin. Among the education, training, and work-related experiences that should be analyzed and recorded are the following:

1. High school transcripts and portfolios

2. Standardized tests (state, ACT, and SAT)

3. Worksite learning experiences (internships, apprenticeships, work study assignments, and so forth)

4. Postsecondary courses, certificates, and degrees

5. Continuing education, including courses, seminars, and study tours to enhance work skills, introduce new technology, and develop financial, business, and management abilities

The best criteria by which to evaluate career credentials are the academic, skill, and SCANS standards.

Other Ways Community Colleges Can Serve Tech Prep Students

Community colleges can also provide unique services to young people and adults in Tech Prep programs by doing the following:

1. Giving priority admission status to high school Tech Prep graduates

2. Providing scholarships for all Tech Prep high school graduates admitted to community colleges

3. Providing workplace internships for high school and community college faculty members

4.   Establishing and promoting a bridge program for adults
     wanting to enter community college Tech Prep
     programs[4]

No matter which course community colleges chart for
change, there is no question that the course must be embarked
on, and now is the time to do it. Tech Prep is here to stay, and
students expect community colleges to offer the advantages in
instruction and content they have become accustomed to in high
school Tech Prep programs.

---

[4] Hull, *Opening Minds, Opening Doors*, pp. 144-146.

Chapter 10

Developing Partnerships

Elaine D. Edgar

Issues

Tech Prep prepares students for the technology-based careers of the future—careers that will require at least associate degrees, advanced technical skills, and mastery of higher-level content in mathematics, science, and communication. Partnerships within Tech Prep consortia among educators, employers, and community leaders result in exciting new career pathways to the technology-based occupations of the future.

Providing educational opportunities for students after high school is a critical part of the vision and success of Tech Prep. Because of collaboration among secondary education, higher education, business, and labor, Tech Prep students can pursue uninterrupted curricula through high school and college to earn associate degrees. Tech Prep programs integrate students' educational experiences, foster high academic attainment, and, with the help of industry and labor, establish and verify technical and academic competencies. Tech Prep graduates are both employable and college ready.

A key goal and outcome of Tech Prep is to reduce remediation rates among the program's students. Students in high school Tech Prep classes must acquire competencies in mathematics, science, and communication equivalent to those required of college-preparatory students. This ensures that Tech Prep students will enter colleges and universities "college ready," that is, without need for remediation or developmental courses.

An exemplary Tech Prep program has been established at the Firelands Campus of Bowling Green State University. High school students enrolled in the engineering and industrial technician Tech Prep program take all their classes at the college campus. High school teachers travel to the campus to teach the high school classes; full-time college faculty members teach college-level courses in mathematics, electronics, and manufacturing. High school juniors entering the program take college assessment tests and are placed in a combination of high school and college courses. All of the high school graduates of this Tech Prep program have been able to enter the associate degree program without remediation.

The Firelands program shows that Tech Prep is more than articulation agreements aligning traditional high school vocational programs with college associate degree programs. Tech Prep involves business, industry, and labor partners working together to identify the competencies needed by associate degree graduates, and high school and college faculties working together to develop Tech Prep curricula that meet employers' needs.

Collaboration of this kind is taking place at Cuyahoga Community College (CCC), where faculty members responded to a need for educated technicians in the graphic design/digital imaging/printing industry. After industry representatives identified the required competencies, participating high school instructors realized they needed professional development to help students acquire those competencies. Accordingly, CCC's faculty developed a customized educational program with state-of-the-art digital imaging/printing equipment. The equipment serves as a portable classroom that rotates among high school sites.

The first step in Tech Prep's excellent beginning in Ohio was the formation of an ad hoc committee to establish the state's Tech Prep vision and mission. The committee comprised community and technical college presidents, school superintendents, and representatives of the Ohio Board of Regents and the Ohio Department of Education. The committee decided to make systemic educational change the heart of Ohio's Tech Prep initiative and funded demonstration sites to drive the change at the institutional level. The committee also agreed that Tech Prep would be jointly administered by the Ohio Department of Education and the Ohio Board of Regents. The first five years of implementation have focused on creating Tech Prep consortia throughout the state through competitive grants.

Ohio now has twenty-eight Tech Prep consortia comprising forty-four public colleges, universities, and regional campuses (including all community and technical colleges); all ninety-two vocational education planning districts; over four hundred secondary school districts; and six hundred business, industry, and labor partners—all working together to ensure excellence and the relevance of coursework to the competitiveness of tomorrow's workplace.

Curriculum development in each consortium has been a collaborative process between the state and the local Tech Prep consortium; together these two entities identify and incorporate relevant competencies into school and college programs. The state's role is to help local consortia anticipate needs and problems. Industries with an interest in the proposed program contribute industry-specific information to the consortia, which then develop curricula that address labor market needs in high-technology fields in their regions. For example, plastics is one of Ohio's fastest-growing industries. Members of the Polymer Processors Association, the Society of Plastics Engineers, and plastics industry leaders asked the Ohio Department of Development to develop qualified and highly skilled plastics/polymer technicians for the industry. The Department of Development collaborated with Ohio's Tech Prep program to develop a statewide plastics core curriculum for students in high school and college. First, more than ninety representatives of plastics companies and their education partners identified the core academic, employability, and occupational skills needed by students headed for careers in the plastics industry. Second, a comprehensive statewide plastics/polymer training curriculum for students in high school, apprenticeships, and college was developed and implemented. Then the Plastics Technical Competency Profile, a list of academic and occupational competencies identified by the plastics industry, was published and provided to all participating schools, colleges, universities, and plastics employers. As a result, more than fifty high schools and colleges are implementing the curriculum.

Strategic Plan

To guide the Ohio Tech Prep initiative into the twenty-first century, Tech Prep partners in Ohio developed a plan with two purposes:

1.   To establish a framework—a set of goals and a measurable path of progress—that will ensure the long-term viability of Tech Prep, and

2.   To provide guidance to all Tech Prep stakeholders so that they will share an overall view and direction.

The Ohio Tech Prep plan has four major goals:

1. To provide a seamless education path, including early career exploration, starting in high school and leading to an associate degree, with expanded and enhanced competencies in mathematics, science, communication, and technologies beyond current high school and associate degree programs.

2. To expand the enrollment of Tech Prep students to better serve Ohio's labor market needs. Fifteen percent of all eleventh- and twelfth-grade students in public education will be enrolled in Tech Prep by the year 2000. Sixty-six percent of students completing the high school portion of Tech Prep will directly enroll in state-assisted colleges and universities by the year 2002. Five percent of students enrolled in Tech Prep will be from groups traditionally underrepresented in technology-based occupations.

3. To ensure that teaching and learning reflect the needs of all students.

4. To maximize the opportunities afforded by relevant initiatives, resources, and participating partners.

Communication and management components are being added to the strategic plan. Clear and effective communication is vital to the development of a strong and flexible organization, and the management plan will allow us to monitor our progress in achieving our four goals and in adopting new strategies as required by changing circumstances.

Elements of Success

Several elements are vital to Tech Prep's future in Ohio (and other states). One is to increase student participation in Tech Prep in high schools *and* in colleges and universities to better serve labor market needs. Each consortium needs for all of its members to commit time, energy, and creative thought to this issue. Each local consortium needs to develop local plans to attain the remaining goals and objectives of the Ohio Tech Prep strategic plan. To help local consortia develop their plans, the state is considering a proposal to provide strategic planning assistance. Local strategic plans will be tailored to specific consortium needs and characteristics.

Another vital element is to construct an effective assessment system that will show us how well our students are performing in the new programs. Assessment data are invaluable in maintaining highly effective programs.

The final piece of the puzzle is to define a process for creating curricula in a new manner. To promote systemic educational change, the state has developed a curriculum-creation process called the Technical Competency Profile (TCP). TCP is a method of identifying the occupational, academic, and employability competencies that must be learned during grades nine through twelve and the two years of the associate degree. TCP ensures that all consortium partners agree on the required competencies, so that an uninterrupted curriculum can be created to carry students from high school through the associate degree. All participants in the process commit to meet annually to update the competencies and evaluate their implementation. This commitment means that close relationships must be maintained with local employers. TCP also ensures that students who leave Tech Prep after high school graduation are prepared for work, while students who are going to college enter with higher entry-level occupational skills. These skills enable the students to enroll in advanced courses during their associate degree programs.

As soon as the competencies have been designed, each consortium examines how best to deliver the curriculum while building on local strengths. Colleges share laboratories, facilities, classrooms, and equipment with high schools. This reduces costs by avoiding duplication of expensive resources.

Interdisciplinary teams of high school teachers work together to develop competencies based on industry standards and to shape their classrooms to deliver the competencies. In most consortia, the teams include academic and vocational education high school teachers who, during a shared three-hour block of time, use applied academics and contextual learning methods to teach mathematics, science, and occupational competencies. Many Tech Prep students in these consortia are staying on the cutting edge with summer internships. Such is the case in the Lakeland Consortium.

Lakeland Tech Prep Program

Lakeland Tech Prep Consortium, located twenty miles east of Cleveland, includes thirty-five school districts, four vocational education planning districts, one community college, and one state university. Programs are designed to provide high school students with rich opportunities to prepare for high-tech careers in manufacturing, electronics, health care, and computer information systems technologies. In the eleventh grade, students select one of these four occupational areas along with high-level courses in mathematics, science, and communication. Almost 50 percent of the Tech Prep high school graduates are pursuing associate degrees at Lakeland Community College (LCC).

As part of the consortium's internship program, about forty Tech Prep students have summer jobs related to their career interests. A Tech Prep career services liaison contacts participating companies and provides mentorship training and follow-up consultations throughout the summer. Students get hands-on experience in their chosen fields at twenty-eight companies, ranging from a billion-dollar corporation to a one-person sole proprietorship. Students earn between $6 and $10 an hour, and the companies get great workers. In fact, owners and managers are so enthusiastic about the quality of the students' work that many pay for tuition or provide scholarships to LCC.

Most of the companies continue to employ the students part time while they attend college.

> *Having Tech Prep students working for us may reduce the cost of training for our company because of the wonderful education they had before coming here.*
>
> Leslie Smudz, STERIS Corporation

Additional Activities

To help businesses, LCC, the Center for Business and Industry, and the Lakeland Tech Prep Consortium developed a video and workbook entitled *Mentoring—Cultivating Youth in the Workplace*. A copy is provided to each employer who hires a Tech Prep intern.

A one-page ad thanking employers who hired Tech Prep student interns and hosted teacher externships was placed in the *Lake County Business Journal.* The ad also listed the consortium's web site and the names of the persons who should be contacted for additional information.

> *The Lakeland Tech Prep Consortium extends its heartfelt thanks to those employers who hired Tech Prep student interns and hosted teacher externs during the summer of 1997. These employers nurtured the students by helping them understand the transition from school-to-work and helped the teachers better understand the current needs of business and industry.*
>
> *Lake County Business Journal,* Vol. 7, No. 5, October 1997

Local government economic-development coordinators enacted a tax-abatement agreement that applies to employers who hire Tech Prep interns and/or pay some or all of the students' tuition at LCC.

Higher Education Adaptations

Since Tech Prep students enter college with higher levels of mathematics, science, communication, and technology competencies, colleges and universities are now offering courses with advanced skills. Ohio's program is an advanced-skills model, so the college portion of the curriculum is not abridged. LCC has developed three new introductory courses for all non-Tech Prep students in computer-integrated manufacturing technology. These courses were developed to bridge the gap between Tech Prep students and students with no technical background (Figure 1).

Manufacturing Engineering Technology

MFG 095 Introduction to Machine-Tool Technology   3 Credits
This course is designed to provide students with a thorough and practical working knowledge of the following: shop safety, gauges and calipers, applied shop math and machine tool operations. (5 contact hrs.) (NOTE: Not for Tech Prep Students.)

MFG 096 Introduction to Machine Tool Set-Up and CAM   3 Credits
Prerequisite: MFG 095 or permission of instructor
This course is designed to provide students with a thorough and practical working knowledge of the following: basic jigs and fixtures, machine tool operations, introduction to CAD drawing and basic CNC manual programming. (5 contact hrs.) (NOTE: Not for Tech Prep students.)

MFG 097 Introduction to Electrical Devices and Controls   3 Credits
Prerequisite: MFG 096: MFG 097 may be taken concurrently with MFG 111
This course is designed to provide students with a thorough and practical working knowledge of the following: electrical safety, shop floor electricity, electrical measurements, motors, transformers, controls, and basic PLC installation and program and maintenance. (5 contact hrs.) (NOTE: Not for Tech Prep students.)

NOTE: MFG 111 and 121 require prior exposure to applied technologies or Tech Prep status from high schools. Deficiencies can be made up by taking all or part of a sequence of MFG 095, 096, 097. Non Tech Prep students with prior manufacturing experience should contact the Engineering Technologies Office to schedule proficiency exams for MFG 095, 096 and 097.

Figure 1. Sample page from *Lakeland Community College Catalog 1996-1997*

To provide a seamless path for Tech Prep students pursuing baccalaureate degrees in technology, LCC's engineering technology faculty and administrators developed and signed articulation agreements with Cleveland State University and the University of Toledo for a bachelor's degree in technology.

Shared Facilities, Shared Ideas

LCC shares its laboratory facilities and instructors' expertise with area high schools free of charge as part of the Tech Prep initiative. Over ninety eleventh- and twelfth-grade high school students are bused to the college to use its state-of-the-art laboratory facilities. Students attend the college for three hours each day to take applied physics and communication courses and a course in computer-integrated manufacturing electronics technology or computer information systems. The technical and academic high school teachers interact with LCC faculty members, sharing not only the equipment and facilities but their ideas about Tech Prep. This ensures that the transition from high school to college will be a coherent one.

Since professional development for faculties is critical to the success of Tech Prep in higher education, the Lakeland Tech Prep Consortium developed a series of teaching technology seminars for its faculty. The luncheon seminars are convenient and allow faculty members time to discuss issues related to their classroom teaching and to learn more about Tech Prep. Seminar topics include the following:

- Teamwork (cooperative learning strategies)
- Advanced technology
- The integration of academic and technical concepts
- Instructional strategies (contextual teaching strategies, applied academics)
- Multiple learning styles

- Student assessment techniques (portfolios)

- Principles of TQM

To provide additional professional development opportunities to the college faculty, Tech Prep links with the Excellence in Teaching Committee at the college and with the local public broadcasting station via satellite. Luncheon programs with topics ranging from critical thinking skills to planning for educational technology provide a forum for the faculty to share technology tips and practical information. Other colleges and universities also offer professional development models. For example, Youngstown State University offers a graduate-level course entitled Principles of Conceptual/Applied Teaching and Learning.

Steps for Success

Establishing and sustaining effective partnerships is critical to Tech Prep's success. Steps for sustaining partnerships include the following:

- Share ideas.

- Be honest and truthful.

- Get beyond past issues and barriers.

- Keep focused on Tech Prep students and look at what works best for them.

- Always have a balance of employers and educators on all committees.

- Set realistic goals.

- Develop a strategic plan.

- Implement comprehensive professional development activities for all partners.

- Forge positive relationships with other reform initiatives.

- Keep pushing for change at local, regional, and state levels.

- Keep a sense of humor.

Benefits, Outcomes, and Measurements

When secondary school teachers and college faculty members collaborate in the development and close articulation of Tech Prep programs, everyone benefits. When colleges collaborate with high schools, both provide richer and more coherent educational opportunities for students. Similarly, the professional development opportunities created by colleges, not only for their own faculties but also for high school colleagues, result in positive outcomes for all. Raising the academic rigor in mathematics, science, communication, and technologies is accomplished most effectively when people in both secondary and higher education work together building Tech Prep curricula and learner assessments.

> *I've learned to drink coffee, I'm making money, I haven't missed a day, and I'm enjoying myself!*
>
> Vincent Thomas, Tech Prep student

A key to making systemic change and creating opportunities for students is to work with all partners to develop and implement a strategic plan. First, it is important to establish a framework—a set of goals and a measurable path of progress to ensure the long-term viability of Tech Prep. Second, a strategic plan provides guidance, ensuring that all stakeholders share a common vision and direction.

Evaluation

Program evaluation is another critical component. To assess the strengths and weaknesses of the Tech Prep initiative, the state leaders launched a five-year comprehensive longitudinal study of Tech Prep in Ohio. Each year, evaluators meet with the local governing board, business, industry, labor, and educators during a two-day visit to each of the consortia. Recently, in the third year of the study, the evaluators randomly visited high school and college classrooms in each consortium to determine whether teaching and learning methodologies are changing.[1]

Each year the state funds local consortia competitively through a request for proposals (RFP). This process dictates desired outcomes. For example, grants awarded to consortia require not only an in-kind match but a cash match. The cash match increases each year, ensuring that consortium partners are truly committed to Tech Prep and helping to institutionalize Tech Prep. This year the RFP will reward consortia that prepare students to exit high school "college ready" (not requiring remediation or developmental courses). This is a desired, measurable, and rewarded outcome.

Tech Prep is one of the most promising education reform initiatives Ohio has experienced to date. It has a solid infrastructure and a solid strategic plan. But its future is literally in the hands of educators, employers, parents, and community leaders. If these people do not act together to bring about lasting change, Tech Prep will not reach the success of which it is capable. A vision alone cannot sustain the movement's positive momentum. Tech Prep's partners—working together—can!

---

[1] See the summary of evaluation findings on Ohio's Tech Prep web site—http://www.bor.ohio.gov/techprep/evaluation.

Breaking the Mold

in Teaching and

Learning

Overview

The goal of educating more students with better academic knowledge and workplace skills has been at the heart of the Tech Prep movement since its inception. By expanding the scope of vocational education and focusing on the "neglected majority" of students, Tech Prep consortia have been striving to improve achievement within a more diverse population of learners since the mid-1980s. As vocational education was reexamined in light of the changing workplace and, in particular, the growth of technology, applied learning methodologies evolved. Vocational education sought to broaden the base of academic knowledge and skills gained by vocationally oriented students while retaining its traditional strengths—especially hands-on and experiential learning.

The historical and unapologetic association of contextual learning practices with vocational education has been a barrier to their broader acceptance. Societal aspirations to status and biases against nonprofessional work have been among the reasons a more contextual approach has been resisted.[1] More recently, however, the impetus to adopt a more contextual approach has come from educators in the general movement for school reform, with support from researchers in brain-based learning. There is now a greater understanding of the way the human brain organizes and processes information; this research tends to support contextual approaches to learning. With this recognition, Tech Prep strategies appear to come together somewhat with those developed by school reformers who espouse a constructivist approach. "Constructivism" is defined as an approach to teaching based on research about how people learn.[2] At the core of constructivist thinking is the

---

[1] Kenneth C. Gray and Edwin L. Herr, *Other Ways to Win: Creating Alternatives to High School Graduates* (Corwin Press, 1995), pp. 30-31.
[2] J. Lynn McBrien and Ronald S. Brandt, *The Language of Learning: A Guide to Education Terms* (Alexandria: ASCD, 1997).

notion that students learn best when they gain knowledge through exploration and active learning, often using hands-on materials. Sound familiar? Strategies for problem-based learning associated with constructivist learning are similar to the project-based learning that is increasingly being incorporated into contextual learning practice. The point here is not to present these ideas as equivalent, and certainly not to present a full discussion of constructivist teaching and learning. However, the convergence of these two approaches— constructivism and contextual learning—creates a unique historical moment and a great opportunity. Academic education and vocational education have developed—for the most part separately—innovative approaches that have much in common. Thus the path is open to a more integrated educational system, one in which contextual and constructivist approaches can begin to mingle, inform one another, and evolve together with strong support from both the vocational and academic sides of the schoolhouse.

Evidence that this is already happening can be seen in John Souders' chapter, "Academic Courses Taught in Context," as well as in Arnold Packer's exposition on project-based learning. Souders explains how contextual learning addresses differences in learning styles as well as other educational needs. He describes innovative practices that have evolved in contextual learning, in part, he maintains, through the modeling and support provided by textbooks and the assessments designed by educators. Packer describes the kind of thinking supported by the innovative contextual strategy of project-based learning and how projects support the development of thinking and employability skills.

Carolyn Prescott shows how telecommunication and technology enable teachers and students to go beyond the classroom walls to accomplish some of the more innovative contextual practices, such as project-based learning. She shows how students can go virtually to the workplace and the

*community—in search of mentors, experts, and audiences. She
makes it clear, however, that technology is a tool in the hands
of, primarily, the teacher, whom she describes as the agent of
change. Julie Hull Grevelle and Sharyl Kincaid pick up that
banner with their chapter entitled "Professional Development,"
in which they describe strategies that go beyond one-time
workshops to make a deeper impact on the teacher's
understanding and practice. Nancy Zimpher, in "Contextual
Learning Practices in Higher Education," addresses the
challenge of redesigning the educational experiences higher
education institutions deliver. By and large, these institutions
still adhere to the teaching practices and milieu of fifty years
ago. Although they do include practitioners of enlightened
teaching, these are still fairly few. Accordingly, Zimpher
summarizes concepts and strategies to guide instructors
through a process of rethinking the curricula, integrating
contextual learning and teaching, and designing field-based
learning experiences.*

*The consensus represented by these writers should
encourage us. They call for us to change ourselves and our
collective mind-set about teaching and learning, getting away
from our respective "turfs" to reshape schools. The emphasis is
overwhelmingly on students and teachers, with administrators,
technology experts, textbook and software developers, and
university professors working in support of teachers. The
movement is clearly toward teacher empowerment, with the
goal of content- and context-rich school experiences.*

Chapter 11

Academic Courses Taught in Context

John C. Souders Jr.

> Another look at the clock revealed that only two minutes had passed. To Eric, it always seemed that, while he was in school, time almost came to a standstill. Once again, Ms. Aguilar was filling the blackboard with meaningless symbols. This time they supposedly described what she referred to as "the properties of a right triangle." Instead of understanding these "properties," Eric saw an endless stream of terms that had no meaning to him and yet, according to Ms. Aguilar, held the key to his future.
>
> As geometry played out at the front of the class, Eric slipped into a daydream. He imagined that he was at work, surrounded by the hum of large machines. In front of him was a set of complex blueprints with detailed measurements for fabricating an engine intake manifold. Eric surveyed the blueprints, quickly discerning the relationships between the figures on them. Working with a master

> machinist, he used these relationships to program a computer-controlled milling machine. Eric glanced at the clock on the factory wall. Hours had passed and he was tired but felt very satisfied with his work.
>
> When Eric awoke from his reverie, he looked at the clock again. Only a minute had passed.

The above scenario is all too typical. Many students in today's classrooms are not reaching their potential because they see little connection between school work and "real" work. Most students like Eric have a strong desire to succeed and participate in the world of work, and often they are particularly interested in advanced technology. They want to be on the cutting edge, to have an impact on the lives of others, and they are enthralled with the challenge advanced technology presents. However, a barrier stands in their path—school. For students like Eric, school is not a help but a hindrance. As Ms. Aguilar tells her students, education holds the key to a student's future. But because they don't *see* the connection between education and their futures, too many Erics end up on the scrap pile of education, never realizing their dreams or reaching their potential.

This tragedy is not just personal but national in scope. For America to stay competitive in today's global economy, its most valuable resource, its people, must be empowered to the fullest. Economist Lester Thurow sums up the urgency of empowering America's workforce in this way: "In the 21st century, the education and skills of the workforce will end up being the dominant competitive weapon."[1] Eric's situation has serious and far-reaching implications. If America is to continue to compete, it cannot afford to allow Eric and countless other

---

[1] Lester Thurow, *Head to Head: The Coming Economic Battle Among Japan, Europe, and America* (New York: William Morrow, 1992).

young people like him not to develop the skills they will need to succeed in the workplace.

It is never enough simply to point out the causes of a problem; something about the *process* that allows the problem to arise must be changed. One reason the management philosophy called total quality management (TQM) has been widely adopted by businesses and industries during the last few years is that it focuses on *processes*. A fundamental tenet of TQM is that processes must be constantly improved so that more value is added and less product is rejected.[2] This tenet is just as applicable to education as it is to business and industry, but, by and large, the American educational system does not follow it. As John A. White, former assistant director of the National Science Foundation, puts it, "Unfortunately, little or no attention is given to developing human potential. The true 'value added' by the educational system must be questioned."[3]

Educators would do well to give serious consideration to this tenet of TQM, setting their sights not only on determining why students fail but on what changes in *process* will reduce the failure rate. They should not be content to identify causes that contribute to student failure, and they should refuse to accept failure as a fact of life. Following TQM's lead, educators should change the educational process, introducing educational approaches that address a variety of student learning styles.

One such approach is contextual learning.

The contextual learning approach is based on the premise that learning is most effective when information is presented within a framework that is familiar to the student. This

---

[2] R. Aqudyo, *Dr. Deming: The American Who Taught the Japanese About Quality* (New York: Carol Publishing Group, 1990).
[3] John A. White, Speech to the First National Symposium on the Role of Academia in National Competitiveness and Total Quality Management, Lake View Resort, Morgantown, West Virginia, July 1990.

definition is readily understood if we think of knowledge as a puzzle. Each piece of the puzzle represents some piece of knowledge acquired in the past. At any given moment, the puzzle represented by the sum total of our knowledge forms a kind of mosaic. When we attempt to learn a new concept, we are attempting, in a sense, to add a piece to our puzzle. If the concept is presented to us in a context that is within our frame of reference, it "makes sense"—the puzzle piece fits perfectly, not merely filling a spot of its own but shedding new light on the pieces around it. However, if the concept is presented to us abstractly or in an unfamiliar context, we may not understand it and consequently we may reshape it to fit our puzzle. This reshaping causes the concept to lose some of its meaning and depth. This loss is the inception of misunderstanding and makes adding new puzzle pieces—related concepts—even more difficult. Many students, like Eric in our scenario, experience school learning as a disjointed succession of puzzle pieces with almost indistinguishable shapes, so "trimmed down" to their essence and devoid of context that they cannot be grasped and put in place.

The contextual learning approach provides an alternative means of meeting students' learning needs. The contextual learning approach is based on an understanding of learning as a complex process that cannot be addressed adequately through drill-oriented, stimulus/response methodologies.[4] As suggested by the puzzle analogy, the assumption underlying a contextual approach is that the mind seeks meaning through searching for relationships that make sense and fit with past experiences.[5] With this approach, educators are encouraged to choose and/or design learning environments that incorporate as many different forms of experience as possible—social, cultural, physical, and

---

[4] Howard Gardner, *Frames of Mind: The Theory of Multiple Intelligences* (New York: Basic Books, 1983).
[5] Caine and Caine, *Making Connections: Teaching and the Human Brain.*

psychological—in working toward the desired learning outcome.[6] Such diversity provides educators one means of building a flexible educational environment that can be adapted to students' backgrounds and needs.

In general, the contextual approach to learning addresses at least three identifiable needs of today's students:

1. Students need a set of expanded skills with which to get along in contemporary work and society.

2. Students need help to develop a sense of meaning and purpose in school learning.

3. Students need teaching strategies that take into account the different ways in which they learn.

The Need for Expanded Skills for Employability and Citizenship

"Expanded skills" refers to the fact that narrow skills training in one area is no longer adequate for most of today's jobs or for living in a complex society. The skills needed for work and citizenship, especially in today's rapidly changing, technology-driven workplace, include thinking skills such as logic, multiple strategies for problem solving, and interpersonal skills such as working in teams, as well as the habits of mind that promote lifelong learning. Such skills were documented and organized into a useful framework by the Secretary's Commission on Achieving Necessary Skills (SCANS) under the direction of Dr. Arnold Packer of Johns Hopkins University. Traditional teaching—with its emphasis on rote learning; on abstract, neatly structured problems and solutions; and almost exclusively on individual performance—has not adequately met

---

[6] D.A. Kolb, *Experience as the Source of Learning and Development* (Englewood Cliffs, New Jersey: Prentice-Hall, 1983).

the need for these skills. Contextual learning methodologies such as project-based learning and cooperative problem solving, by their nature, foster and support the SCANS skills.

The Need for Meaning and Purpose in Schooling

Many students in our current system, including many who may be categorized as abstract learners, are confused about the meaning and purpose of their schooling. For many students, high school is simply an obstacle to be hurdled in order to get to "real life," rather than a site of serious learning. High school students often feel themselves to be in a state of protracted deferment; real life is always on the horizon but they never get there. Learning is not taken seriously as part of life; at best, it is seen as a means of going to college, and at worst, as with students such as Eric, it is an unfathomable barrier. Establishing the connection between schooling and the larger world outside school is critical for adolescents, who want to join that world. Contextual approaches to education help to make explicit the connection between school learning and work, adult decision making, and membership in the community.

The Need for Teaching Techniques That Accommodate Different Learning Styles

The contextual approach is significant in its accommodation of different learning styles. Much work has been done in the area of learning styles,[7] defining and underscoring the important variations in the ways people receive and process information.

---

[7] D.A. Kolb, *Learning-Style Inventory Technical Manual* (Hay/McBer, 116 Huntington Ave., Boston, MA 02116, 1976, revised 1978).

One way people receive information is by experiencing physically real situations that provide sensory data. Feeling the heat produced by friction and measuring a room are examples of receiving information physically or experientially. A different mode of receiving information involves reading or hearing verbal (i.e., abstract) information without benefit of the physical reality. Listening to a lecture and reading a textbook are common examples of this process.

Once a person receives the information, there are different ways the brain processes it. One type of processing is introverted; the person thinks about and analyzes the information internally with little or no interaction with the equivalent physical reality. People who prefer this way of processing information watch, observe, and contemplate the information within their own minds without interacting physically with the external world.

On the other hand, a person with an extroverted processing style prefers to interact with physical applications of the information through hands-on experiences. Laboratory work and projects cater to this processing style. Team activities and group work that produce physical results are effective with extroverted learners.

These two approaches to receiving and processing information define the spectrum of variation in learning styles. People who prefer the abstract, introverted approach function comfortably in passive learning environments in which lecture and individual work are emphasized. People who prefer the concrete, extroverted approach learn best in active learning environments in which experimentation, discovery, and group work are the main instructional modes. Our current educational system has done a laudable job of meeting the needs of abstract learners but has not been flexible enough to adequately meet the educational needs of people like Eric.

Contextual learning provides a means of meeting the needs of a much broader range of learners. The following defines different modes of contextual learning that can be combined to support a wide diversity of learning styles.[8]

- Relating: learning in the context of life experiences

- Transferring: learning in the context of existing knowledge—using and building on what students already know

- Applying: learning in the context of how knowledge and information can be used

- Experiencing: learning in the context of exploration, discovery, and invention

- Cooperation: learning in the context of sharing with, responding to, and communicating with other learners

These forms of contextual learning provide a flexible set of strategies for reaching students with diverse learning styles. Imagine visiting a geometry classroom where the Pythagorean theorem is being taught. If the teacher is using a contextual learning approach, students may be found working all around the room using string and tape measures to lay out the foundation of a rectangular shed, or they may be out in the school parking lot calculating its grade. These hands-on activities provide students a means of *experiencing* the Pythagorean theorem while *cooperatively* working in groups. It is also likely that students will be working in groups *applying* the Pythagorean theorem to such real-world problems as calculating the length of a ramp for a wheelchair. These classroom exercises place the Pythagorean theorem within the context of its use and help students develop an understanding of its meaning by building on (*relating and transferring*) existing knowledge. As this geometry lesson indicates, contextual approaches to learning can transform classrooms into

---

[8] Hull, *Opening Minds, Opening Doors*, p. 41.

environments where students interact with each other and actively engage with course material.

As the idea of contextual learning has evolved, new strategies have been added. The following list is not comprehensive, but it illustrates the spectrum of activities that can provide a context to learning.

- *Hands-on learning*—This refers to active learning—other than pencil-and-paper activities—in which students experience concepts and/or skills. Hands-on learning may involve using tools and devices, handling or quantifying the properties of materials, observing physical events, or assembling or repairing equipment. Hands-on learning builds on a traditional strength of vocational education and of laboratory exercises in the sciences.

- *Project-based learning*—Project-based learning involves activities, usually requiring several steps and some duration (more than a couple of class days and up to a semester) and cooperative group learning. Projects may focus on the development of a product or performance, and they generally call upon students to organize their activities, conduct research, solve problems, and synthesize information. Projects are often interdisciplinary. For example, a project in which students draft plans for and build a structure, investigate its environmental impact, document the building process, and develop spreadsheets for the associated accounting would involve the use of skills and concepts drawn from courses in English, mathematics, building trades, drafting and/or design, and biology.

- *Contextual connections*—Connections between an academic concept or skill and the context in which it is embedded and used can be made in a variety of ways: by means of a text introduction to the subject; through media technology such as video, CD-ROM, and Internet connections; or through student activities such as interviewing someone in a related occupation. For example, a teacher might introduce a lesson on Ohm's law by arranging for students to talk with a technician from a natural gas utility company. Connections can be made to the workplace, to research institutions, to public agencies, and to museums. Through them, the student sees that classroom learning has meaning and application in the world outside school.

- *Applications*—Students work with some aspect of the knowledge as it is typically applied, such as working mathematics problems that would be used by a pharmacy technician, conducting water quality tests that are used as indicators by an environmental agency, or developing machine drawings as a CAD designer would in an engineering setting. The assessment criteria and the format for presentation may be drawn from professional or industrial examples, such as developing a laboratory report according to protocols and even using the same type of reporting form that is used by a public agency or private laboratory. In some cases, students collect and report data as part of a larger network, as with one project that engages students worldwide in mapping the earth's magnetic field.[9]

- *Mentoring and consulting*—Arrangements can be made for students to communicate and consult with subject matter experts (SME) from the workplace who are well informed about specific academic concepts and skills. The curriculum connection can be made in a variety of ways: SMEs can participate in assignments or assessments, tutor or coach small groups of students on difficult concepts as they are applied in the workplace, and/or mentor

---

[9] Judi Harris, *Design Tools for the Internet-Supported Classroom* (Alexandria: ASCD, 1998).

individuals or groups in project work. Increasingly, mentoring and other connections between students and adults outside school are carried out via videoconferencing and the Internet.

- ***Connections to a wider audience***—Students experience a form of contextual learning whenever their work gains a wider audience. Writing for publication, comparing data on the Internet, presenting scientific data on a relevant issue to a public body such as the city council, and developing web pages on subjects of study are ways of extending the audience for students. And when students gain a public audience, they understand the significance of their work and take it far more seriously.

Some critics argue that courses presented in a contextual or applied manner are "watered-down"; that is, they are said to lack the rigor of more traditional courses. To support this argument, these critics often point to an applied course such as "consumer math," which focuses on life skills such as balancing a checkbook or figuring a household budget. Obviously, these skills are more elementary than algebra competencies such as solving quadratic equations or analyzing systems of equations. This mismatch in content and level of difficulty—a comparison of apples to oranges—is interpreted to mean that applied courses are universally elementary and lacking in academic rigor. This type of comparison is neither fair nor legitimate. A meaningful comparison of a traditional algebra course with one that is contextually based yields a more positive interpretation that reports on the effectiveness of the two different learning approaches.

A well-designed, contextually based algebra course covers the same competencies as a traditional course. The mastery of these competencies is as rigorous as their mastery in a traditional course. However, the contextually based course has the added dimension of real-world problem solving. Anyone who has taken applied courses at the postsecondary level knows that such courses are among the most difficult in the curriculum. Unlike theoretical courses in which assumptions can remove difficult aspects of a problem, an applied course requires that these difficult aspects be treated and properly modeled. Thus, in an applied course, the concept being taught becomes the tool for solving the problem and students must learn not only how to use the tool but also its limitations. Rather than being watered-down, contextually based academic courses challenge students in ways traditional courses are not capable of doing and demand problem-solving strategies that match the rigor of the real world.

Increasingly, there is recognition among educators within the academic disciplines that contextual or applied learning is important to meeting student needs. Standards set by the National Council of Teachers of Mathematics (NCTM) advocate building relevancy and application into the teaching of mathematics. These standards represent widespread recognition of the efficacy of applied learning and its potential to increase learning among a broad cross section of students while maintaining the required rigor.

However, major hurdles involving educational biases and practices must be overcome before contextual learning realizes this potential. The following are suggested strategies for overcoming these hurdles.

- Postsecondary institutions cling to traditional ways of teaching and are slow to embrace new learning techniques that emerge from educational reform movements. Postsecondary faculties need to develop an appreciation of the power of contextual learning. High schools throughout the country are offering mathematics, science, and language courses based on contextual learning theory and seeing very positive results in student performance. Dialogue between postsecondary and secondary teachers must be encouraged so postsecondary faculty members understand that contextual learning is effective and that many students entering postsecondary institutions will demand its use.

- Schools of education around the country are primarily housed in four-year postsecondary institutions. Though contextual learning is beginning to make inroads in preservice training, it remains a minor part of the overall curriculum in most schools. For contextual learners at all grade levels to gain the most from their education, an ample supply of teachers well versed in contextual learning is needed. Schools of education need to be encouraged to reexamine their curricula, and introduce ways to devote adequate course hours to contextual learning theory and methodology. Schools of education need to work closely with teachers who have succeeded with the contextual learning model and to provide students the opportunity to see this model in practice.

- Educators should invest in faculty in-service training programs that emphasize contextual learning. Experience at the secondary level has shown that faculty members who have attempted to teach contextually based courses with no training often become frustrated. This is understandable. Contextual learning adds new dimensions to a teacher's responsibilities and a change in the teacher's fundamental role. Contextually based courses are usually more interactive, applied, and laboratory oriented than traditional courses. They involve cooperative learning scenarios and require teamwork of all students. Faculty members cannot be expected to blend these elements into an effective strategy based on single in-service experiences; they need ongoing support from peers and mentors who are working to achieve or have successfully implemented contextual learning.

- Educators should support the development of curriculum materials that are contextually based. As an example, the American Mathematical Association of Two-Year Colleges has just published a draft of its new standards, entitled *Crossroads in Mathematics: Standards for Introductory College Mathematics Before Calculus.* These standards clearly delineate content, and intellectual and pedagogical competencies. Interwoven throughout these standards is an appeal to present concepts within the context of real-world applications, to provide students with hands-on learning, and to allow students to work collaboratively. These standards complement those produced by NCTM and provide clear direction for building student-centered postsecondary mathematics curricula. Educators should endorse these standards and work with publishers to develop materials that embody the standards and their contextual learning base. It should be acknowledged that some educators currently eschew textbooks and prefer teacher-designed curricula that are not textbook-dependent. Contextual learning advocates, who have worked with both vocational and academic teachers who come to the classroom ill-prepared to design curricula and unable to find the time to do it, generally believe that textbooks carry out important functions: They provide a basic resource for content as well as context. Many teachers are teaching mathematics and science without adequate preparation in the field, let alone a rich contextual base. For example, how many teachers can tell their students how a knowledge of the electromagnetic spectrum might be used to solve problems in an industrial situation? Textbooks can provide this kind of information about the context in which information and skills are embedded or applied. Textbooks also model effective teaching strategies through suggested lesson plans and support materials. More recently, multimedia materials have become available and provide simulations in which students solve problems. Such contextual learning simulations can also act as a catalyst for projects.

- Back in the early eighties, CORD recognized the need to develop textbooks that provided students a rich, contextually based learning experience. To meet this need, CORD allied itself with the state directors of vocational education. Over a ten-year period, this alliance produced three highly innovative sets of curriculum materials— *Principles of Technology*, *CORD Applied Mathematics*, and *Applications in Biology/Chemistry*—that ushered into high school science and mathematics classrooms a new wave of optimism. Students who previously struggled with mathematics and science topics were now mastering these concepts and setting their sights on high-tech careers.[10] Through 1997, over 3.5 million students across the country had taken these trend-setting courses. Based on this acceptance and an expanding demand for contextually based materials, CORD created in conjunction with South-Western Educational Publishing the next generation of applied academics. *CORD Algebra* and *CORD Geometry* retain the contextual, hands-on workplace orientation of the original CORD mathematics materials, but include major changes suggested by field users. Another major change is that the new books come in both modular and hardbound formats. The main purpose of moving to a hardbound format was to make contextually based mathematics materials available to students in the twenty-three states where textbook adoption processes demand this format. CORD felt that the educational reform movement that it and the state directors of vocational education initiated could not be sustained if nearly half the students in our country did not have access to contextually based materials. The production of these books provides momentum for moving contextual learning into the twenty-first century.

- Educators must address issues of assessment as they relate to contextual learning. Although one metric for measuring

---

[10] Hull, *Opening Minds, Opening Doors*, pp. 57-63.

the success of contextually based academics is the standardized test, it should not be the only one. As stated earlier, contextually based courses contain elements—laboratories, real-world problem solving, group projects—that are not necessarily present in traditional courses. Consequently, an authentic assessment of student achievement in contextually based courses should go beyond standardized tests and evaluate performances and products based on these unique elements. Methods of authentic assessment have been developed.[11]

Authentic assessment can provide valuable and specific information about student progress through several avenues.

- *Projects:* Participating in projects allows students to demonstrate their abilities to use academic tools to solve real-world problems. Assessment is often based on the products and/or performances related to the project.

- *Portfolios:* Portfolios are a collection of products such as laboratory reports, interviews, and project summaries. Kept over time, a portfolio provides concrete evidence of progress in knowledge and skills as well as attitudes about producing work.

- *Demonstrations:* A major component of contextual learning is experiencing new knowledge or concepts from a hands-on perspective. Laboratories are the centerpiece of this component, and demonstrations are an effective way for students to show their skills and discuss the knowledge gained through laboratory experience.

- *Case studies:* In a contextually based course, students are constantly exposed to real-world situations. Through these, they become adept at assessing the performance of others in certain tasks such as planning, allocating resources, leading

---

[11] See Table 1 in chapter 3.

teams, and solving problems. Case studies can provide students scenarios for testing their ability to carry out these tasks under conditions that cannot be simulated in a classroom. Assessing students' performances on these case studies will provide educators insights into how adaptable students are in performing these tasks in new situations. The degree to which students can adapt is a measure of their mastery of the tasks.

- *Paper and pencil tests:* A main goal of any contextually based academic course is to convey knowledge. Assessment must include a component that tests students' knowledge against some set standards. Such testing provides valuable feedback to the educational system and establishes a means of gauging student progress.

- *Structured observation:* Contextual learning supports the use of cooperative education. Throughout a contextually based course, students should constantly be interacting within groups and building interpersonal skills. To fully assess students in this type of course, it is imperative that their abilities to work in groups are observed and feedback is provided to promote continued growth.

Eric cannot believe that the geometry period is almost over. During this period, he has worked with his classmates in laying out the perimeter stakes for a rectangular foundation. Eric is particularly proud of his contribution to the team. With his teacher, Ms. Aguilar, Eric has created a clever way to construct his team's data tables so the collected data can be easily analyzed. To ensure that the foundation has square corners, his team used the Pythagorean theorem. Though one of his teammates did most of the calculations, Eric assisted and now feels comfortable that, after a little homework, he will be able to do these calculations on his own. During a break at work, Eric begins to daydream. He wonders how the geometry lab could have been done better.

The transition of Eric from the beginning of this chapter to the end is the dream of all educators. Eric now has a positive attitude about education and sees it not as a barrier but as an escalator to his future success. America needs a large supply of Erics. The lifeblood of the American workforce is a continual infusion of technically competent people with the ability to learn quickly and apply new skills. In the past, people like Eric have not contributed significantly to this infusion. However, they now have the opportunity to play a critical role in revitalizing America's competitive edge in the global marketplace. The educational system is key to developing these students into versatile and skilled workforce members, and the dedication of educators to this task will be greatly enhanced by adopting, developing, and supporting contextually based academic courses.

Chapter 12

Project-Based Learning

Arnold Packer

The New Competencies

The skills needed in the twenty-first century A.D. have a lineage that can be traced back to the twenty-first century B.C. Indeed, the "new competencies" have a familial resemblance to the skills that humankind has demonstrated ever since *Homo sapiens* learned to use tools and communicate with one another. Forty thousand years ago, humans had to plan their hunts, read the signs that disclosed their prey's habits, fashion hunting weapons, communicate and agree on their assignments, and learn from their experience so that the next hunt would be more successful than the last one. Those who could not solve the hunting problem starved. Those communities that succeeded at the hunting and gathering tasks began to redefine the problem: how to abandon the nomadic life by securing a dependable food supply from a stable location. Humans had entered the Agricultural Age.

Success in the Agricultural Age depended on similar skills, redefined for the new era: planning, reading the signs (now the signs that affected crops), developing agricultural implements, communicating among workers and family members to agree on assignments and rewards, and learning how to improve crops so that each year's yield was better than the last. Failure at these tasks also had dire consequences—a couple of bad years often spelled famine. Success once again provided an opportunity to redefine the problem. If survival—food, shelter, clothing—was more assured, humans could aspire to higher living standards. A factory worker expected three meals a day, a single family house, and a car or two. Humans had entered the Industrial Age.

Success during the Industrial Age called again for applying the same five fundamental skills in a new context:

- Plan the enterprise,

- Read the signs (now about markets rather than prey or crops),

- Develop machine tools,

- Communicate and come to agreement with the workers, and

- Learn how to improve production and marketing each year.

There were differences, too. Specialization, as Adam Smith pointed out in the late eighteenth century, and as Frederic Taylor institutionalized at the beginning of this one, made for a more efficient industrial enterprise. The planning, sign-reading, tool-design, communication and agreement, and system-modification functions could be left in the hands of managers and specialists. The ordinary production line worker could survive with only a modest (if any) command of these skills. Universal education came into being, but did not need to universally produce graduates skilled in these five competencies. As long as a worker hooked up with an enterprise that had these skills, he or she would survive and indeed prosper.

As the twentieth century wanes, the Information Age is beginning. Industrial success brought mass production and higher levels of consumption. Once again, societies had the freedom to redefine problems and seek a higher standard of living. Many could now aspire to have healthy and tasty meals, multiroomed, temperature-controlled houses, and designer clothes—not to mention new cars, exotic vacations, and home entertainment centers. The five fundamental competencies endure, albeit transformed once again. Workers with aspirations for the consumer goods noted above are finding they need to have the five competencies. The era of union-protected consumer-society wages for unskilled work has ended, except for a lucky few. Technology, international trade, and the weakening of unions conspire to change the wage structure characteristic of the industrial age—a wage structure that a generation ago provided a middle-class income to unskilled workers.

Rewards of Education

As in previous epochal changes, those who have the skills required by the new age are prospering, while those who do not, suffer. In the United States between 1980 and 1996, the median real wage of those with only high school diplomas fell by 6 percent while those with college degrees had an earnings increase of 12 percent. In 1982, the total compensation (including fringe benefits) of the top 10 percent of workers was 4.6 times greater than those in the bottom decile ($35.16 versus $7.72 per hour in 1997 dollars). In the next fourteen years, compensation for highly paid workers increased by $1.73 per hour while that for the low-end workers fell by 93 cents per hour. The ratio had increased to 5.4.[1] (*NY Times, 6/14/98*).

Each age put different demands on learning. A hunter-gatherer society had few specialists. There was a tribe leader and maybe a witch doctor, but everyone needed to know some facts and concepts and be able to do certain tasks. Things changed slowly in the Agricultural Age. Although some began to study science, philosophy, and trade—and some societies built centers for learning—the vast majority remained ignorant and illiterate. This education system was inadequate for the Industrial Age. A much larger proportion of the population needed "higher-order" skills, and the masses needed to become at least literate and modestly numerate. At the end of the twentieth century, societies are searching for the education and learning system for the Information Age.

Today's search for an education system begins with a reexamination of what has to be taught and how to teach it; or, better yet, with redefining what must be learned and how to learn it. Perhaps it is not too surprising that the five fundamental competencies that have shaped humankind's success over time are still the necessary skills, once again redefined for a new age. Humans will continue to work with others to solve meaningful problems and negotiate solutions. This will require planning, obtaining and interpreting information, and using technology (tools). Humans will also have to assess and learn from their experiences and apply that knowledge to future challenges.

SCANS Defines the Five Competencies

The five competencies were more explicitly defined early in the 1990s by SCANS. They are:

---

[1] *New York Times*, June 14, 1998.

- **Planning Skills:** Allocating financial, temporal, spatial, and human resources—preparing a budget, schedule, space layout, and staffing plan. (For example: When will we hunt? How many hunters will we take?)

- **Information Skills:** Acquiring, evaluating, organizing, and communicating information. (For example: Which seed works best? When is the last hard freeze likely?)

- **Technology Skills:** Using, choosing, and maintaining equipment. (Shall we use spears or bows? Do long hoes or short work better? What kind of machine tools are needed?)

- **Interpersonal Skills:** Working with others, negotiating, teaching, working with diversity. (Can we jointly decide how to apportion the work? Can we agree on the division of rewards at the end of the hunt, harvest, or fiscal year?)

- **System Skills:** Understanding, monitoring, improving, and designing systems of all kinds. This most complex and important of the competencies is the most difficult to define. Most basically, workers need to work with processes that operate over time. The process can be hunting or farming or manufacturing or installing or constructing. One can understand systems built by others or by nature (such as the system of seasons as seen in the stars). Systems will be biological, physical, social, or economic in nature. At a higher level, one can design or build a system and find a metasystem to improve it as experience is gained and reflected upon. (What can we do differently to make sure the deer does not get away next time?)

Project Characteristics

School can provide an opportunity to acquire these competencies if students are engaged in the "right" way in "appropriate" projects. Moreover, it can be done without sacrificing the content of academic subjects. What is the right way, and what projects are appropriate? The SCANS/2000 Center at the Johns Hopkins University is searching for the answers to these questions. The hypothesis is that students can learn the required competencies and academic skills within projects that are:

- **Sustained:** They require five to ten weeks of sustained reasoning effort to complete.

- **Technology supported:** Modern work tools—primarily computers—are used to do many of the tasks.

- **Collaborative:** Students function in teams with structured roles, assignments, and codes of behavior.

- **Relevant:** For students over fourteen years of age, they simulate the work done by a large number of American workers whose earnings are middle class or better.

- **Multidisciplinary:** To develop a solution to the problem, students will need to draw on knowledge from a number of disciplines.

The SCANS/2000 Center is producing eight CD-ROMs. These provide scaffolds or frameworks on which teachers can build projects meeting the five criteria to test the hypothesis. By the middle of 1998, six have been completed and alpha tested. The seventh is scheduled to be completed later in 1998 and the final one in the first half of 1999. These project scaffolds take the form of *electronic scenarios* or *case studies* in which students play the roles of decently paid workers. Each CD uses a different scenario. They include developing a business plan for a retail store, designing information systems, locating factories, developing budgets for a new product, applying statistical process control, and creating an error-correction team.

City Tours

The *Marketing for Tourism* project provides a good example of how the CD-ROMs incorporate the required competencies and academic skills in project-based learning. In it, students work in teams and "become" project associates (paid $17,000 plus fringe benefits as a starting salary) at a fictional tour company, *City Tours.* They must develop a weekend tour of Baltimore City for a family of four with two teenage children. Each team must produce a spreadsheet and a marketing brochure. On the spreadsheet, students must calculate the revenues, costs, and profits associated with planning and marketing the tour. They must also conduct research, write the prose, choose the graphics, and produce the marketing brochure using a publishing program on the computer.

Three Baltimore City Public High Schools piloted the CD-ROM in the spring of 1998. Ninth-grade teachers in two or more subjects collaborated to implement the project across disciplines in the last (eight) weeks of the semester. Student teams traveled together from class to class, completing the research and writing in their English class, learning about graphic design in their art class, learning about the culture of Baltimore in social studies, and so on.

Prior to engaging in the project, the students' English class taught grammar rules, the techniques of expository writing, and research techniques. Through the project, students learned to function cooperatively—developing team names and assignments and, most importantly, a team code of behavior (very different from the unproductive interaction demonstrated in full-class behavior). They also acquired technology skills by using a word processor, spreadsheets, a publishing program, and the Internet.

In June, two of the implementing schools, Northern and Forest Park, connected via teleconference for a contest. Two experts, Bob Helsley, a graphics arts instructor at the Maryland Institute College of Art (MICA), and Kathy Southern, director of the Children's Port Discovery Museum of Baltimore, judged the students' final brochures. Prior to the contest, the judges developed a scoring rubric, which analyzed a team's ability to communicate a theme through the use of color, pictures, graphics, and well-written, intriguing text. They then used the rubric to score each team's brochure.

During the contest, the judges discussed the scoring criteria with the students. Mr. Helsley showed examples of exemplary work from his advanced graphic design class at MICA; Ms. Southern explained what she looked for in advertising copy for a campaign for the museum (whose layout is being designed by Disney). An interactive video arrangement allowed the attendees at the schools to exchange ideas and see and discuss the students' work and Mr. Helsley's examples.

The winning team came from Northern High, a high school that had been designated "reconstitution eligible" by the state for poor performance on standardized tests and other measures such as dropout rates and attendance. The team's brochure extolled the virtues of eating in Baltimore's restaurants. It was awarded most of the twenty-five points allotted for communication—choosing and staying with a theme, researching (via the Internet) the possibilities, and writing a set of descriptive paragraphs. The team gained points for creative use of color and for composition, but lost some points for squeezing text to make it fit in the layout by using a smaller font. The other three criteria were ideas and content, typography, and graphics.

The contest was the capstone lesson in using the SCANS skills, especially the interpersonal and planning skills. Students had to accept criticism (which is not easy) and *reflect* on the product during eight weeks of work; they learned how to improve the next time they had to develop a marketing document.

The mathematics component of the project will be completed in the fall of 1998. Students will use their mathematics, research, and communication skills to plan a tour and develop a budget for a marketing campaign while maximizing profit. They will see where two lines—one representing revenues and another costs—intersect and where profits are maximized. They will come to understand the economic concepts of a break-even point and profit maximization. Simultaneously, they will learn and use algebra through slopes and intercepts of lines and maximization of functions. They will also have a chance to practice and apply simpler concepts such as percentages and fractions, reading and making charts and tables, and arithmetic (including estimating). All this will be done using advanced technology and business software applications such as spreadsheets. Finally, students will learn how to communicate mathematically by writing memos to the "boss," explaining various marketing and pricing recommendations.

Project-Based Learning Kits

Several other organizations, including the Center for Occupational Research and Development (CORD), Classroom, Inc., and the Learning Team, have created such CDs to bring real-world relevance to the classroom. For example, CORD has a five CD-ROM series called *Math at Work* that is geared to students in grades five through twelve. These CD-ROMs set the users up in adult role situations and ask them to use mathematics skills and other academic, occupational, and employability skills to complete their given scenarios. The situations range from running a small business as a vending cart operator to running a race as part of a bicycle racing team, building a swimming pool as a contractor, putting out a forest fire as a smokejump spotter, or remediating a diesel spill at a train derailment as the incident commander.

No matter what the scenario, students are expected to act responsibly as they use various skills to analyze and solve the given problem or set of problems. They use such math skills as estimation; reading graphs, charts, and tables; managing resources; calculating ratios and proportions; using a protractor to measure angles; measuring shapes in two and three dimensions; reading scale drawings; converting units of measurement; adding vectors; reading topographical maps; calculating slope; using a number line; solving formulas with powers and roots; and choosing the correct formula for a given situation.

Additionally, many of these CDs are available as components of an entire project-based learning kit that will use the technology to introduce students to an even bigger project. This project will use more extensive resources including community guest speakers, computer applications, and research.

In addition to the *Marketing for Tourism* CD-ROM, the SCANS/2000 Center at Johns Hopkins is developing CD-ROMs for Entrepreneurship in Retailing, for Information Technology in Health and another in Manufacturing, and four others with manufacturing contexts.

Designing Project-Based Learning

Both the design and implementation of project-based learning—at least as defined here—pose significant challenges. In the SCANS/2000 case, a team of organizations requires many months of effort to develop a single electronic scenario. The challenges are that:

1. each scenario must address a relevant and authentic problem;

2. students should be required to use high-level skills and knowledge from at least one academic discipline, and the project must fit the schedules and teaching styles of the selected course(s);

3. the solution should require information technology;

4. it must engage students in a sustained effort;

5. the problem should be solved using teams (as this mimics how problems are solved in real workplaces); and

6. the CD-ROM technology must be effectively exploited.

Selecting a relevant and authentic problem demands knowing something about the world of work, the academic discipline(s), and the teaching environment. The problem should not be too narrow or one that very few graduates are likely to encounter. Many millions of twenty-first-century American workers will work in tourism or marketing (or solving the other seven electronic scenarios). Far fewer than one million will have careers in pure science or mathematics.

Developing a realistic scenario demands creativity and imagination. If the problem is authentic, its solution will unfailingly demand some of the SCANS competencies. The same is not true regarding the academic disciplines. In the case of the *Marketing for Tourism* CD-ROM, project designers used Maryland's Core Learning Goals (CLG) to define which academic skills to cover. To meet Maryland's goals, the designers needed to incorporate slopes and intercepts and expository writing into the story in a believable way. The designers found it impossible, however, to both include all of the learning goals and maintain a realistic level of authenticity. This is the reverse of standard process of curriculum design where applications are only an afterthought and have no authenticity (e.g., If Jane is twice as old as her aunt, who is four times older than her parrot . . .). The designer also has to look for ways to divide the "assignments" into class-long sessions. Finally, real problems are inevitably multidisciplinary. Getting administrators and teachers to cooperate so that two or more disciplines can be brought to bear simultaneously (interdisciplinary teaching) takes luck and effort. Administrators must make accommodating schedules and teachers must make accommodations to each others' personalities if it is going to happen.

The third criterion is easily met. As is the case for the SCANS competencies, weaving the use of technology skills into the project comes naturally. Computers are ubiquitous in today's workplace. The designers found it easy to weave the use of spreadsheets, word processing, desktop publishing, and the Internet into the dramatic flow of the electronic scenario.

If the students are emotionally involved, the designer has succeeded in making the problem "real." The designer's challenge is to engage students and maintain the involvement over a sustained period of time. Learning must entail hard work—but it does not have to be boring. The hypothesis is that using computers in a real-world scenario provides a welcome departure from standard methods of classroom instruction. Evidence from the first implementations supports this hypothesis. When the actor who played *City Tours'* president visited one of the implementing high schools, students approached him for a job. This authenticity led to student engagement in the work. Teachers had to tear students away from their computers when the bell rang. This does not happen often enough in today's schools. It did happen at both the high school and community college levels with these projects. Intellectual rigor and interest were sustained.

Authentic scenarios produce the challenge of teamwork. People rarely complete tasks alone in the workplace; more often, projects are done as a team. To mimic this, designers need to guide teachers in the effective use of teams to solve a problem. Teachers must then relay the information to their students. In one of the electronic scenarios, the "CEO" asks the class to divide into teams. Each team must develop a budget for a new product (in this case, one of five variations of an electric car). In the other scenarios, the direction may be less explicit but the support for working in teams remains. Collaboration skills such as negotiation, consensus building for decision making, and compromise are stressed. In the *Marketing for Tourism* project these skills are crucial to producing the brochures, financial spreadsheets, and stand-up presentations.

Finally, design is no trivial task. Scripts and production values count. Programming (in Authorware in this case) is still a challenge. Students can always "click" their way through multiple-choice problems. The CD-ROM provides a framework for a problem and a core set of information, usually available in "file drawers" or on the "computers" in the simulated workplaces. These core data provide a starting point that lets students solve the problem within a reasonable time.

The project helps teachers and faculty provide rich applications in core academic disciplines. Teachers retain the primary teaching role, supported by "tutorials" and prompts in the module that allow students to review and practice the key academic skills needed to undertake the project. The CD-ROM brings all this to the students' desktops in a way that would be impossible for a single teacher to do. It neither spoon-feeds students with all the data they need nor undertakes the main teaching role.

Can all this be accomplished without the CD-ROM? Presumably, if the teacher has the time and the paper-based resources to meet the first five criteria listed above. This would be easier if the teacher had a VCR and access to an appropriate video to establish the scenario. Can it be done without access to technology, thereby ignoring the third criterion? It would be more difficult but not impossible. The remaining criteria are, however, essential: a relevant and authentic problem, a require-ment for applying high-level academic skills, a sustained effort, and working in teams. Whether they are designing their own projects or implementing one with the use of a scaffold such as the CD-ROMs, teachers need support to be successful at it.

Faculty Development for Implementing the Project

Using a new method of instruction requires a change of teaching style and classroom organization. This can be a difficult task. The first attempt at implementing the mathematics component of the *Marketing for Tourism* project was unsuccessful. The researchers had underestimated just how far this kind of learning departed from standard teaching practice and how much faculty support was needed. They found that, to be successful, teachers had to learn how to:

- Establish and motivate teams and assess individual performance,

- Navigate their way through the CD-ROM and become proficient in the software tools,

- Solve the problem posed to the students,

- Apply a long-term management system to their classes,

- Become comfortable with the idea of not having all the answers, and

- Fit the project into an already crowded curriculum.

Each one of these departures from current practice is hard work. One of the SCANS/2000 team's partners is the Center for Technology in Education (CTE), part of the Education Division at Johns Hopkins. CTE carried most of the faculty development load at the high schools and also participated in the faculty development at the community colleges. The SCANS/2000 Center recently received a $1 million grant to continue the effort (a follow-on to the $1.3 million used to develop and test the first five community college scenarios) and build an electronic learning network for community college faculty who want to implement SCANS-type project learning.

CTE has a patented approach, *Team Research and Learning (TRL),* for guiding teachers to successfully establish team learning. Team learning serves three purposes: It's an effective way to learn the academic skills, teamwork is an important SCANS competency, and it is the only way to keep most students engaged over a multiweek period. Yet, despite the benefits, collaborative learning is far from successful all of the time. It requires techniques, such as those embedded in TRL, for forming and motivating teams, assessing individual performance, and providing the guidance needed.

Using a computer is another challenge. Students often find navigating through the CD-ROM more intuitive than teachers and faculty who have less computer experience. The same thing may be said about the various software products that the students must employ during the project. Faculty members must become proficient in both to make the project work. In addition, teachers must learn to plan, organize, and manage computer access by student teams. They require planning and preparation time to accomplish all this.

Teachers may find solving the problem posed in the project as substantial a difficulty as mastering the technology. Math teachers familiar with problems that can be readily handled in ten to twenty minutes may not know how to organize and attack an authentic assignment that requires a sustained effort and includes dozens of steps. English teachers comfortable with expository writing about character development in *To Kill a Mocking Bird* may be uncomfortable guiding students in writing a decision memo. Neither may feel as if they know how to assess an oral presentation about quantitative data—or teach their students how to deliver one.

"Become a guide at the side instead of a sage on the stage," is a cliché of modern pedagogy. It is not easy. When the students' travel brochures were critiqued by outside experts, teachers were uncomfortable admitting they did not know all the answers. Large, SCANS-type projects will raise this discomfort level frequently, especially the first time a teacher takes his or her students through it. There are pitfalls at each step—forming the teams, using the technology, and attacking the problem. Unless teachers learn how to handle this change in roles, the project will not succeed.

Perhaps the most difficult challenge of all is integrating the project into an already demanding set of curriculum requirements. Projects support application and do not usually provide direct instruction. They, therefore, do not help teachers who are struggling to "cover all the material in the syllabus." They may be best placed as an end-of-semester capstone effort to be undertaken after the didactic teaching is accomplished for the term. This requires discipline on the part of the teacher who, rushing to complete the syllabus, may not allow enough time for project development and completion. A better approach may be to use the project as a laboratory assignment in conjunction with didactic lessons given during class hours. This approach was used successfully by a community college physics teacher when implementing the *Locating an Environmentally Sensitive Factory* project.

Beyond the Classroom

The successful applications—in both the high school and community college settings—had support from outside the classroom from deans, principals, and other administrators of the education system. Administrators provided the technology, the time for training and planning, the scheduling flexibility, and some relief from the tyranny of curriculum requirements.

Why should administrators provide these resources to enable project-based learning? Because it is key to their students' success in the new Information Age. Employers are demanding that schools do a better job of preparing workers for the twenty-first-century workplace. They are calling for the competencies imparted by the projects. At one community college, local businesspeople are helping the faculty assess student presentations. Several have commented, *"I wish all my employees could do as well."*

On the academic side, influential organizations like the National Council of Teachers of Mathematics (NCTM) are demanding that schools adapt curricula to meet employers' demands. These projects meet the demands. NCTM wants students to value mathematics, become confident in their ability to do mathematics, become mathematical problem solvers, communicate mathematically, and reason mathematically. They want graduates to be able to apply these capacities to real problems. In a similar vein, the National Research Council's (NRC) standards for science seek to enable students to become workers who can learn, reason, think creatively, make decisions and solve problems.

Neither NCTM nor NRC gave the school system guidance on reconciling these lofty goals with the subject coverage issue. In the case of Baltimore's high school math teacher, completing the project while facing extensive, rigid coverage requirements was more of a challenge than she could meet in a single semester. Instead of the project, she had to drill students on factoring polynomials—something students will never encounter again after high school. Administrators have to help her decide what is more important. The decision should be obvious, given the current propensity of high schools to turn out students who "hate math and science." The goal is to motivate students to learn enough so that they have the confidence and capability to use these disciplines. But old ways die hard. It is easier to test students' ability with factoring polynomials (an ability that will fade quickly from inevitable disuse) than their capacity to attack an authentic problem.

Ultimately, administrators will have to decide whether they want to meet NCTM's and NRC's lofty goals or continue with the current curricula that deal primarily with remembering how to solve algorithms, including those regarding factoring polynomials. But algorithms—of all kinds—will increasingly be solved by computers in the twenty-first century and not by well-paid American workers. Demand and wages for file clerks, bank tellers, and telephone operators are in decline. Instead, well-compensated workers will be required to do reflective work, facing novel problems without clear answers. They will have to follow a Darwinian process of experimenting with alternative solutions, reflecting on the efficacy of the alternatives, discarding the inferior process, and replicating the best approach. This is the essence of project-based learning. It is a lot easier to teach how to compute a square root than to develop a superior marketing plan. The twenty-first-century economy, however, will have very little use for the former and generous rewards for the latter.

Chapter 13

Telecommunication and Technology

Carolyn Prescott

School reformer Neil Postman poses several questions for educators who are contemplating the uses of technology in the classroom. He begins by asking: What is the problem to which this technology is the solution?[1] Historically, Tech Prep programs have faced several problems, or challenges, that information and communication technologies may help to solve:

- How can schools and workplaces connect more easily and with a more meaningful link to curricula?

- How can vocational and academic education be more fully integrated?

- What is the best way to teach for the transfer of learning?

---

[1] Carolyn R. Pool, "Perspectives/Centuries of Learning," *Educational Leadership*, Vol. 55, No. 3, November 1997, p. 5.

- How can high schools best equip their graduates to begin career pathways or continue schooling?

- How do we address the needs of students who enter our programs unprepared?

Technology in the Classroom—Four Stories

A number of schools have applied the tools of technology in ways that address these problems. The classrooms described in the following four scenarios are composite pictures based on school visits, teacher interviews, and research reports. These descriptions are technology intensive because they are intended to convey a vision of how a variety of learning technologies can be used to support curricula and to meet the challenges of Tech Prep.

Project-based learning with a workplace connection

In their science and technology (Sci-Tech) class, Julia and her team members are designing a small mechanical car to meet certain criteria, among them the ability to cross into a given area of a field, drop a Ping-Pong ball into a target, and return to the edge of the field. Using a CAD shareware program to create its design, Julia's team also keeps a detailed log of daily progress, including reports on the team's group dynamics. Members will use a spreadsheet to record and display trial run data, and they will write documentation for the operation of the car. Before actual building takes place, however, Julia's team, along with the other teams in the class, must present its design to a panel of professional engineers who will evaluate the plan and provide a written critique. Designs and critiques will travel between students and engineers via E-mail. By the way, where are the teachers? You can't see Ms. W., the physics teacher, because she is surrounded by a group of students listening to her minilecture on force and work. Mr. B., the

> shop teacher who teams with her, is coaching a student on the CAD program.

Tools for the learning continuum—from individualized remediation to teamwork for problem-based learning

> Ms. G.'s geometry class is organized as a learning laboratory. Students work in small groups using manipulatives, pencil and paper, and, often, one of the classroom's four computers. Today, Todd and Janelle are playing a simulation game in which they build a swimming pool. Todd explains, "It's like you're a contractor; you have to schedule people to come in and work and you have to figure out the geometry so you know how much material to order." At another computer, Jamie is using an interactive tutorial on basic geometry concepts. Ms. G. comments that Jamie entered the class unprepared because of early learning disabilities that are only now being addressed. "This software gives him a great deal of practice and the tutorial support that he needs to work through the problems as many times as needed. The repetition is essential for him, and we've both been encouraged by his progress, which has helped him become an active member of his class team." The class team to which Ms. G. refers is working on an actual building project—a greenhouse for the school. Two team members, Pilar and Valerie, are creating a spreadsheet for project costs, using one of the class computers. The construction project is being carried out in cooperation with the construction framing and biology teachers. Ms. G. explains that, at one time, so many things going on in one room would have been too much to consider, but that her basic teaching method has changed over time. "I do most actual instruction in small groups or minilectures. Students take more initiative on projects and more responsibility for their skill-building." She credits the students' capability and her own shift in teaching methods to several developments, chief among them the use of authentic assessment and electronic portfolios in the school and a telementoring professional development program in which she participated for two years.

Classroom investigations extended to the workplace and the web

In a corner of Ms. J.'s chemistry class in the community college, five students huddle over a list of questions; the students are scheduled for an interview today in the school's videoconferencing center. They will be talking with a power plant operator sitting in the control room of a power plant about 100 miles away. Besides a number of general questions about the power plant and the various jobs associated with it, the students will ask the operator about how an understanding of the gas laws and states of matter is critical to daily operations there. They also hope to have the operator agree to be a content reviewer for the multimedia tutorial that the class is producing on the behavior of gases. Other activities that will be integrated into the tutorial are photographs (taken with a digital camera) of two laboratory exercises on gases. The tutorial will include written material on the gas laws, downloaded from an on-line science museum on the Internet. The students expect to put their completed tutorial on the college's web site, which is linked to an on-line chemistry course developed by a coalition of community colleges.

Career preparation with an authentic and immediate purpose

Ms. W.'s systems administration class includes students at three different levels of competency in systems administration; most of the seniors have been in the class for three years, working their way through a prescribed program of study. The class is a study in transmitted knowledge and culture, in which students who are only marginally experienced in computer use, like Jane, who does not have a computer at home and therefore haunts the lab after school, are mixed together with young hackers, like Alejandro, who grew up with computers at home. Through a methodology of cooperation, collaboration, and camaraderie, both groups become competent and responsible guardians of the system. Motivation to excel in this program is high; some students even add to their credentials by obtaining network certification through a community college program, which they attend through a videoconferencing link. Students are driven by the status and responsibility of being in "sys-admin" for the school, as well as by the promise of job offers from local firms that recruit from the class. For the school, the class provides the expertise needed to run a technologically equipped school.

Analyzing the Vision of Technology Integration

About the foregoing scenarios, many teachers will ask: Whose dreams are these? With four computers per classroom, a videoconferencing center, web sites, distance learning links, and electronic portfolios, the classrooms described here cannot be considered typical. The degree of realism that should be granted to anyone's visions of technology may be fairly questioned—for example, by teachers who have been told for three years running that the school is soon to "get wired," or by teachers who have yet to receive a single computer for a task as fundamental as classroom record keeping, or by teachers who have been thrown into teaching a computer applications class without prior training. The horror stories of technology implementation in schools are legion. These realities cannot be ignored, but neither should they discourage us so completely that we do not look at what technology *can* do to solve our problems. Every technological application mentioned in the scenarios above already has been implemented at numerous sites around the country. Unquestionably, these success stories are not the norm, and the technology itself brings many problems—the most critical being the need for teacher support and training for technology. However, a recent report indicates that the most important leadership for the implementation of technology occurs at the school level and usually involves a small cadre of innovative teachers, led by one of its own members, or, about half the time, assisted in some pivotal role by the principal.[2] This is consistent with findings that technology is most successfully implemented when it is part of a larger instructional vision.[3] Although our envisioned classes are not real, they are constructed of the technological applications of many classes and thus contain within them viable solutions to the Tech Prep problems raised earlier, which we can now revisit and analyze.

How can schools and workplaces connect more easily and meaningfully to curricula?

Tech Prep programs have long been concerned with identifying and helping students understand the connection between what they learn in school and earning a living. Tech Prep programs undertake to help students mature by exposing them to good role models and encouraging them to choose areas of concentration for their high school studies. The latter focus helps to increase student motivation and interest as well as to move students toward potential careers. In practical terms, however, it has proven difficult to create connections with the workplace that are really compelling for students. For reasons of security, liability, proprietary information, transportation, and time, linking to the workplace has tended to be expensive and difficult to achieve. Moreover, internships and mentoring do not necessarily link curriculum—through everyday classroom learning activities—to the workplace.

---

[2] Barbara Means and Kerry Olson, SRI International, *Technology and Education Reform* (Washington, D.C.: Office of Educational Research and Improvement, U.S. Department of Education, April 1997), p. 115.
[3] Barbara Means, Kerry Olson, and Ram Singh, "Beyond the Classroom— Restructuring Schools with Technology," *Phi Delta Kappan*, September 1995, p. 71.

Telecommunication links—via the Internet and videoconferencing—can make workplace connections available to more students—especially valuable to those isolated in rural areas or urban ghettos—and can make workplace connections more routine and integrated into the curriculum for all students. In the science and technology class described in the first of our scenarios, the primary communication between workplace and school occurs via E-mail. The course is designed to include tasks performed in many workplaces—scheduling, design, testing, documentation—and the students' work is evaluated and commented upon by outside professionals. This lends a seriousness to the classroom project that test scores or teacher approval cannot duplicate. As Meredith White, who teaches the science and technology class at LBJ Science Academy in Austin, Texas, commented, "The students know that they can't build—they can't even get their materials—until their design is approved by the engineers [from a company in the community]."[4]

In Ms. J.'s chemistry class (third scenario), the outside world comes into the school via a videoconference with a power plant operator and an Internet-based investigation of the gas laws. The power plant operator will tell stories that vividly demonstrate the importance of temperature, pressure, and volume in the power plant, while acting as a role model and a source of career information. Videoconferencing, discussed in more detail later in this chapter, is becoming increasingly affordable and user friendly. As with other technologies, the primary issue for educators will be not the technical aspects but the uses to which videoconferencing can be put, that is, how people in the workplace can interact with students in ways that clarify academic content, demonstrate employability skills, and allow students to identify with them in their occupational roles. The interview of the power plant operator is only one of many

---

[4] Interview with the author, fall 1997.

strategies that might eventually be developed. Interviews with people in the workplace give students a sense of reality, of a link to the adult world outside the school that they find very exciting. As one student participant in the WORKTECH project (a project that brought high school students together with employees at Sony Technology Center in San Diego) exclaimed, "I can't believe I'm getting to interview a real person!"[5] The strategies for student-workplace connections can go beyond the interview format; other types of connections include students solving a work problem as presented by workplace mentors, students observing or participating in a workplace meeting, and workplace representatives coaching students in problem solving.

Internet Research Benefits

The Internet brings not only E-mail but a giant library into every connected classroom. The immediacy and sense of discovery associated with finding information on the World Wide Web is appealing to Ms. J.'s students, who may have previously regarded research as a static activity. Using Internet resources (in conjunction with printed material) properly, her students truly construct their own understanding of essential concepts. They are taught to become critical appraisers of the material they find on the Internet. Retrieving, evaluating, and synthesizing information from the sea of information available on the Internet involve learning at its most profound level. Internet searching requires fundamental research tools: Boolean logic, an understanding of search engines, easy reference tools that help students get started and understand how information is linked, and the use of concept maps to clarify information linkages, to name a few. However, as James McKenzie of *From Now On—The Educational Technology Journal* has so eloquently pointed out, the search for information on the

---

[5] Interview with the author, 1997.

Internet is a profound search for truth. He explains some of the issues in this excerpt from his essay, "Culling the Net: A Lesson on the Dark Side."

> When you don't know what you don't know, it is difficult to determine what it is you need to explore or what you can safely throw away. When we fish from the concrete piers of our certainties, we hook mostly bottomfish of the most ordinary kind. It is when we head for the open seas with our lines trolling behind us that we are apt to land the big fish like Hemingway's Old Man. How do we sort through a menu of thousands of files? Since bias and personal comfort both rely upon the screening of information to match misconceptions, it is easy to fall into the trap of opening and retaining only those articles which support our point of view. If we hate the timber interests, we delete their data. . . . If we hate the environmentalists, we delete whatever the Sierra Club posts over Internet. . . . The search for truth requires discipline, courage and intuitive skill.[6]

Using the Internet challenges students to think, assess information, and solve problems in the complex context of the world outside school, but with the safety net and guidance of teachers. Entities represented on the web include businesses, trade groups, nonprofit organizations, government agencies, museums, and universities. All these sites represent current connections to the workplace and the community, and all these entities engage in activities that can be integrated into curricula.

Two links mentioned in the earlier classroom scenarios are different in that the electronic portfolio and the school web site are links from the school to the outside world. The electronic portfolio is easily shown to prospective employers or colleges; it

---

[6] "Culling the Net: A Lesson on the Dark Side," *From Now On—The Educational Technology Journal*, http://fromnowon.org, 1998.

is designed to go out into the world. It appeals to students for that reason and because of its format. The web site allows students to share their work and ideas worldwide, which they take pride in doing. As Bill Handlin, the webmastery teacher at Spring Woods High School in Houston, Texas, has stated, "Students are very proud to create something that becomes part of the World Wide Web, something that can be seen by people in the community and beyond."[7] In addition, the process of web page building, as described by Bill and his colleague, Patricia McCulloch, involves continuous problem solving by students.

How can vocational and academic education be more fully integrated?

Tech Prep programs continue to be plagued by the traditional division between vocational and academic programs. This division is likely to be blurred as technology allows more connections to the outside world and school becomes less separate from work and community life. In both academic and vocational courses, students will be able to witness and participate in activities that link concept and application, theory, and practice. Eventually, vocational teachers and students, long stigmatized in many high schools and community colleges, will not be considered academically second-rate because of their interest in future work because that concern will be shared by all teachers and students. The understanding of future work also is likely to be broadened by exposure to connections between school and work. Occupational opportunities will be seen as more varied than they were previously thought to be; for example, the division between working "with the head" and "with the hands" may break down when the realities of the workplace are scrutinized more closely.

---

[7] Interview with the author.

The information explosion—as brought into the classroom by the Internet—will also put more pressure on educators from every sector to identify and emphasize the most fundamental ideas and skills, rather than trying to teach everything. As the scientist E.O. Wilson recently observed, "The ongoing fragmentation of knowledge and the resulting chaos in philosophy are not reflections of the real world but artifacts of scholarship."[8] Wilson was referring to the divisions between great branches of knowledge, but his statement applies as well to what has previously been termed "academic" and "vocational" learning. Increased contact with the real world of work and real-world problems may help us to develop more unified approaches to problem solving across the disciplines; to identify fundamental theoretical frameworks that apply across many different types of systems, from manufacturing to pond life; and to educate students to have what Wilson calls "fluency across the boundaries" between the humanities and the natural sciences.

The use of technology tools will also help to integrate academic and vocational learning. In the science and technology class described in the first scenario, students learn about physics through a hands-on project, and they enjoy methodologies that are typical of both academic and vocational classes: building, documenting, reflecting, and listening to lectures, to name a few. The course incorporates the use of technology tools of the workplace—a simplified CAD program and spreadsheets. These tools alone will not accomplish integration, but, by their nature, they tend to bring together concepts and practice. Software tools such as these as well as multimedia programs and web page builders can be highly motivating factors in learning that can transfer to academic content. For example, if a student is avid about multimedia production, she will surely learn more about covalent bonding by describing it in a multimedia format.

---

[8] "Back from Chaos," *Atlantic Monthly*, Vol. 281, No. 3, March 1998.

Technology skills such as multimedia production, computer graphic arts, web page creation, and systems administration (mentioned in the last scenario) are now being offered both as career preparation classes and as general technology electives, and the fact that these courses are taken by students on both sides of the vocational-academic divide also helps to break down that boundary.

How can schools teach for the transfer of learning?

Teaching for the transfer of learning is a challenge that most Tech Prep teachers understand, but structuring classes to enhance transfer is still not easy. Teachers need contextual examples of the concepts they are teaching, an understanding of how skills are used and evaluated in the workplace, and, often, some version of the tools of the occupation. The point is not that the classroom should become a replica of the workplace, but that selected features of workplace practice, when incorporated into classroom activities, will later function as familiar landmarks when students enter unfamiliar work environments. The transfer of learning can be supported by applying at least three types of technology tools in the classroom: real workplace software tools, simulation software, and the involvement (via telecommunication) of workplace mentors to guide and evaluate student work.

The use of real workplace tools in the classroom—in our earlier examples, a shareware CAD program and a spreadsheet in the science and technology class—allows students to experiment with formats that they will recognize when they are called upon to use them again on the job, albeit in a more sophisticated form. Word processing software, spreadsheets, presentation software such as PowerPoint, and basic drawing tools often come bundled with computers or are part of a basic package purchased by the school. Using the tools of the workplace motivates students, who enjoy seeing their work in a professional format and can often see their own errors more clearly in such presentations.

In the geometry class described above, students play a software game that simulates construction math and problem solving. With its variations in problem solving, geometric forms, and dimensions, the game lends itself to replay. Students thereby enter into multiple learning strategies that enhance the transfer of learning: they are immersed in a complex situation they must process in order to perform a task (building the pool), as they are provided with advice and reflective thinking about the task from an advisor within the game. This learning experience simulates and helps students to anticipate what would be expected of them in a real work situation.[9] The notion of simulating workplace environments in order to teach for the transfer of learning is the basis of software created by CORD as well as by the SCANS/2000 group led by Dr. Arnold Packer at the Institute for Policy Studies at Johns Hopkins University, and others. As the rationale and methodology become more widely understood and disseminated among software producers, more software of this type should become available, allowing teachers to select simulations tailored to the standards and content of their instruction.

Finally, when students present their work for scrutiny by professionals outside the school, they experience the standards, the vocabulary, and the rigor associated with evaluation in the workplace. In such a situation, the learning that takes place not only is likely to be transferred from the workplace exposure to future work, but also affects school performance.

---

[9] Center for Occupational Research and Development, *Math at Work Series Pooling Around User's Guide* (Waco: CORD Communications, Inc., 1997).

Providing adequate opportunities for career preparation

Articulation agreements in Tech Prep programs have created new opportunities for high school students to take advanced and specialty courses at community colleges, which have in turn made arrangements with local industries and/or affiliated advanced technology centers. However, as the technology of distance learning advances, opportunities for career preparation in the specialty areas will greatly expand.

How will this be possible? Because of satellites, distance learning has been a reality for some time, but satellite courses become cost-effective only when larger numbers of people participate. More recently, videoconferencing, which uses high-speed data lines to transmit voice and image, is allowing for more flexible and varied distance learning opportunities. Videoconferencing units are now available at prices that many schools and small businesses can afford (as low as $6000 per unit as of this writing), and the network of videoconference sites is growing. Consequently, face-to-face connections among schools and workplaces will become more routine and cost-effective. This, in turn, will allow the connections to be made at the curriculum and the classroom level, as in Ms. J.'s chemistry class described earlier.

A current initiative by a company called Teledesic, spearheaded by Bill Gates and Craig McCaw, to build a constellation of low-earth-orbit (LEO) satellites will surround the earth and provide a low-cost, highly accessible telecommunication network. The LEO satellites, in contrast to higher-orbit, geostationary satellites, would make ground-based telecommunication wiring and fiber-optics unnecessary and would presumably offer consumers low-cost, user-friendly connections adequate for the Internet and videoconferencing. If realized, this project has the potential to make distance learning routine. The full implications are beyond the scope of this chapter, but one of the most important aspects of this technology is that excellent teachers may come to the forefront as educational service providers. Especially at the community college level, those who have demonstrated the best practices and most effective teaching will have the potential to connect to a vast and distant audience.

Distance learning has long been plagued by its "talking heads" reputation, so we must remind ourselves that more choices—of courses, subjects, and teachers—whether in person or via videoconferencing, will not guarantee more learning. Interactivity in distance learning is often heralded but less often achieved, not because of the technology but because the traditional methods that most teachers used also lacked interactivity. Some new models are emerging that address this perennial teaching problem, using both synchronous and asynchronous telecommunication (the latter does not require both parties of an interaction to participate at the same time). The Virtual High School, funded by a Technology Challenge Grant from the U.S. Department of Education and developed by the Concord Consortium (a nonprofit educational research group) through a regional consortium of schools, is a cooperative of fifty-five high schools in thirteen states and four countries. Each school contributes outstanding teaching talent to a pool augmented by volunteers from businesses and universities. With the help of outside experts, teachers in the pool design and offer innovative courses over the network. These electronic seminars, each with an enrollment of twenty students drawn from far and wide, demonstrate how excellent course offerings and opportunities can be offered to students across distance.[10] The Virtual High School model is addressing questions of interactivity, assessment, and teacher preparation that will be instrumental in developing netcourses of the future.

---

[10] Carla Melluci, "The Future Is Now," *CONCORD.ORG* (newsletter of the Concord Consortium), spring 1997, p. 3.

The Internet is already beginning to play a significant role in training and development for teachers and other professionals. The Appalachian Regional Commission's (ARC) Contextual Teaching and Learning Network, a project carried out through a partnership between ARC and CORD, employs interactive videoconferencing, E-mail, web sites, and voice mail to provide professional development for teachers in rural and widely scattered communities in Appalachia. The technology provides opportunities for extending learning, applying it in the context of everyday work, and working through the problems encountered with support and guidance.

Addressing the needs of unprepared students

Teachers would welcome a world in which all students enter high school or community college prepared for the curriculum, but few have had that teaching experience. In most of our high schools and community colleges, the percentage of unprepared students is substantial. In the past, many vocational programs were the proverbial "dumping grounds" for unprepared students, and, today, some Tech Prep programs are subject to the same administrative practice. In the geometry class described in the second scenario, software plays an important role for one unprepared student. Interactive educational software, if it's well designed, has been shown to be effective.[11] It can provide the extensive practice that many students, especially those with learning disabilities, need in order to master skills.

Recent research into human brain function has demonstrated that the brain is a dynamic, continuously self-organizing organ. This characteristic is known as brain

---

[11] Richard Cooley, Policy Information Center, Educational Testing Service, *Computers and Classrooms: The Status of Technology in U.S. Schools* (Princeton, New Jersey: Educational Testing Service, May 1997), p. 34.

plasticity.[12] This understanding of how our brains develop new processing patterns is being applied to software development. For example, Scientific Learning Corporation has developed a comprehensive program called Fast ForWord to address the needs of children with maladaptive brain processing patterns, such as dyslexia and other learning disabilities. Fast ForWord makes use of computer-generated artificial speech, digitized human speech, and digital tones and sounds that modify the characteristics of speech to train children's brains to process information differently and more successfully.[13] The use of computer software is particularly appropriate for this kind of training because software can adapt to the learner's changing pace and never gets fatigued or bored throughout a lengthy session of training that, although challenging for the student, would be tiring for even the most dedicated teacher. In the future, the collaboration of brain research and software development can be expected to provide teachers with additional tools and resources that address the needs of unprepared students.

The Path to Implementation— Guidelines and Cautions

We've described how technology can be applied to some of the problems and challenges of Tech Prep programs. Neil Postman's question—What is the problem to which this technology is the solution?—was the starting point of this visioning process and the ensuing discussion. Postman urges educators to go beyond this initial question, however, and to ask further questions, among them: Whose problem is it? Who will

---

[12] Paula Tallal, "Language Learning Impairments and Brain Plasticity," *Curriculum/Technology Quarterly*, Vol. 7, No. 2, spring 1998, p. 9.
[13] Sheryle Bolton, "Auditory Processing and Fast ForWord," *Curriculum/Technology Quarterly*, Vol. 7, No. 2, spring 1998, p. 3.

benefit, and who will pay for it? Suppose we solve the problem. What new problems will result?[14] Schools and school systems would do well to incorporate such tough questions into the technology-planning process. The long history of failed uses of technology in schools attests to the fact that hardware and software alone will effect few or no solutions to educational problems. Empty computer labs, closets packed with broken computers, and libraries of unused software found in many schools are sad evidence of the cycle of enthusiastic embrace, rapid implementation, and failure that has attended many attempts at technology integration. This cycle should not surprise us when we consider that the emphasis in the past has been on hardware to the exclusion of pedagogy and without adequate support for the technological infrastructure.

Imagine, for a moment, the confused scenario in the banking and financial world if computers had been introduced without systematic training of employees or technical support. Loan officers and stockbrokers receive notice of the introduction of technology. A few weeks later, they enter their offices to find them equipped with desktop computers. After half a day of training, they are left with a manual, a help number, and the promise that a technical support person will visit their banks weekly. Employees know that, even as they determine how to use the new machines, productivity must be maintained and corporate objectives must not be compromised.

Such a scenario has been played out repeatedly in the education field. As reported to the president recently by the Panel on Educational Technology of the President's Committee of Advisors on Science and Technology, teachers currently receive little technical, pedagogic, or administrative support for the fundamental changes of the technologically transformed classroom and are left "largely on their own as they struggle to

---

[14] Pool, p. 5.

integrate technology into their curricula."[15] Much has been said about teachers' resistance to technology, yet, given the circumstances of implementation in many schools, resistance could be considered a healthy response. Amazingly, many teachers have had quite a different and more positive response, and that is to take whatever technology is available and create a dynamic learning environment. These teachers, the makers of lemonade out of what were often technological lemons, are the innovators represented by the teachers in the scenarios presented here. They have shown us the ways technology can be used to improve learning.

The goal of the integration of technology into Tech Prep programs is to improve student achievement and to help students become lifelong learners. If technology is to be integrated effectively, the classroom teacher must be recognized as the primary agent of change in the learning process. Implementation thus should be centered around the needs of the classroom teacher. These needs, described earlier, are summarized in the following guidelines for technology implementation:

- *Teachers must be collaborators in the integration of technology into instruction from its inception.* Teachers must be involved in the development of the instructional vision into which technology use will be incorporated. As stated in *Technology and Education Reform*, "good curricular content comes first."[16] Teachers must also be given time to plan for changes in the pedagogical approach

---

[15] President's Committee of Advisors on Science and Technology, Panel on Educational Technology, *Report to the President on the Use of Technology to Strengthen K-12 Education in the United States* (March 1997).
[16] Office of Educational Research and Improvement, U.S. Department of Education, Technology and Education Reform, Washington, D.C.: U.S. Department of Education, p. xii.

and to participate in the evaluation, especially formative evaluation, of changes.

- *Teachers must have support for learner-centered approaches that technology can facilitate.* Technology can facilitate and, in some cases, promote learner-centered approaches to teaching such as project-based learning and independent investigation. If teachers are to exploit technology in these ways, they need support as they shift from a directive, teacher-centered approach to a more interactive, learner-centered approach.

- *Teachers must have adequate training in the "hands-on, how to" aspects of technology.* Teachers need training and support to become knowledgeable about and comfortable with the software they use.

- *Teachers need adequate support for the technological infrastructure.* Teachers cannot be responsible for the maintenance, repair, and replacement of the system or its components. Technology planning must account for these functions.

A process of implementation based on this list will raise some of Postman's questions. "Whose problem is it?" "Who will benefit?" The list also gives the considerations that must be included in order to answer the question, "How much will it cost?" Educators must be realistic about costs and must honestly address the question of who will pay for it. Educators as well as the public are right to ask whether technology will be implemented at the expense of other educational priorities. For example, Tech Prep teachers will not want to trade equipped laboratories and machine shops for computers, and for good reason. The hands-on aspects of contextual learning remain an important component of the Tech Prep approach, and hands-on-the-computer is not a replacement for hands-on-actual-materials.

Finally, Postman cautions educators to consider: Suppose we solve the problem. What new problems will result? One way educators can build in protection against the new problems that result is to implement change at a reasonable rate; another is to build in formative and summative evaluation at appropriate intervals throughout the implementation process. Formative evaluation may include one-on-one observations and interviews with teachers and students using technology, as well as self-evaluation of the learning process. Within the structure of implementation, there should be opportunities for reporting on and revising the technology plan.

In summary, technology can support the Tech Prep vision and the overall philosophy of school reform. Technology can provide tools for independent and cooperative learners and can extend the context of learning beyond the physical boundaries of the school. For the promise of technology to be realized, the basis for technology implementation must be the instructional vision, the experience of the learner and the curriculum content must remain central to that vision, and the teacher must be recognized and supported as the agent of change.

Chapter 14

Professional Development

Julie Hull Grevelle and Sharyl Kincaid

Let's assume that a new vision for Tech Prep has been adopted in your consortium. Administrative agreements have been made. Your curriculum has been redesigned, and new text materials have been purchased. Planning is done, and adjustments in courses are complete.

But . . . what happens when the teacher closes the classroom door?

Do we really know if change has occurred? If so, will it result in a better learning environment for more students?

Will student achievement levels go up or remain the same?

The answers to these questions often lie in the preparation and support system in place for the teacher. If the teacher receives notice two weeks prior to the beginning of school that he or she is going to teach a new type of course using "the latest in contextual teaching materials" but has little more than half a day of training, by the third or fourth week of school the teacher will probably have put the new tools and materials on the shelf and pulled out his or her old lesson plans. However, if the teacher spent some time other teachers learning about contextual learning and has participated in a sound professional development program that provides follow-up and a system for networking with peers during the school year, significant and positive changes can occur in the classroom.

There is little doubt that professional development has the potential to improve practice. Mounting evidence suggests that high-quality, focused professional development can lead to marked increases in student achievement.[1] However, attempts at education reform with poor training are little more than ideas on paper. As schools attempt to incorporate new teaching styles and curricular change, methods of teacher professional development should be reconsidered, restructured, and even, in some cases, overhauled. A common misconception in the education community is that a two- or three-hour training session is adequate for teachers to adjust teaching methods that have been a part of everyday practice since the beginning of their professional careers. This adjustment includes changing the methods of classroom management, instructional strategies, assessment strategies, and expectations of student behavior. The one-shot training workshops are usually of little long-term benefit, and often do more harm than good.

Tech Prep consortia should consider various methods of professional development that will sustain comprehensive, long-term efforts to change curricula and pedagogy. Studies of Tech Prep, including the National Assessment of Vocational

---

[1] Sharon P. Robinson and the National Research Policy and Priorities Board, *Building Knowledge for a Nation of Learners: A Framework for Education Research* (Washington, D.C.: Office of Educational Research and Improvement, U.S. Department of Education, 1997), p. 30.

Education[2] and the National Evaluation of Tech Prep,[3] support the need to expand professional development efforts and improve training methodologies. In their teacher training experiences, CORD and SREB *High Schools That Work* have also found that poor teacher professional development frequently leads to failure in the implementation of applied academics. Dan Hull states, "Teachers should be helped to find connections between theory and practice. They can excel in the knowledge and presentation of subject matter and be woefully lacking in applications of the concept."[4]

Overcoming Attitudes and Beliefs

Given the above facts, it is difficult to understand why we don't invest more effort in the professional development of teachers. Yet, the nation's schools spend a meager percentage of their budgets on staff development (often 1 to 2 percent). The answer may be in the attitudes of the education community about reform and about the purpose of professional development.

For the past two decades, the slogan, *all students can learn*, has echoed in faculty meetings, headlined mission and goal statements, and decorated walls of classrooms and offices in the nation's public schools. The wording of the slogan may vary slightly, but many a district has used it in some version. But, perhaps because of personal biases about learning, very few

---

[2] *National Assessment of Vocational Education* (Washington, D.C.: Office of Educational Research and Improvement, U.S. Department of Education, 1994).
[3] *Heading Students Toward Career Horizons: Tech-Prep Implementation Progress* (Princeton, New Jersey: Mathematica Policy Research, 1997).
[4] Daniel M. Hull and Leno S. Pedrotti, "Changing the Way We Teach to Match the Way We Learn," *Teacher Education and Practice*, Vol. 11, No. 2, fall/winter 1995, p. 26; Gene Bottoms, "Why Isn't Applied Mathematics Working in My School?" *Connections*, January 1996.

really believe that *all* children can learn, and maybe these personal biases about learning are the underlying problem.

Cognitive researchers Caine and Caine describe these personal biases among educators as "mental models."[5] Many educators shape new concepts of reform to conform to their own mental models of teaching and learning. Mental models become a filter for discerning what aspects of a new pedagogy will be accepted. Because their mental models tend to filter out fundamental changes, many educators develop a "fix-it philosophy," limiting change to simple modifications or specific techniques. The result is often a "quick-fix workshop" that neither improves teaching practice nor motivates the teacher to instigate systemic change.

Mental models of teaching and learning will continue to create barriers for progress in Tech Prep if steps are not taken to address individual biases and differences in perception of contextual learning through professional development. Attitudes that are barriers to change often stem from negative experiences resulting from failed attempts to incorporate new teaching methods. Education reformers must recognize that teachers have been pressured, cajoled, and bribed into making changes in the classroom for years. Most of the time, their own interests, concerns, experiences, and attitudes were not considered. To be successful, professional development designers should first listen to teaching professionals and then treat them as an important part of the change process. This is a critical step that must be taken before any individual teacher can feel open to change.

Designers of Tech Prep professional development should be aware that the following beliefs and attitudes are common among educators.

1. We learned things in a traditional abstract lecture method and believe it served us well.

2. We define success by those who respond to traditional lecture methods first because that is what is taught at the university.

3. We have to prepare students for standardized tests—there is too much detail to address this preparation in a contextual way.

4. There is not enough time nor is it practical to manage a classroom through nontraditional means.

5. We identify with the top 25 percent of students because they are already motivated to learn the way we learned in school.

6. We can explain concepts in our areas of specialization skillfully but find it difficult to give students credible instances in which the concepts are used in the world of work.

7. Learning in context of the world of work is not useful and is too limiting. It will stifle students' creativity and imagination.

A fundamental reason for these attitudes is that teachers are naturally prone to teach the way they were taught. Most teachers are part of a self-perpetuating cycle based on one type of pedagogy—lecture/abstract—the one they are most familiar with from their own education. Most of the attitudes and beliefs listed above are born out of this cycle, which does not give teachers the experience or the knowledge to feel comfortable with new methods.

---

[5] Renate Nummela Caine and Geoffrey Caine, *Education on the Edge of Possibility* (Alexandria: ASCD, 1997).

Teachers are not the only educational professionals who have traditional views about pedagogy. Contextual teaching is still a new idea to many educators. Many a campus administrator still believes that the old ways are the best ways. For this reason, some aspects of professional development should include administrators. There is very little chance that a teacher will adopt contextual teaching if the campus administration doesn't support this pedagogy. To benefit students, teachers not only have to believe in contextual teaching's worth; they must also have the time, resources, and training to make the necessary changes in their classrooms. A teacher can attempt adjustments in the classroom structure, but, if the principal or administrator does not provide positive support, especially during the transition period, most efforts will be in vain. Teachers need the confidence of their principals to feel comfortable attempting new methods that may take some trial and error before successful outcomes are achieved.

Starting with a Base of Research

The best means of persuading educators to adopt new teaching methods is to present forceful evidence from research studies relevant to classroom practice.[6] Educational research can have its greatest impact when concepts are derived from experience. Research should be based on the realities of all learners as well as the flow of classroom life. In other words, convincing arguments for teachers must reflect a study of issues that stems directly from classrooms and includes the testimony of their peers. Teachers do not have time to test every new idea in their own classrooms. They are more likely to consider changes if the changes are based on case studies.

---

[6] New York City Public Schools, "Making Staff Development Pay Off in the Classroom" *Research Brief #4* (New York: New York City Public Schools, April 1991).

The lessons learned from studies on learning styles and brain research have finally revealed more effective methods of teaching and learning. The fact that a student has a different learning style from his or her peers does not make him or her less intelligent. Howard Gardner has emphasized this over and over with his research and writing about multiple intelligences. Gardner follows up all of his recommendations for teaching to fit multiple intelligences with authentic models and research in classroom practice. Many other researchers in the cognitive sciences, such as Caine and Caine, use the experience-based approach in their studies and reports.

Specific to Tech Prep and applied academics, many studies have been conducted to compare the results obtained in an applied academics classroom with results obtained in a traditional mathematics or science classroom. While these studies have been isolated, the authentic experiences upon which they are based provide ample evidence for teachers to accept the validity of the curriculum and pedagogy. The following independent research studies demonstrate the success of the applied academics courses:

Baker, Richard A., James Noel Wilmoth, and Beecher Bert Lewis. "Factors Affecting Student Achievement in a High School *Principles of Technology* Course: A State Case Study." Center for Vocational and Adult Education, College of Education, Auburn University.

Center for Occupational Research and Development. "A Report on the Attainment of Algebra 1 Skills by Completers of *Applied Mathematics* 1 and 2." Waco, Texas, 1994.

Center for Occupational Research and Development. "*Applications in Biology/Chemistry:* Evaluation of an Applied Science Curriculum." Waco, Texas.

Center for Occupational Research and Development. "*CORD Applied Mathematics* Series: Evidence of Effectiveness." Waco, Texas, 1997.

Culver, Steven M. "Evaluation of Applied Math Courses at Franklin High School." Roanoke, Virginia: Roanoke Area Tech Prep Consortium, 1993.

Lightner, Stanley Lee. "A Comparison of the Effectiveness of Applied and Traditional Mathematics Curriculum." Dissertation, Oklahoma State University, 1997.

McKillip, William, Edward J. Davis, Thomas R. Koballa Jr., and J. Steve Oliver. "A Study of *Applied Mathematics* and *Principles of Technology* Relative to the College Preparatory Curriculum: Final Report." University of Georgia, 1993.

MGT of America, Inc. "An Evaluation of Tech Prep in Ohio: Year Two Final Report." Tallahassee, Florida, 1996.

National Tech Prep Network. "NCAA Approves Applied Academics Courses for Core-Course Credit Eligibility Requirements." *Connections* [NTPN newsletter], August 1996.

Northwest Regional Educational Laboratory. "The Boeing Company Applied Academics Project: 1991-1992 Evaluation." Portland, Oregon.

Northwest Regional Educational Laboratory. "The Boeing Company Applied Academics for High Schools: Year 2 Evaluation Report." Portland, Oregon.

Pebble, Jerry, and Frank O'Connor. "An Evaluation of the *Applied Mathematics* and *Applied Communication* Demonstration Sites in Indiana." Indianapolis: Indiana Department of Education, 1992.

Souders, John C. Jr. "NCAA Approves Geometry Credit for *CORD Applied Mathematics* Curriculum Series." *Connections* [NTPN newsletter], January 1997.

Wiseman, Kim D. "Identification of Multiple Intelligences for High School Students in Theoretical and Applied Courses." Dissertation, University of Nebraska, 1997.

Teachers need a big-picture perspective on the application of educational research in the classroom. Before teachers will attempt to put new methods into practice, there must be a clear reason for change. Often teachers find this motivation through experiences at state and national conferences, where they hear from other teachers who have found success in new practices. Sometimes teachers have opportunities to experience the workplace firsthand; this helps them understand the logic and purpose of introducing concepts within the context of authentic situations.

Round Rock Independent School District in Texas involves business partners in its Tech Prep professional development offerings. Teachers choose from half- to full-day visits to industry sites, while the businesses determine how many educators they can accommodate within a given time period. From twelve to twenty offerings are open to any educator within the district, including counselors and administrators. The goal of these activities is to give educators a context for teaching and preparing students.

Elements of an Ongoing Process

It is one thing to hear about educational research and to realize that your teaching methods need considerable improvement; it is quite another to have the information, tools, and support system necessary to make changes. In fact, if all these are not available, teachers who have become aware of better teaching methods but are unable to use them may be frustrated. Some Tech Prep consortia, such as the those in the

Central Texas region, have implemented study groups to meet this challenge. Teachers are divided into groups and, either by consensus or as an assignment, read a particular article or book relating to issues and research in education. The groups meet periodically, usually weekly or biweekly, to discuss what they have read. Of course, this activity takes time, but the support and opportunity to discuss important issues with a group whose members understand the issues can be invaluable.

The National Association of Secondary School Principals report, *Breaking Ranks,* stresses the importance of ongoing peer support and follow-up in professional development. The report makes two relevant recommendations:

1. Every high school will be a learning community for teachers and for the other professionals it employs, and

2. The high school—with the help of the school district— will provide adequate funding, time, and other resources to ensure that professional development is a continuous, ongoing process.[7]

Through group discussions, all teachers—the best teachers, new teachers, tired teachers, and uninformed teachers—can collectively address concerns or barriers, learn from each other, and nurture new ideas for contextual learning.

When barriers begin to diminish, teachers and administrators should have plans for ongoing professional development and its implementation. It is extremely important for campus administrators to understand the process—first, so they don't hinder it and, second, so they can nurture it. While the administrators may not need an in-depth workshop, they at least need an overview. As a campus and/or district makes plans

---

[7] NASSP, *Breaking Ranks: Changing an American Institution* (Reston, Virginia: NASSP, 1995).

to offer training on contextual teaching, several factors should be considered.

1. *Is the training part of a systematic campus-wide change process, or is it the "training du jour" to be replaced the next year?*

   There is nothing more detrimental to teacher morale than to build excitement and support for a new idea, begin the training and implementation process, and then scrap the whole thing the following year.

2. *Does this training relate to and support other campus improvement initiatives?*

   It is important to understand how all the puzzle pieces fit together. If an educator doesn't see the connection between the training and the educational process as a whole, the tendency is to view the training as an add-on or "just one more thing they want me to do."

3. *Is there a long-term plan for ongoing training and use of materials?*

   Before any new training begins, plans should be made for follow-up training. Frequently, one-shot training results in useful information, but nothing is done with it. There must be an expectation that the training will be implemented, and the procedures for follow-up and evaluation should be explained in the initial training. Time must be provided for the teachers to discuss successes and failures with each other and the "experts." As implementation proceeds, higher levels of training may be desirable.

4. *Are necessary supplies available?*

   Make sure that the implementers have all the supplies necessary. Since contextual teaching generally involves hands-on projects, supplies beyond those required by conventional teaching are usually needed. While the cost need not be excessive, it should be accommodated in the budget.

Methods of Teacher Training

Methods of teacher training should follow proven ideas about contextual learning in the classroom. As one teacher trainer put it, "Teachers are people too, and should benefit from a broad spectrum of activities that lets them discover and solve real problems, then reflect upon their experiences and collaborate with others." Effective methods of teacher training should include combinations of theory, demonstration, practice, feedback, and coaching. Teacher training programs designed with these various elements will result in a dramatic increase over traditional methods in the transfer of skills from the workshop to the classroom.[8]

A study of the transfer of training to the classroom, by Joyce and Weil, reinforces the need to make training programs more contextual. As shown in the following chart, the inclusion of each training component increases the amount of skill attained as well as the transfer of skills to the classroom. If all training components are incorporated, the likelihood of full implementation increases from 5 to 90 percent. Feedback and coaching significantly improve the transfer of skills to the classroom. Without the opportunity for teachers to internalize and participate in their own renewal, it is difficult to bring about any sort of change.

---

[8] Bruce Joyce and Marsha Weil with Beverly Showers, *Models of Teaching* (Needham Heights, Massachusetts: Allyn and Bacon, 1992).

Table 1

Research on Teacher Training Methods		
Training Components	**Skills Attained**	**Skills Transferred to Classroom**
Theory	10-20%	5-10%
+		
Demonstration	30-35%	5-10%
+		
Practice	60-70%	5-10%
+		
Feedback	70-80%	10-20%
+		
Coaching	80-90%	80-90%

In a recent survey of a group of thirty applied mathematics teacher trainers, CORD's staff gathered observations on what should be included in any professional development program.[9] Trainers felt strongly that there should be more and better ways for teachers to communicate with other teachers. Follow-up sessions were unanimously considered important; suggestions for follow-up included electronic mail, videoconferencing, visitations, six-month surveys, and phone calls.

When asked for the top three most effective means of getting teachers to attend and participate in workshops, the respondents agreed on the following: 1) compensation (money, time, and graduate credit), 2) release time, and 3) flexible scheduling. They followed these responses with a list of the most frequent complaints of teachers. Among these were loss of time with class and family, little time to network with other teachers, lack of compensation, lack of follow-up, and the location of the training.

[9] Private conversations with Ms. Pam Fails and Ms. Sara Mynarcik, Center for Occupational Research and Development.

At the conclusion of the teacher trainers' survey, small-group discussions were conducted to formulate the following top ten rules for delivering successful professional development programs:

1.   Realize that teachers are experts and involve them in the workshop.

2.   Model contextual teaching techniques.

3.   Provide follow-up activities such as E-mail, videoconferencing, site visits, and phone calls.

4.   Offer tested, up-to-date, hands-on activities that are ready to use when teachers return to class.

5.   Provide compensation (money, time, graduate credit), release time, and a choice of days to attend.

6.   Organize peer groups so that teachers can support each other on an ongoing basis.

7.   Share experiences and make the material relevant to each teacher's classroom situation.

8.   Monitor progress, adjust agenda, and be flexible to the needs of teachers.

9.   Offer a variety of training activities such as theory, demonstration, practice, feedback, and coaching.

10.   Do not lecture.

As we move forward with reform efforts, we must maintain focus on our primary purpose: Is what we are doing or planning to benefit all students? If we maintain this focus, teachers will want to pursue new methods of teaching. Professional development can be a positive experience for teachers, giving them the renewal needed in an environment that usually points the finger before assessing the real issues of reform. We have to make every effort to adequately prepare and support teaching professionals in this process of change.

*   *   *

Staff development: West End Tech Prep Consortium

The West End Tech Prep Consortium of Claremont, California, was formed in 1992. The effort is supported by several school districts as well as the Employment Development Department, West End Selpa State Rehabilitation, San Bernardino Private Industry Council/JTPA, the National Alliance of Business, and several hundred employers who serve on local and regional program advisory committees.

In the consortium's second year, members chose to focus on staff and curriculum development. Out of this effort, the strategy of a site leadership team institute emerged; nine high school principals were involved.

To ensure that all teams would be developed according to their site needs, three start-up dates, corresponding to three levels of program development, were made available to the schools. Participating principals formed site leadership that included the following players: academic teachers (one representative from each of the applied academic core areas of mathematics, communication, biology/chemistry, and physics), two technical subject area teachers, a counselor, a career-center technician, and the principal. All thirteen high schools, the regional occupational program, and the community college completed the institute.

Session topics included the following:

Session One:

- paradigm shifts and how to deal with change
- developing a site team and team building
- identifying components of a Tech Prep model

Session Two:

- developing career pathways

- the role of applied academics
- developing a seamless curriculum
- articulation process

Session Three:

- job market and future jobs
- what skills employers are asking for (SCANS)
- business/employer panel

Session Four:

- job-shadowing experience and reports

Session Five:

- role of career guidance
- student identification and follow-up
- marketing and student outreach
- developing employer resources
- overcoming barriers
- developing and implementing a site action plan

The institute included a series of five all-day workshop sessions that were held approximately thirty to forty days apart. Each session focused on the components of Tech Prep; assignments were given to participants, with progress reports presented by teams at the next session. The consortium's fiscal agent provided institute organization and planning. Outside resource people and successful examples were used, and several effective instructional techniques were modeled during the institute sessions that could then be used by the teams at their school sites or in a teacher's classroom.

As the institute evolved, two of its innovative features became the most effective in changing the attitudes of participants: education about the workplace and networking sessions with fellow educators. For example, four employers were invited to participate in a panel discussion on the skills they look for when hiring employees, descriptions of their workplaces and positions, and their perceptions of how well education is preparing students for the world of work. Following the panel discussion, all institute participants were required to participate in half-day job-shadowing experiences in community businesses. Participants returning from the worksites reported on their experiences and identified their relationship to Tech Prep. *This was the first recent time the majority of the teachers had had any contact with business or industry.* The learning experiences and testimonials were significant, and the experience alone made believers of several teachers, counselors, and administrators.

Working with other educators motivated institute members to complete the assignment on time and to derive the maximum benefit from their worksite experiences. Time was given and activities were designed to help teachers network with teams and faculty members at other school sites. Participants from the community college and the regional occupational program interacted with secondary educators, and the sharing of successful examples among participants and schools helped to broaden the resources available to sites.

Institute materials, meals, and facilitation costs were the responsibility of the Tech Prep consortium. Each school site assumed the responsibility of teacher release time using a variety of funding sources.

Additional technical assistance is available upon request to former workshop participants; in many cases, the consortium leaders have conducted follow-up visits to sites. Two institute follow-up workshops have been held, providing an opportunity for school sites to share their progress, successes, and barriers and to network with other leadership teams.

Educators have found the institute approach to be very effective in staff development. Institute leaders claim that the key to the success of a leadership team approach is the support and direct involvement of the high school principal and support from the assistant superintendent or director of educational services to assist teachers with release time. The institute approach may also be used at a single school site, but this limits the networking opportunity that would be available in a larger group.

Chapter 15

Contextual Learning Practices in Higher Education

Nancy L. Zimpher

Signs of the need for a change in the instructional practices of higher education are numerous. In the 1990 report *Scholarship Reconsidered,* Boyer observed, "knowledge, for all its glory and splendor of the act of pure discovery, remains incomplete without the insights of those who can show how best to integrate and apply it."[1] More recently, the Carnegie

---

[1] Ernest L. Boyer, *Scholarship Reconsidered: Priorities of the Professoriate* (Princeton, New Jersey: The Carnegie Foundation for the Advancement of Teaching, 1990), p. 10.

Foundation for the Advancement of Teaching investigated the learning lives of undergraduate students in higher education. The authors of the report[2] charge that "universities are guilty of an advertising practice they would condemn in the commercial world." Undergraduates, it says, are promised access to top-rated professors, splendid facilities, and groundbreaking research, but upon arrival are provided only limited opportunities to engage directly with professors.

The report concedes that recent initiatives in higher education have "turned some large lectures into smaller discussion classes, linked undergraduates with prominent professors for one-on-one work, and established institutes to help professors and graduate students refine their teaching skills."[3] However, it notes that few of these accommodations have fundamentally changed the teaching and learning context of higher education. One remedy appears to be an expansion of conceptions of scholarship to integrate teaching as a form of scholarly activity. As Boyer notes:

> When defined as scholarship, however, teaching both educates and entices future scholars. Indeed, as Aristotle said, "Teaching is the highest form of understanding." As a scholarly enterprise, teaching begins with what the teacher knows. Those who teach must, above all, be well informed, and steeped in the knowledge of their fields. . . . Teaching is also a dynamic endeavor involving all the analogies, metaphors, and images that build bridges between the teacher's understanding and the student's learning. Pedagogical procedures must be carefully planned, continuously examined, and relate directly to the subject taught. . . . With this vision, great teachers create a common

[2] "Reinventing Undergraduate Education: A Blueprint for America's Research Universities," *The Chronicle of Higher Education*, Vol. XLIV, No. 33, April 1998.
[3] *The Chronicle of Higher Education*, April 24, 1998.

ground of intellectual commitment. They stimulate active, not passive, learning and encourage students to be critical, creative thinkers, with the capacity to go on learning after their college days are over.[4]

Shifts in the expectations of students and parents for more engaging instructional practices in higher education are increasingly evident in K-12 settings. More contextual and applied instructional practices in high schools will place strong pressure on college teachers and program designers to change teaching practices in the academy. Accordingly, this chapter summarizes a series of concepts and strategies to guide the redesign of higher education curricula, the nature of teaching and learning, and the academic support functions that undergird instruction in higher education. The ideas expressed in this chapter are meant to stimulate thought. The hard work lies in concretizing these constructs, exposing them to dialogue within and across universities, and then identifying means of testing alternative approaches to more contextual teaching and learning curricula, instructional strategies, and instructional support systems.

Attributes of a Coherent Contextual Program

In providing a receptive context for contextual teaching and learning, all aspects of program design and delivery must be reexamined. Accordingly, a framework for viewing the nature of programs was constructed from recent research (survey[5] and selected case studies[6]) on the attributes of coherent teacher education programs. These constructs were further validated

---

[4] Boyer, pp. 23-24.
[5] Howey and Zimpher, 1989.
[6] *Research About Teacher Education*, 1986-1994.

when probed in about a hundred teacher education programs across the nation.

In these studies, exemplary programs were selected as case sites so the authors could determine which attributes seemed to contribute to program effectiveness. These attributes were then assessed by a larger stratified random sample of over 100 schools and colleges of education to determine the degree of consensus. Many of the attributes are essential to an understanding of the design of curricula in higher education. To be able to adapt attributes more conducive to contextual teaching and learning, there must be an understanding that a curriculum is more than its component parts.

Typically, higher education curriculum design is derived from a set of course outlines or syllabi. These are forwarded to some central routing station (i.e., the department chair's secretary), ordered in some time sequencing strategy (e.g., MWF, 1-3 P.M.), and announced in the daily bulletin. Accordingly, students arrive on day one, receive the syllabus (often a one-page printout of the dates of class sessions and session topics), and move through the term according to the schedule. At least twice during the term, they stop by to take a mid-term and a final exam. A more ideal scenario would be a form of curriculum development, typically derived from the interactive discussions of faculty, students, and external constituents, wherein course development is organized around some conceptual framework or intended outcomes for the program. Then, sequential decisions about didactic, field, and laboratory experiences would flow from this curriculum framework.

Ideally, coherent programs of learning come from a shared conception of the curriculum, typically derived by a team of faculty and sometimes, although infrequently, assisted by students and external constituents. The curriculum for a subject field is constructed around a clear idea of that field. If, for instance, the field is teacher education, this conceptual frame comes from a shared understanding of certain important variables of the discipline. These include the common beliefs, values, scholarly underpinnings, and assumptions that undergird the discipline. In education, these fundamental tenets would focus on shared understandings about teaching, learning, schooling, and learning to teach. These conceptions are debated amongst the faculty. Competing views and philosophies are negotiated and fine-tuned, so that a decision can be made about which views are to be highlighted in the program and which are to be secondary. If there are major intellectual disputes in the field, these are taken into account in some thoughtful sequencing of the curriculum. This can be done only after hours of conversation, scholarly discourse, and alternative structuring of the curriculum.

After this shared or consensual curriculum is decided upon, its coherence is enhanced by an articulated set of themes or core values woven into the curriculum like threads in a cloth. In the scientific disciplines, for example, if a concept such as inquiry or scientific method is critical to an understanding and appreciation of the discipline, it occurs in the curriculum on multiple occasions. The same is true if a key theme of the curriculum is be focused on issues of equity, cultural competence, or diversity.

Focusing on a set of integrated themes and core values requires the faculty to calibrate or organize the curriculum in some logical, developmental fashion. They have to share their course plans, determine overlap in the design of syllabi, and ensure intended repetition of core concepts to students. Students should be able to identify common themes that reflect the shared understandings of the faculty.

Other attributes that guide a more contextual approach to program development include the organization of the curriculum into alternative formats. Certain aspects of the curriculum—such as an array of survey or lecture classes—would continue to be important to its design. However, more curriculum time would be devoted to laboratory opportunities, both on campus and in natural settings off campus. Historically, some disciplines—biological and physical sciences, health sciences, fine arts, and the professions—have been laboratory based. But, even in these, situated learning may be more limited to the campus laboratory than to real-world sites.

Beyond these disciplines, aspects of contextual teaching and learning also apply to the liberal arts and sciences. This suggests that more curricular experiences for all disciplines be defined by both classroom *and* laboratory experiences. While many colleges advertise cooperative, extern, and field-type experiences, these are still generally limited to disciplines traditionally thought of as field based. A new or more contextual curricular approach assumes a more widespread use of field-based experiences, and more hands-on opportunity to experience concepts in their everyday context.

Consideration must be given to other facets of a contextual curriculum. For example, would the length and time for study have to be adjusted to meet the contextual demands of the curriculum? If more field and contextual experiences were integrated in the curriculum, would a student still be able to matriculate and graduate in four years? Some students would graduate sooner, some later. One can imagine important and necessary changes in the largely eight-to-five, Monday-Friday mentality of academic institutions. And, of course, the obvious impact of information technologies must be considered. These can change the learning context to any time, any day, any place. However, such curricular adjustments are still not in the mainstream of higher education curriculum designs.

Finally, providing a contextually coherent curriculum requires that students be prepared to experience such a curriculum. Traditional higher education curricular models are created largely for the student as an individual consumer. Students enroll on an individual ticket, passage for one, booked through the registrar, and deposited one course at a time until the owner's card is filled. The new contextual curriculum might look otherwise. Students would be admitted to the university in a cohort of not more than twenty to twenty-five students. This model already exists at the University of Texas at Austin and, in larger cohorts, at the University of Maryland. At these institutions, to name but two sites, students have a shared organizational structure. This enables them to experience intellectual development collaboratively, form supportive study groups, engage in a form of group socialization, and—if maintained in the discipline major—experience the life of the professor as scientist, artist, professional, or humanist. A cohort arrangement strengthens the group's interaction with faculty as well, providing valuable feedback to the professor about the effects of the curriculum design. Student cohorts regularly inform professors that topics have already been covered in previous course experiences.

In summary, the attributes of coherent programs are intended to create a more contextual curriculum design. As such, faculty becomes more conscious of the impact of curriculum design on student opportunity to learn and do. Contextual teaching and learning mean that the messages sent through curriculum design and the construction and sequence of courses are as important to the learning context as the dissemination of knowledge. Further, the ways students experience the curriculum—whether in cohorts, externships, or some other manner—send a strong message about acquiring knowledge relevant to a specific discipline, and knowing what knowledge counts when and where. These attributes will undoubtedly define the new contextual curriculum over time.

Attributes of Contextual Teaching and Learning

Beyond the design of curricula, contextual teaching and learning will demand a reconsideration of new and more contextually based teaching methodologies. Major shifts in our understanding of teaching and learning processes have evolved over the past several decades. However, in higher education the prevailing perspective on teaching and learning has for too long been viewed by many as a relatively obvious phenomenon: Professors talk and students listen; I teach and you learn. In contrast, reviews of the current literature on teaching and learning reflect a confluence of research on how and why individuals learn "in a deep and conceptual manner, alone and in groups."[7] From the perspective of cognitive psychology, several observations can be made about more learner-centered approaches to knowledge acquisition. These have been articulated for the American Psychological Association as five learner-centered principles:[8]

1. Existing knowledge serves as a foundation for future learning (the knowledge-base principle);

2. To develop new learning requires reflection and regulation of one's thoughts and behaviors (the strategic-processing principle);

3. Motivation and affective factors, such as personal goals, play a significant role in the learning process (the motivation/affect principle);

4. Learning proceeds through common stages and is influenced by inherited and experiential/environmental factors (the development principle); and

---

[7] Howey and Zimpher, in press.

[8] Patricia Alexander and P. Karen Murphy, "The Research Base for APA's Learner-Centered Psychological Principles," in *Issues in School Reform: A Sampler of Psychological Perspectives on Learner-Centered Schools*, ed. N.L. Lambert and B.L. Combs (Washington, D.C.: The American Psychological Association, 1998).

5. Learning is as much a social shared undertaking as an individually constructed enterprise (the context principle).

While institutions of higher learning are increasingly staffed by professors and instructors who exhibit teaching behaviors that reflect a deep appreciation of teaching for understanding, they are nevertheless uncommon. The following observations offer a framework for thinking about teaching and learning as a more interactive phenomenon. As such, teachers (faculty) and learners (students) would become partners in the learning process. Professors would become students, and students would become teachers. The goal would be for learning to become more self-regulated and for learners to assume more responsibility for their own learning. Learners would form teams and acquire information collectively. Sharing knowledge would replace hoarding knowledge; collaboration would override competition on the academic playing field. Meaning would be constructed, not "delivered." And technology would change everything, including the way learners are stimulated, the way we seek and display information, the way we think about what is possible to learn and remember, and the ability to access information when we need it.

Thus, the following shifts in teaching practice will likely evolve:

- Teaching will become more public. Professors' classrooms will be open to other professors; professors will teach in teams; students will assist more regularly in the instructional as well as the learning process. Faculty members will regularly explain to their faculty colleagues why they choose a particular teaching practice in their classes.

- The nature and quality of the assessment of teaching will change. Public accountability will enter college lecture halls; students will become partners in the critique of teaching. Authentic, instructionally embedded student assessment will more closely link to the curriculum; that is, what is taught will relate more closely to what is learned. The mid-term and final exams, two archaic forms of assessment typically wholly detached from the learning experience, will begin to fade away.

- Processes for professional judgment will change. Instead of the typical unidimensional reports of teaching practice and review, professors will build teaching portfolios containing examples of their teaching skill. These might include video clips of their teaching and more dynamic forms of student feedback, collegial critiques, and personal reflections on their teaching practice. Syllabi will become "living documents" displaying the teaching context of the course or class.

- All teaching will become increasingly enabled by technology. Classes will become more reliant on the Internet, more web based in design. Students will regularly communicate during out-of-class time with their professors through E-mail, and just-in-time responses will become common practice.

- Faculty efforts at curricular sequencing and "coverage" will yield to helping students use class time to "select" important understandings. (It will no longer be possible to cover all the information segments of a field of study.) Thus, class time will require facilitation to guided study, helping students select what is most important and useful for advanced applications of knowledge from masses of information.

- Faculties will become guides in helping students accommodate diverse approaches to and cultural perspectives on knowing and doing. As access to and assimilation of knowledge are increasingly influenced by one's world view, the faculty's role of helping students deal with contrasting philosophies will impact the student's ability to integrate complex forms of knowing.

- Increasing diversity in the classroom—from a diverse student population and a shrinking of the global context—will require professors to accommodate a more culturally complex context for student learning and help students acquire diverse cultural competence.

- Contextual teaching and learning will require new views about where teaching and learning occur. The classroom of the future will probably be wherever the learning needs to occur, and will be enabled by virtual classrooms rather than on-campus classrooms.

- Faculty members will become students of their own teaching. Scholarship about teaching will become as prominent as scholarship about disciplinary interests. In other words, as the classroom changes and responds to a more contextual view of teaching and learning, it will focus on inquiry.

Creating an Infrastructure for Contextual Teaching and Learning

By and large, the infrastructure of most universities cannot easily accommodate contextual teaching and learning practices. The system of instruction on most campuses is driven by traditional faculty needs where teaching is concerned. Large chunks of instruction are delivered in unidimensional lecture halls typically equipped with bolted desks, a chalkboard, a podium, an overhead projector, and possibly a television. Room after room reflects a paradigm of teaching and learning that is largely passive in nature. Room design works against the formation of student conversation groups, limited technological equipment keeps the Internet at bay, and class bells still regulate most teaching halls.

This is just the tip of the iceberg. Following is a list of changes that must be made to support effective contextual teaching and learning:

First, the faculty must be more vocal about instructional needs, and must convey these needs every time a course is reviewed and put in place.

Other issues to be considered include: What will it take to teach a more contextually driven course? What kinds of facilities, what new structures in the use of time will be needed? What off-campus sites will be required? What is the relationship between contextual teaching and learning and concepts of service learning? How will faculty development programs offer opportunities for faculties to grow and learn about new forms of teaching and learning? Probably all forms for and regulations about what must be submitted to curriculum review committees will have to change to accommodate important shifts in teaching stance.

Second, teaching facilities and resources to support new forms of instruction will change.

With regard to facilities, "smart" classrooms will probably be needed. This raises new questions: What is a "smart" classroom? How much technology is enough? What can appropriately be done in class, and what out of class? How will rapid changes and rising costs in the delivery of technology-based instruction be accommodated? With regard to resources, how will teaching loads and work-load descriptions be adjusted to make room for team teaching and faculty cohorts for curriculum planning and implementation? How will budgets driven by student credits become more responsive to new delivery systems?

Third, how will the university provide for "just-in-time" instructional delivery systems, where offerings must be adapted to fit consumers who need flexible learning schedules? How can instruction be delivered in more instantaneous modes and formats, using the full benefit of electronic communication between students, faculty, assessment and grading practices, and resource information?

Finally, what will tenure and promotion look like in the contextual teaching and learning climate? How will we examine and assess teaching? How can faculty and students become more equal partners in the teaching and learning process? How will standards for and the documentation of good teaching and learning shift in response to contextual formats? If tenure and promotion standards are adapted to meet new modes of teaching and learning, what rewards and incentives must be put in place?

These and other questions will continue to arise as our understanding of new modes of teaching and learning unfolds. Ideas of curriculum development will change; instructional practices will shift; and, ultimately, university infrastructures will create a capacity to accommodate new modes of teaching and learning.

The time has come; students will see to that!

Employer

Support

Overview

The partnering of business and education is one of the emerging success stories in recent Tech Prep efforts. As a result of this partnering, the education and business/industry sectors are talking and listening to each other. An understanding is developing among educators that not only colleges and universities but also business and industry are the "end-users" of the "product" of education—students.

A new role

As end-users, employers are assuming a new role in education as they work to ensure a flow of qualified workers to their businesses and industries. Their "return on investment" comes from higher performance from new workers and lower training costs during their first three years on the job. Employers are discussing different cooperative efforts with educators to give students exposure to careers and experience in work-based programs. They're also striving to give educators information about current industry standards and practices and about current and future labor markets to help educators guide their students better.

In assuming this new role, employers are not attempting to "control education." Any employer will tell you that he or she has enough responsibility just making the business profitable. Employers would be happy with their old role: pay taxes, give advice, and criticize. But most employers now know that the profitability of their businesses is heavily dependent on highly qualified, well educated, flexible employees. And for the educational sector to produce this result, it needs employers to assist in the teaching and learning process.

The increased communication between business and education is also helping overcome one of the challenges Tech Prep and other school-to-career programs face: helping students, teachers, parents, and employers understand that the

*programs are, and must continue to be, academically rigorous.
It has provided greater understanding of each sector's work
and challenges and has allowed teachers to participate in
summer internships in business/industry so they can experience
and learn in high-performance workplaces. From these
internships, they can take back to their classes a new
understanding of what such workplaces require. Better
communication has also helped businesses realize that, without
their clearly defining expectations of potential employees,
educators are "flying blind" in their effort to prepare students
for meaningful careers.*

Different program offerings

*A number of programs have been structured to offer the
different career-discovery and -exploration options that should
be open to young people, some starting in kindergarten, others
in middle school or junior high, and many in high school. To
encourage business and industry to become involved in these
efforts, the National Employer Leadership Council has
developed and published* The Employer Participation Model:
Connecting Learning and Earning, *which offers employers
guidance in developing education partnerships. The document
lists fifty-six steps for involvement in workforce preparation.
Businesses of all sizes can choose the level of involvement
appropriate to their resources and capacity.* [1]

*The educational programs established by Siemens, General
Motors Corporation, and Devro-Teepak demonstrate an
apprenticeship approach to the education of future employees.
While these three companies represent the large end of the
scale, it is important to note that many of the operating
companies of Siemens are small and mid-size employers, and*

---

[1] National Employer Leadership Council, 1996. Copies can be obtained by
calling 800-360-NELC.

must operate within the budgetary and employee constraints of smaller companies. Similarly, the dealerships involved in GM's program are often smaller independent businesses.

The approaches of all three parent companies have been shaped by the company cultures and the industries they represent. Each offers something that can be learned and replicated by others. Each has clearly outlined the steps it took to establish its program. Like many smaller businesses, each company was motivated to become involved in education by the belief that it had something of value to share with educators and students, and by its continuing need for—and commitment to helping prepare—highly skilled workers.

For educators, it is both encouraging and challenging to find out about companies that want to use their experience to provide input into the curriculum and into educating students. Encouraging, in that they must take comfort from the fact others are willing to bear the burden of educating students. Challenging, in that it takes educators with open minds, a willingness to work hard, and the ability to change from knowledge deliverers to facilitators of learning to reap the benefits of employer involvement in Tech Prep programs.

As Tech Prep leaders, we must constantly remind ourselves and others that the goals of public education are much broader than job preparation or career focus; the goal of education is to prepare youth for all aspects of life, and properly structured work-based experiences can contribute to this broad agenda. There is now a body of evidence, both statistical and anecdotal, to show that Tech Prep and other programs geared to introduce students to and prepare them for careers are worth the effort. "The Teaching Firm," a study conducted by Education

Development Center, Inc.,[2] *indicates some of the benefits educators and students derive from work-based experiences. The study examined the effects on teachers and students of the informal learning that takes place in work-based experiences, and the value added to the curriculum by such experiences. Benefits to educators and students included the following:*

1. *Increased student appreciation of subject matter*

2. *Increased teacher understanding of the "hands-on" approach to learning*

3. *More positive response to educational change from both students and teachers*

4. *Increased student interest in pursuing a four-year degree*

5. *Increased student confidence*

    The study also suggests a strong link between formal and informal learning, and reveals critical gaps between school-based and work-based learning. Into these gaps fall the following:

- *goal-directed learning*

- *an understanding of quality*

- *critical thinking*

- *individual initiative*

- *professionalism*

- *teamwork and communication*

    Employers also reaped benefits from work-based learning efforts, as The Employer Participation Model: Connecting

---

[2] Center for Workforce Development, *The Teaching Firm: Where Productive Work and Learning Converge* (Newton, Massachusetts: Education Development Center, January 1998).

Learning and Earning *indicates in its list of the returns on investment employers can expect from workplace education programs, including:*

- *An increased pool of qualified applicants to meet current and future workforce demands*

- *A reduced cost of employee recruitment, selection, and training*

- *Strengthened links between work and learning as well as labor market supply and demand*

- *Collaboration between employers and educators to support workforce development*

- *Enhanced employee morale and relationships between employer and employees*

- *Support for employees in their role as parents*

- *Enhanced company reputation from involvement in education reform*

- *Improved community relations through participation in partnerships*

Thus Tech Prep and other education and workforce preparation programs provide clear benefits for all stakeholders—employers, teachers, students, the local community, and even the nation, which benefits from being able to compete on a global scale.

No longer can people dismiss workforce preparation as lacking academic rigor or as unworthy of attention. It can have life-changing effects. Ask Ebony Baldwin, who says, "I thought getting into a Tech Prep program was a way to escape college. Then I started getting to troubleshoot and repair televisions, power supplies, and computers, and found I wanted to go on to college. Now I'm about to graduate with an associate of applied science degree. After I work for a while, I may complete a four-year degree."

Ebony is a nontraditional student, a female in the male-dominated world of electronic engineering technology at Sinclair Community College in Dayton, Ohio. Ebony is delighted with the career options that are now open to her—career options she might not have even considered without Tech Prep, without devoted teachers, and without employers who gave her the opportunity to experience a work environment.

Chapter 16

Workplace Experiences for Students and Educators

Juan R. Baughn, Sue Magee Cahill, and Karen R. Holmes

Students benefit from exploring the workplace in a structured environment with clearly defined learning goals. Although many students have part-time jobs, most of these jobs have little to do with what the students are learning in school, and even less to do with the way they want to earn a living after they graduate. By participating in work experiences at one or more workplaces, high school students gain a wider grasp of their options and can better plan an academic program with realistic career goals. When students see their options for the future, they connect their learning and their goals to the world of work. The educational benefit of a high school student's work experience is usually far greater than the technical skills learned to perform a job; it's the experience of the environment and culture of working, and how it affects the student's attitude regarding personal accountability for quality, problem solving, teamwork, responsiveness, and relating the academics of school to useful applications in life and work.

When educators, too, experience the workplace as part of a professional development program, they learn about specific businesses, advanced technology, employers' concerns, and the interpersonal skills their students will need. Educators gain the understanding necessary to design and implement projects based on the workplace environment their students will enter, and to integrate interpersonal and job-related skills into the fabric of their curricula. Their new understanding of the business world and the challenge of implementing a career-relevant curriculum prompt them to bring contextual learning into academic subjects and renew their enthusiasm for teaching.

When students participate in workplace experiences, parents learn more about the opportunities open to their children and can help them plan academic programs based on their career goals. Parents whose children participate in workplace experiences or otherwise benefit from business-education partnerships see real changes taking place in their children. Motivated, enthusiastic, and purposeful, students have a vision that propels them toward successful careers.

An integrated, academically rigorous curriculum developed by educators in conjunction with business and industry representatives prepares graduates to compete in a global workforce. Contextual, hands-on learning methods can blend the technical and soft-skill requirements of a career path with the theoretical learning that underlies them.

How Do Schools and Businesses Connect?

In many cases, the school district and a few educators envision a business-education partnership. In other cases, businesses approach the school district. Someone in one of these groups has to make the first contacts and call the first meetings. The degree of success of these efforts depends on a number of factors:

- the commitment of key educators

- the commitment of representatives of the business and industry community

- a shared vision about the need for and benefits of the initiative

- a focused, dedicated effort on the part of a core group whose job it is to make the partnership work

- the active support of the local chamber of commerce

Many manuals, workbooks, and articles detail ways to develop partnerships, and samples of forms and letters are easily obtained. The success of partnerships, however, does not depend on the availability of materials. Success depends on the leadership of the school district, business or industry, or chamber of commerce to engage the interest of educators and/or business representatives who can focus on establishing a partnership. The key ingredient of this process is time—time to make contacts, investigate opportunities for involvement, develop a plan, and take action.

Employers are more likely to become involved in partnerships when they are given a specific role for a defined period of time. The level of employer involvement varies, depending on the nature of the program, the resources required, and the capacity of the employer to meet those needs. Obviously, programs such as worksite tours require less time and the involvement of fewer employees than other programs that are more resource intensive.

Steps to Forming Partnerships

Establishing a school climate that views business-education partnerships as important and a business climate in which cooperation with educators is considered advantageous sets the stage for successful partnerships. When teachers, administrators, guidance counselors, and others are familiar with Tech Prep and other national workforce education movements, they are more open to integrating work experiences into the curriculum. When businesses realize that training a student before she or he enters the workforce is less costly than training an incumbent worker, they are eager to select representatives who want to help shape future employees.

To start a partnership, consider these steps:

1. Identify one or two spokespersons who will be ambassadors to the business sector (or, if business is leading, to the education sector) to "market" the proposed partnership. Their names, faces, and style will have an impact. They must understand the idea of the partnership thoroughly and present the right image.

2. Offer a menu of options (Figure 1) for business participation—apprenticeships, internships, mentoring programs, career shadowing, career study/co-op programs, worksite visitations, career camps, and interdisciplinary projects. The size, staff, interest, and nature of the businesses as well as their proximity to the school all help determine the nature of the partnership. But the most critical factor is having clear goals. *If a business can envision its contribution, it is more likely to become involved.*

3. Offer opportunities for program participation in four areas: students in the workplace, educators in the

workplace, employers in the schools, and business advisory groups. The first three are self-explanatory; the fourth, business advisory groups, establish articulation agreements and help arrange applied academics and career study/co-op programs.

Students in the Workplace
Initiatives:
Apprenticeships
Mentorships
Career Study/Co-op
    Programs
Career Shadowing
    Opportunities
Career Camps
Interdisciplinary Projects
Workplace Tours

Business in the School
Initiatives:
Interdisciplinary Projects
Career Days
Classroom Presentations
Career/Job Fairs

Educators in the Workplace
Initiatives:
Internships
Career Shadowing
Worksite Visitations

Business Advisory Groups
Initiatives:
Task Forces for
    Development of
    Articulation
    Agreements
Advisory Board for
    Academic Academies
Advisory Board for Career
    Study/Co-op Programs

Figure 1. Partnership Programs

Programs for Students in the Workplace

Apprenticeships

Apprenticeships give students a long-term, work-based experience in one environment, preparing them to earn a living in a specific business or industry. Students typically enter apprenticeships in their junior or senior year of high school. In some apprenticeships, students work half a day and attend

school the other half. In others, students work all day for a set
number of days and then return to the campus for several days.

Mentoring programs

Mentoring programs provide sustained career or project
advising and guidance on a one-to-one basis. An ideal
mentoring relationship between a student and a qualified person
from business or industry entails several levels of activity and
commitment. In one or more academic course(s), a student
selects a topic for a project or identifies a career aspiration. A
teacher or counselor locates a business person interested in
being part of the program, and a commitment is made. The
business person serves as the student's mentor for a
predetermined amount of time, during which the student spends
a scheduled part of each day or week working on a project under
the mentor's supervision. The student reports to the mentor's
workplace and observes or works with him or her there.

The mentor exposes the student to careers and opportunities
within the corporation the mentor represents. Additionally, the
mentor provides experiences and information to help the student
complete his or her project. The student is responsible for
defining the project, developing a hands-on approach to it, and
formally presenting the project at both the business and the
school. Mentoring projects often focus on a career interest or
specific topic and have research, speaking, and writing
components as well as a final demonstration.

Other mentoring programs are less structured, but the
common thread is the one-on-one guidance of a student by a
mentor working in the career field in which the student is
interested. Three factors are important to success in mentoring
programs:

1.   The provision of a teacher or counselor to act as an
     intermediary between the student and the mentor and to
     help with the operational details

2. An accountability standard for the student and the mentor

3. At least one visit by the mentor to the student's school

Beyond these guidelines, each program is designed according to the student's and the business's interests, the staff assigned to administer the program, and agreement as to what constitutes completion of the program. Tenth grade is usually targeted as the first year of mentoring programs because many businesses have age limits and freshman schedules are often predetermined.

Career shadowing

Career shadowing experiences for students last anywhere from half a day to five days. During this time, the student accompanies, or "shadows," one or more employees throughout the day, observing what they do and how they interact with others in the workplace.

Before a shadowing experience is set up, the business plans a schedule for the student and contacts the employees who will work with the student. Having several employees work with the student can benefit both parties: The student is exposed to a broader base of information and to different perspectives, and no one employee feels unduly burdened.

Career study/co-op programs

In a career study or co-op program, students spend part of each school day working at a job that is related to their career interest. They are monitored by a certified co-op teacher, receive academic credit for the experience, and are often paid for their work. Students complete time-card reports and weekly reports. The co-op teacher not only meets with the students in school but also visits the worksite. This type of program is subject to state regulations and thus varies from state to state. The co-op program more closely mimics the experience of holding a "real"

job than simply exploring or researching a career or special
topic. Co-op programs generally involve students in grades
eleven and twelve.

Career camps

Career camps, held during off-school time, allow students
to explore careers in an environment that exposes them to a
variety of career pathways and worksites. Career camps
encourage students to participate in multiple activities. In one
model for a summer career camp, students do the following:

- Discover methods of researching career opportunities

- Select career interests

- Identify personal and academic strengths

- Tour area businesses

- Interview business partners and senior adults about their
  careers

- Learn team-building skills

- Design plans for their academic studies

- Explore diversity in today's society and in the workplace

A summer career camp may operate six hours a day for one,
two, or three weeks. This time frame permits field trips to
businesses, museums, parks, and cities beyond the school
district boundaries. Students participate in workshops,
teleconferences, computer-based learning, and seminars.
Actively engaged in critical thinking and problem-solving
processes, they begin to develop the interpersonal skills needed
in the workplace.

To be successful, a career camp must be fun and provide
experiences that differ from classroom learning. It may include
one or more field trips that expose students to careers in local or
state government, aeronautics, transportation, retail, food

preparation, or anything else regionally available. The camp may include a teleconference, which gives the students an experience with twenty-first-century technology and links them with students in another location. A visit to a senior residential facility can give students the opportunity to ask both residents and staff about the career choices they made. Art, music, writing, computing, and physical fitness can all be included in the camp experience. Career camps are ideal for students in seventh, eighth, and ninth grades.

Interdisciplinary projects

Integrated curricula and hands-on contextual learning are the backbone of Tech Prep and other education reform movements. Projects that involve integration of curricula and contextual learning connect academic disciplines and include resources beyond the classroom—such as the corporate environment. These projects, which can be done on a large or small scale over differing periods of time, are most successful when woven into the curriculum and perceived as integral to it. Students see the relevance of what they do in the classroom by making connections between the concepts they are learning and the ways they are implemented in the real world of work.

Successful interdisciplinary projects combine diverse elements: academic components such as science, reading, history/economics, mathematics, art, music, technology, and human services/consumer science; a workplace experience; field trip(s); guest presenters from the business community; and a diversity component. All students from kindergarten to grade twelve can benefit from such projects. The earlier they are introduced, the more the learning that will occur throughout the grades.

Workplace tours

Traveling to local businesses helps students understand the demands and expectations of a job. Before planning any field trip for students from kindergarten through grade twelve, consider the career implications of the experience. Businesses can be enlisted to give tours focused on the career opportunities in their organizations. (Be sure to check their age restrictions.) Even a third-grade trip to a zoo offers the opportunity to discuss and explore careers.

Educators in the Workplace

Teacher internships

In a teacher internship program, educators are placed in a business or industry to complete a work assignment. They work for five to seven weeks during the summer and, in the process, identify a range of career opportunities about which to inform students, other teachers, and guidance counselors.

To participate in a teacher internship, a teacher submits an application that includes a curriculum vita and identifies areas of interest. Concurrently, participating businesses identify projects or areas in which they need assistance. This enables the program director, who is responsible for enlisting the businesses needed to participate, to place the teacher in an appropriate setting and establish him or her at the worksite.

To enable teachers to gain credit for their experience, cooperating universities hold seminars at the businesses where teacher interns are working. A university faculty member works with the interns on education reform topics—team building, conflict resolution, diversity, and others—that pertain to both business and educational environments.

Since the teachers are expected to apply the learning they derive from the work experience to their teaching during the next school year, they complete a curriculum-impact project. The teachers receive a stipend for their summer's work. Funding for stipends can come from several sources: the participating businesses, the school district, private organizations, or government agencies. Businesses benefit from the work done by the teacher; teachers benefit from the stipend, graduate credits, and workplace experience; students benefit from the project implemented by the teacher and from his or her increased understanding of workplace issues.

Career shadowing for teachers

Career shadowing for teachers is similar to career shadowing for students. Participating teachers receive a stipend and are required to design a curriculum-impact project for the following year. The teachers maintain a log of daily activities and observations.

Worksite visitations

Days designated for in-service professional development offer an ideal opportunity to send teachers into the workplace for a limited time. In small groups, teachers spend a morning or afternoon at a business focusing on career options. Before the visit, a list of questions and issues is given to both teachers and business representatives. Through dialogue, teachers learn the interpersonal skills needed and the work ethic in the business environment; then they debrief as an entire faculty or by department/grade to identify common threads among the workplaces. Through these visitations, many teachers become interested in participating in extended internships or shadowing programs.

Steps for a Model Partnership Program

A strong partnership brings business and industry representatives into the classroom and into the planning of curricula and programs. Strategies for establishing and operating a partnership program vary with the needs of a school district and local businesses, financial resources, and the demographics of a community. Following are the ten key steps to designing a partnership:

1. Establishing a commitment to the partnership

2. Defining the stakeholders

3. Identifying key players

4. Designing a multiyear plan

5. Procuring financial support

6. Implementing the plan incrementally

7. Publicizing and marketing the partnership program

8. Generating reports, including an annual report for the business community

9. Evaluating the program

10. Revising and expanding the program

Each of these steps requires personnel and documentation so the program can continue over an extended period of time. Since the goal of partnership is long term, each step requires thoughtful planning and energetic implementation. Constant, open communication between the business and educational partners is essential.

During the pilot year of any initiative, a video showing different perspectives should be made. The video, which should provide a "big picture" look at the program, can be used to promote the program and to inform your current and potential business partners.

In a shadowing program, it's important to send sample itineraries or schedules of activities to your business partners. In your orientation materials, provide a handout that describes strategies for successfully communicating with students.

To encourage continued business participation in partnerships, education partners should award certificates or plaques of appreciation that can be displayed at the businesses and the school. Holding an event such as a recognition dinner or golf tournament may encourage others to join a community of partners.

All stakeholders in worksite learning programs—students, educators, parents, and the business community—benefit from the programs because, where they are in effect, the educational system more clearly reflects society as a whole. Annual reports and publicity inform the public about the cooperative effort, so both businesses and the school district are credited with partnership success. School districts and communities working together enable partnership programs to become part of the tapestry of the educational system and the community. The infusion of these relationships into the students' education means that students relate their academic efforts to their career goals. Rather than leave their futures to chance, students choose and prepare for their futures, clearly envisioning their place in a global society.

Chapter 17

Ensuring Excellence

John P. Tobin

Businesses and industries across the nation agree that today's high-performance workplace requires employees with academic and technical skills and the "soft" skills outlined by SCANS. They need employees who are willing and eager to learn and to apply their skills in a constantly changing technological environment.

Unfortunately, such employees are still relatively few in number and are also very much in demand. Training and retraining programs have been instituted to help bring the skills of incumbent workers up-to-date and to teach SCANS skills. But such training and retraining programs are costly, since the workers have to be paid and continue to receive benefits while they are being trained but are not productive. It is far less costly and time-consuming to train prospective or part-time employees to a standard either prior to full-time work or early in the entry-level phase of work.

With this in mind, companies such as Siemens of New York have formed partnerships with educators to effect change at the high school level. They expect this change to prepare students for work and for lifelong learning.

Business-Education Partnerships

Business-education partnerships such as these enable employers and educators to understand the challenges each sector faces, and to come up with curricular and program solutions. But it's not always easy to form such partnerships, or to know exactly what role employers should play in the education enterprise. To provide guidance in this area, companies such as Siemens, BellSouth, and Eastman Kodak have formed the National Employer Leadership Council (NELC). This group has worked with other employers, small and large, and with associations such as the National Alliance of Manufacturers and the National Alliance for Business to map out strategies for employer action in education.

NELC Model

The model they have developed, called *Connecting Learning and Earning,*[1] addresses three functions: working with policymakers, other employers, and stakeholders to build a workforce system; providing information and work experiences for students and teachers; and strengthening company commitment to education. Members and affiliates of NELC—small, medium, and large companies—embrace the model because of the return on investment it yields. This return on investment consists of the following:

- an increased pool of qualified potential employees

---

[1] See chapter 19.

- a reduction in the cost of recruitment, selection, and training of employees

- strengthened links between work and learning, and labor market supply and demand

- enhanced employee morale

- enhanced company reputation

- improved community relations

NELC's model provides a menu of employer activities that involve students. These include career awareness, career exploration, and career-preparation activities ranging from employer talks to students about business/industry opportunities to internships, apprenticeships, and mentoring programs. Activities with teachers include project-based learning; school-based entrepreneurial projects; and internships, externships, and sabbaticals. But perhaps the most important activity in which employers and teachers can partner is the development of curricula that are tied to industry standards.

Changing a Mind-Set

One of the challenges involved in doing this is helping educators understand that the education system delivers a product—students, who will one day be the employees of business and industry. Of course, high schools traditionally have other end-users—colleges and universities—and for many years the educational system has prepared its product to meet the specifications of those end-users (though, of course, without using those terms). Now we have to broaden the concept of education to embrace workforce preparation as well as college preparation. And to do that we have to change the mind-set of educators, parents, and even some employers. We must realize as a nation most people will not complete baccalaureate degrees, nor is such necessary for success in many workplaces, although the four-year degree remains the true American dream.

For many companies, potential employees must have a strong academic background, some technical skills, and the ability to continue to learn and apply their knowledge—but they don't initially need four-year degrees. Thus, as end-users of a large number of the schools' products, employers have realized the need to define their expectations of students and to work with schools to help them meet those specifications. However, schools have not traditionally seen themselves as vendors of knowledge or engines of economic development within their regions, and sometimes resent the use of this language. Whatever the words used, the time has come for a widespread realization that the United States is one of the few advanced countries with no formalized system of workforce development—and that it must have such a system if it is to compete successfully with other countries.

The fact that we have waited this long to institute such a system can work to our advantage if we can learn from the successes and failures of other countries. But it can certainly work to our disadvantage if we refuse to face the fact that its time has come.

Economic and Demographic Factors

There are educators and others who are currently saying, "But in a time of low unemployment and high productivity, why should we change anything?" I respectfully suggest that they look at marketplace factors and determine what percentage of our nation's workforce is engaged in making high-value products that demand high-value skills. The higher the percentage of high-value products we make, the more competitive we are. If much of our employment base is involved in low-value products requiring low-value skills, our ability to buy and sell, and consequently our standard of living, declines.

We also need to examine demographic issues. Currently, one baby boomer turns fifty every seven seconds. This will soon result in the loss of our more highly trained and experienced workers. And who will replace them? Unless we change the way we prepare our workforce, those who will fill our workplaces will be a high-minority workforce (of women and others) who lack adequate education and training in science and technology. This may cause high-value work to leave the United States to be done by better prepared workers in other countries. Once exported, this work is difficult to retrieve.

In addition, those who are replacing the baby boomers will have to support a larger population of aging and underprepared workers, as well as retired persons whose pensions are inadequate to sustain a reasonable standard of living.

I estimate that our window of opportunity for turning things around is about five years. During this time, we must help schools understand the economic impact of underprepared workers. It is a clear case of supply and demand. If we fail to produce a supply of students with strong academic and technical skills, with SCANS skills, and with the ability for lifelong learning, we will not meet the demand for skilled workers. America will then lose the ability to develop and maintain high-quality products and employees.

ETAP

Siemens Telecom Networks, a Florida-based operating company of Siemens, believes strongly in tying curricula to industry standards. It developed a Tech Prep/Youth Apprenticeship program called the Electronics Technician Advanced Program (ETAP), through which high school students can begin to acquire fundamental knowledge and applied training in electronics. This is done during a ten-month course entailing five hours per week of work after school. Upon completion of high school, students who have satisfied program requirements are considered for admission to the two-year ETAP, and qualify for $1,000 scholarships, paid tuition, lab materials, and on-the-job training if they are accepted.

ETAP provides a seamless transition from school to career and leads to an associate degree in electronics engineering technology, to electronics industry certifications, and to government certifications. These outcomes are desirable not only for students, but also for Siemens Business Communications Systems and others in the industry, who know exactly what they are getting when they hire a graduate of ETAP. Siemens Telecom Networks recently transferred control of this program to Siemens Business Communications Systems. Both companies continue to be closely aligned in workforce-development activities.

Quality

Siemens believes that the reliability of its products depends on its people. The choices and actions of its manufacturing employees are directly reflected in the products manufactured. Thus, quality products can be produced only by a quality workforce—and education and training are the foundation of quality workforce preparation.

As U.S. employers enter a period of intense global competition, they can look for future generations of skilled workers in Tech Prep and similar programs that combine classroom learning with practical, work-based experience—programs that adapt the best of the system of formal apprenticeships found in European countries to the U.S. workforce. For more than 100 years, Siemens has participated in such apprenticeship programs.

Project ABLE

In conjunction with U.S. secondary schools, community colleges, and local leaders, Siemens has established school-to-career programs such as Project ABLE (Applied Business Learning and Education). ABLE is a "2+2+2" program; that is, it begins with two years of training while the student is in high school, continues through two years at a community college, and ends with two years at a four-year college or university and a baccalaureate degree. Because early education and training by Siemens prepare students to understand the real world of work and to learn where and how they can fit into it before they have to be paid a full-time wage and benefits, ABLE has proven to be a cost-effective investment.

ABLE has several significant features:

1. It emphasizes the best of Siemens culture and business practices;

2. It is structured, with few electives;

3. It is sequential and developmental;

4. It uses an applied curriculum;

5. It is competency based;

6. It has multiple entry and exit points;

7. It has paid work experiences;

8. It is integrated with existing developmental programs; and

9. It can be disseminated through distance learning.

Industry Input

ABLE acts as a conduit for the infusion of industry-specific information into curricula. With this input, educators understand exactly what their students must learn to be successful in the workplace, and companies contain their worker-training costs. Experience has shown that the least expensive training option for potential employees is to train students in high school; the next least expensive option is to train students at community college. The best overall approach to fully training a potential employee is to start with two years of work-based training during high school and continue with two years of work-based training at community college (a "2+2" program). This is a less costly option than training someone with a two-year degree and no work-based experience, since the graduate of the 2+2 program is ready to be fully productive as soon as he or she is hired. The other most cost-effective program is a 2+2+2 program like ABLE, with the additional two years of learning leading to a four-year degree.

Other Programs

In a Siemens Business Communications Systems training/education program at high schools in California, students who want to become field technicians and customer representatives receive paid training at Siemens facilities. They work there six hours a week, with an additional six-week stint during the summer in which they gain crucial basic and specific job skills along with SCANS skills. In the second year of the program, participants earn college credits while working part time for Siemens. Students attend a customer-engineer training the following summer, and spend time at Siemens locations around the country.

In Raleigh, North Carolina, Siemens Power Transmission and Distribution has a two-year apprenticeship program that combines a traditional high school and work-related curriculum with hands-on technical training in manufacturing as well as industrial electronic technologies. After graduation from high school, students continue their training in the program while enrolled in postsecondary studies. Those graduating from the program are trained as either quality-control technicians or electronics technicians. An ABLE program is just entering its second year of operation.

Siemens Energy and Automation operates a similar program in Alpharetta, Georgia, and in Franklin, Kentucky, Siemens Electromechanical Components runs a program that trains future tool and die makers in a program conducted in partnership with the Kentucky Advanced Technology Center and Western Kentucky University. The program's apprentices spend eight hours each week in the classroom, with the balance of their time being spent gaining hands-on experience in building, repairing, and maintaining dies and molds for industrial and automated equipment.

At Lake Mary, Florida, Siemens Business Communications administers a three-year apprenticeship program for telecommunication technicians in which the apprentices spend approximately twenty hours each week studying at Seminole Community College and twenty hours training at the apprenticeship lab and/or the factory floor. Students at local high schools spend two afternoons a week at the apprenticeship laboratory in a paid workplace learning experience.

When student workers graduate from such training programs, they may go to work for the company with which they have trained, go to other Siemens operating companies, or choose to continue their education at postsecondary institutions.

Success Factors

What makes Siemens training programs so successful? At least nine factors contribute to their success:

1. A paid work experience as a core element in a progressive, developmental, on-the-job training program, that is integrated with an academic school-based curriculum

2. A high school curriculum that seamlessly joins to a degree-granting college program. The curriculum is generally based on a Tech Prep-like model of accelerated technical training that results in advanced placement and credit on the college level.

3. A high-performance workplace that requires and instills "hands-on" technical skills that are internationally

benchmarked through rigorous examination and testing
of performance-based protocols

4. The development of employability, management,
    communication, and process-management skills

5. The integration (employment) of key high school and
    community college trainers/teachers into a Siemens
    manufacturing and service environment

6. School credit for worker-training activities in both the
    factory and factory-training center

7. Industry-recognized credentials upon successful
    demonstration of industry-driven proficiencies.
    Emphasis on the integration of national, industry-driven
    standards (not federal standards) with state and local
    educational standards

8. Using the knowledge supply chain to drive systemic
    change and development, enhance long-term company
    benefits, and maximize return on investment and local
    public-sector resources

9. A design tailored to meet the needs of local Siemens
    companies, as evidenced by the customers who are
    manufacturing or service mangers, after meeting an
    appropriate cost-benefit analysis

Benefits of Training

Siemens believes that the relationship among business,
workforce training, and a knowledge-based economy is
improved by programs that educate and prepare prospective and
incumbent workers for a global marketplace. It believes that
curricula should be tied to industry standards, so that a flexible
workforce with transferable skills, trained to meet industry
needs, will result. It believes that it makes sense to work with
high school and community college students, teachers,
instructors, and administrators to establish programs that will
help produce work-ready graduates.

These individuals must have strong mathematics and reading skills; self-esteem; self-motivation; the ability to communicate clearly, solve problems, and work collaboratively; and the desire to work. These skills and attributes are not optional; they are required, not just for success at Siemens, but for the continuing prosperity of our nation. We must upgrade the skills and competencies of our workforce to enable the United States to remain globally competitive.

Employer Considerations

If your company is struggling with whether it should have a role in education, the following issues should be considered:

- Schools are engines of economic development, both locally and nationally.

- Employers compete for business on the basis of cost and quality, and so must control costs to remain competitive.

- Employers recognize that both cost and quality are directly influenced by education and training.

- Since we compete in a global economy, other countries with better trained workforces may take work away from America.

If you are still unsure about whether you should have a role in education, ask yourself and others in your company the following questions:

- Where do we get our employees?

- How skilled are they?

- What is the pool from which we will draw future employees?

- Will demographics, economics, or other factors have an impact on this pool?

- What is the cost of recruiting an employee?

- What is the annual turnover rate now? In the future?

- Do we understand our local knowledge supply chain?

Consideration of these questions should help answer the question of whether your company should be involved in education. What your role should be is up to you. However, realize that there are many options for involvement in the education process. Remember that it is fine to start with small steps, perhaps a talk to a class of sixth-graders about what your company does. Then consider progressing to participation in a careers day or a careers fair to explain what kinds of opportunities your business or industry offers. From there you might progress to tours of your business, or job shadowing opportunities that last half a day or longer. Check the NELC model in chapter 19 for more suggestions. How you get involved with education may well determine not only your company's ability to remain competitive, but that of the United States.

Chapter 18

Employers Take a Teaching Role

Don Gray

In years past, employers assumed that the people they hired, even for entry-level positions, would have both the appropriate employability skills (punctuality, the ability to communicate effectively, respect for supervisors, eagerness to learn) and a solid foundation in basic academic skills, including science, math and English, as demonstrated by an ability to read with understanding and write clearly. What distinguished the successful applicant from the unsuccessful one often was the level of technical skills brought to the table. And for many jobs, such as assembly line work, "technical skills" were a non-issue: The new employee could learn everything he or she needed to know on the job, and the required skills changed very little from one year to the next.

Today, the core skills an employer seeks in a new employee have expanded to include the ability to work in teams and a flexibility that enables the employee to perform a variety of functions. For jobs that require technical skills, the rapid evolution of technology results in a rapidly changing list of needed skills. However, at the same time that requirements are expanding, many employers contend that applicants' basic academic, employability, and technical skills are poorer than they used to be.

For a long time, employers tended to lay the blame on schools for turning out graduates with marginal skills. But those complaints were typically expressed only to other business associates, and rarely discussed directly with the instructors and administrators at the local schools at which the applicants matriculated. The employers were frustrated with the schools, but they didn't feel they had any responsibility themselves to prepare young people for entry-level jobs.

More recently, enlightened employers are recognizing that they can be part of the solution. By taking a proactive role as educators, they're realizing better, faster results than they could possibly expect by waiting for schools to, as if by magic, become enlightened and change their curricula.

What employers are starting to see, with the help of Tech Prep and School-to-Work programs, is that teaching the skills an applicant ought to possess can be incorporated into the curriculum, beginning at early grade levels. Students in schools across the country are exploring career possibilities. They're learning to connect school to work and work to school. Once they make this connection, students are less apt to ask, "Why do I have to learn this?" They already know why. Instead of showing resistance to learning "useless" information, they're eager to learn new concepts and techniques, because they know they'll be using them soon.

More and more, employers are taking a leadership role in making this happen. They're getting involved with educational systems, helping to launch School-to-Work programs and providing recommendations on curriculum. They're encouraging their own employees to become workplace mentors for young students, recognizing fully that only some of their youth apprentices will opt to join their firms. They're collaborating with instructors to make sure the lessons taught in the classroom are reinforced in the workplace. In short, more and more employers are changing their mind-set about hiring. Instead of relying on instant solutions to immediate problems, they're realizing the benefits of becoming part of the long-term developmental solution.

A Case Study: Automotive Youth Educational Systems

Over the last ten years or so, a growing number of automotive dealerships across the country have experienced increasing difficulty in hiring qualified repair technicians. The dealerships run classified ads week after week, but get little response or find that the applicants don't have the needed skills. This situation not only jeopardizes the dealerships' ability to satisfy their customers, it also jeopardizes the customers' long-term satisfaction with their vehicles, and, by implication, with the manufacturer who produced the vehicles.

Why has it been so hard to attract qualified technicians? In part, dealerships are experiencing the same difficulties many other employers know well: The last seven years have seen a rapidly expanding American economy, where the demand for skilled workers outstrips the supply. This situation has been exacerbated in recent years because the number of young, entry-level workers is actually smaller than when the baby-boom generation first went to work. In the middle of this decade, there were seven million *fewer* 21- to 29-year-olds in the workforce than there were in 1980.

Another challenge to filling positions is that a career as an automotive technician lacks the prestige of careers that require more extensive academic qualifications. Youngsters with a great mechanical aptitude are often actively discouraged by their parents, teachers, and counselors from pursuing automotive service careers, in favor of pursuing four-year degrees. Many of those parents and educators would be astonished to learn that experienced technicians earn from $30,000 to $50,000 and more annually.[1] Many dealerships can cite one or two master technicians who regularly earn more than $75,000.

While the supply of available technicians is declining, the demand is growing. Although vehicles are better built than cars of past and therefore need less frequent maintenance and fewer repairs, the increasing complexity of automotive technology means that technicians must be more knowledgeable about electronics, adept at using sophisticated diagnostic equipment, and skilled in interpreting the results. Some older technicians are electing to leave the industry rather than make the effort to upgrade their skills. They must be replaced, and the total number of technicians in the field must be augmented because of new government regulations (in certain areas) related to vehicle emissions and safety inspections and repairs. In 1995, the U.S. Labor Department projected that 60,000 *new* automotive technicians would need to enter the field to meet the demand for the next five years.

Under the typical franchise agreement an auto manufacturer has with its dealers, personnel issues are strictly the province of the dealer; the manufacturer doesn't get involved. But as it is becoming apparent that qualified technicians are increasingly scarce nationwide, manufacturers are seeing the need to step in and provide assistance to their dealers.

---

[1] Parents and high school educators would also probably be surprised to learn that from 35 to 45 percent of those currently enrolled in technical schools and community colleges *already hold bachelor's degrees.* Known as "reverse transfers," these college graduates are now seeking the specific technical training that will help them get jobs!

Although some local partnerships had been struck between metropolitan dealer associations and nearby schools, the first rallying cry that was sounded nationally came in the form of the keynote address given to the National Automobile Dealers Association conference in 1995 by General Motors Chairman John F. Smith Jr. Smith challenged all dealers to help themselves by helping their local schools and local communities. He urged them to forge partnerships with the schools by providing advice on technical curriculum issues; becoming benefactors through the donation of tools, equipment, and dollars; and opening their doors to students for paid worksite learning experiences.

Smith committed General Motors to taking a leadership role in this effort, and several months later, General Motors Youth Educational Systems (GMYES) was launched.[2]

Inspired by the European apprenticeship system, GMYES modified it as appropriate for incorporation into American

---

[2] GMYES was not the first effort General Motors had made in cooperative education. In 1979, GM became the first American automobile manufacturer to establish partnerships with postsecondary schools through the GM Automotive Service Education Program (ASEP). Currently available at sixty colleges across the country, GM ASEP has served as the model for several other successful manufacturer-supported postsecondary programs. In these programs, student technicians pursue associate degrees in automotive technology (complete with the academic achievement this implies) while they concentrate on the specific technologies of the sponsoring manufacturer. They spend approximately half their time in paid positions at dealerships and the other half in the classroom.

Given the continuing success of ASEP, some dealers (and others) questioned the purpose and value of the AYES initiative: Wasn't this a duplication of effort? The answer is decidedly "no." AYES is designed to reach out to younger students, at a stage when more of them are exploring career options, and to encourage them to consider automotive technology careers. In terms of technical training, AYES addresses the basics, while the postsecondary programs focus on the finer points. In some ways, AYES has become a "farm club" or "feeder system" for the postsecondary programs.

school systems. Earlier in his career with GM, Smith had been appointed to a management position in Europe, where he saw firsthand the benefits of integrating classroom and worksite skills. He observed, in particular, the advantages of assigning a workplace mentor to each student to provide one-on-one guidance, thus ensuring the student's successful career development.

As Smith had promised in his presentation, the effort was never intended to be reserved for GM dealerships. In the fall of 1996, the name was changed to Automotive Youth Educational Systems (AYES) to reflect its broad base. Chrysler Corporation has been an active participant since early 1997, and, as this is being written, several other manufacturers have expressed strong interest in taking part. AYES has truly become an *industry-driven* solution to an *industrywide problem.* In this respect, AYES may be unique among Tech Prep and School-to-Work programs, which are typically designed to meet the needs of a single employer at a single location, or, at most, a handful of locations. What's more, the AYES model can be adapted to meet the needs of other industries. Recently, AYES attracted the attention of a well-known computer manufacturer that is contemplating the establishment of a similar system.

The AYES Model

The primary mission of AYES is to act as a catalyst in the development of School-to-Work automotive educational programs at the high school level on a national basis.[3] AYES

---

[3]Such programs might be characterized as an American version of the European automotive youth apprenticeship system. Perhaps the biggest difference is that, in Europe, the system is designed to channel youngsters from an early age into a narrow career field. The American approach, in contrast, is meant to increase exposure to a wide variety of career opportunities.

strives to bring together dealerships and educational systems, thereby providing a source for qualified entry-level technicians. Down the road, AYES anticipates being a developmental source for other service personnel as well, such as service advisors and parts counter clerks.

While the establishment of well-coordinated School-to-Work initiatives is the most visible strategy that AYES has undertaken, two other parallel efforts are part of the AYES mission. The first of these is to enhance the public perception of dealerships as desirable places to work with a wide variety of satisfying career opportunities. Similarly, AYES is striving to elevate the image of the service technician to that of a knowledgeable, dedicated professional. The last major strategy addresses the dealership environment; AYES helps dealerships become "the best they can be" with respect to employee satisfaction. In a booming economy where good employees are hard to find, it makes sense to ensure that one's compensation/benefits package and working conditions are truly competitive with those of the aggressive employer down the street.

Ultimately, AYES envisions an environment in which automotive service is respected and valued as a career choice, where qualified students are eager to join the highly successful educational system, and in which all participating students are fully qualified upon graduation to be hired as entry-level service technicians or to pursue postsecondary education.

Implementation Strategies

Designing an industrywide strategy that can be implemented in a thousand schools and involves several thousand different employers (dealerships) is a huge challenge, but offers certain advantages over strategies that tackle the problem on a local level. A local employer typically draws entry-level employees from just one or a limited number of schools regardless of the quality of education provided at those schools. In contrast, AYES has the privilege of affiliating only with schools that meet certain criteria. Foremost among these criteria is the caliber of the education the school provides. The school's automotive program must be certified by the National Institute for Automotive Service Excellence (ASE), an independent organization that also certifies the skills of professional automotive technicians throughout the United States. The school must have an active Vocational and Industrial Clubs of America (VICA) chapter, with an operative automotive section. Finally, the school must be near a reasonable number of dealerships that can offer worksite opportunities to its participating students. Ideally, the school will be within seventy-five miles of one or more other schools that also meet AYES criteria, so the schools can network with each other in the implementation of AYES. When it's been confirmed that a school meets these qualifications, an AYES representative will meet with school representatives on-site to verify that the school supports the principles of AYES and will actively implement its methodologies and use its materials.

As soon as the school is on board, a kickoff meeting is scheduled at the school and invitations are extended to the dealers and service managers of nearby dealerships. Surprisingly, the AYES opening meeting is the first time a number of these dealership representatives have been on the school grounds, met with the automotive instructors, or seen the school's automotive lab facilities. Even before AYES placed its first student as a summer intern, this "introduction" process could be counted as a solid success. Of course, there's no reason such local dealership/school relationships couldn't have been initiated without AYES acting as the catalyst; in many cases it simply never happened. Schools operated in their own sphere, dealerships functioned in theirs, and their respective worlds rarely overlapped.

At the kickoff meeting, an AYES representative reviews the benefits a dealership can enjoy by taking part, and the respective responsibilities that *all* the stakeholders—including students and their parents or guardians—have in ensuring the success of the AYES initiative. For example, the school commits itself to providing quality coursework to its students, to collaborating with each participating dealership to integrate classroom and worksite experiences, and to overseeing the internship experience to ensure that students do, indeed, develop their technical and soft skills.

The dealership commits itself to providing shadowing opportunities and paid internships for students, assigning a qualified technician as mentor to each sponsored student, providing a tool scholarship to its students (that is, to underwrite the cost of a starter tool set), working with the school on a continuing basis to review student progress, and taking an active role in building awareness of automotive careers among students, educators, and the community at large.

To take part in an internship, the student must agree to be punctual, abide by the work rules established by the dealership, follow safe shop practices, and complete required paperwork.

The student's parents or guardians are also asked to make a commitment to support their child in his or her pursuit of an automotive technology career. This commitment includes ensuring transportation to the worksite during the internship period.

Following the kickoff meeting, the school and dealership representatives get down to work. The first step is to establish an AYES advisory council made up of representatives from each participating dealership and the school. Throughout the year, the advisory council members provide recommendations on the school's curriculum, facilities, and equipment; some councils serve as budget consultants for the school's automotive program. As the time approaches for the summer internship, the council focuses on more immediate details, such as establishing a common hourly wage for interns and determining strategies for placing students in each dealership and providing them uniforms.

For the participating schools also, the successful implementation of AYES is a year-round activity. The schools are encouraged to introduce AYES to their auto technology students no later than early fall of their junior years. The auto instructors point out that internship positions, which begin as full-time positions in the summer following the junior year, are limited in number and are filled on a competitive basis. Students must apply for internships; they are evaluated on the basis of grades in both technical and academic courses, attendance and discipline records, results of drug tests, and the impression made during an interview. For many students, this introduction to AYES is a wake-up call. Suddenly, they can see as never before that what they're doing in school today is directly related to how they'll move forward in a career tomorrow. Many AYES instructors report that their students show a renewed enthusiasm and dedication to both their automotive and academic studies, as they commit themselves to being among the "chosen few" selected for AYES summer internships.

During the late fall or winter months, shadowing experiences are scheduled. Students selected by the school have the opportunity to spend one or two days "on the job" with dealership employees, observing what their jobs entail. Although the shadowing activity emphasizes the technician's role, students are also exposed to positions in the sales department, parts department, business office, and to other service department careers, such as warranty administration. Even students who later decide that they're not cut out to be technicians benefit from shadowing, and some will recognize that there are many other rewarding jobs available in a dealership.

Shortly before the summer internship period, the school and the advisory council schedule their annual mentor/intern training session. The strong emphasis on mentoring is a hallmark of AYES and is credited for much of its success.

The mentor is an experienced technician at the dealership who has earned the respect of his or her peers. The mentor takes on the primary role of worksite educator for the student, during the full-time summer internship period and part-time school-year employment (if available). No less important than the mentor's technical skills are his or her ability to guide and advise the student, to have patience with the young learner, and to be a role model, demonstrating a positive, professional attitude at all times.

Few dealerships provide direct compensation to the mentor for taking on this additional responsibility, and it might seem that the mentor role is a tough one to fill. Fortunately, that hasn't been the case. Typically, a technician will experience a slight dip in earned wages early during the summer internship period, given that much of his or her time is spent in orienting, teaching, and advising the young student rather than in fixing customers' vehicles directly. However, as the summer progresses, the AYES student develops solid skills and new competencies. By the end of the summer, the technician/mentor—with the assistance of the AYES student—is completing some repair work more quickly than would be possible working alone, and is generating more in income than he or she would otherwise be able to do. Of course, the rewards are not only financial, but also professional and psychological, as the technician realizes that he or she has successfully taken on a new challenge and has made a positive difference in a young person's life. A high proportion of AYES mentors take on the same role for new students the following year, and a number of other dealership technicians request an opportunity to serve.

Such success does not happen by accident. Both mentors and interns are prepared to *expect success* during the internship through well-organized AYES mentor/intern training, which is provided just before the summer internship period. This training is divided into three segments over one-and-a-half days. The first segment brings together the new interns, providing them a preview of what life in a dealership is like. The second segment is reserved for the mentors, who are advised of the ups and downs of working with teenagers (most of whom will be embarking on their first paid jobs). The final segment brings together the mentors and the interns so they can meet each other, discuss their expectations, and identify ways to minimize conflict.

One of the most important exercises in the mentor/intern training session is the creation of the developmental work plan. The student details the technical areas he or she has recently covered in school and will take up in the fall semester of the senior year. Together, the student and the mentor outline a progressive work plan for the ensuing ten weeks, ensuring that the new intern will build on existing skills and develop new ones.

During the summer internship, a school representative (typically an automotive instructor or a school-to-work coordinator) makes periodic visits to the participating dealerships to confer with both students and mentors, to advise them on resolving trouble spots (if needed), to verify that the student's work is, indeed, developmental and challenging, and to confirm that the necessary paperwork is being done.

It's appropriate to mention here the wealth of structured materials AYES has created and provides to the affiliated schools, dealerships, mentors, and students. These materials help all stakeholders stay on track and ensure that the AYES experience is consistent across the country.

A dealership/retail facility implementation manual provides the "how to" details on implementing AYES in the dealership. It covers topics such as the dealership's responsibilities in getting involved with the school's AYES advisory council, conducting a self-assessment of factors that contribute to employee satisfaction, providing shadowing experiences, and preparing for paid internships, labor laws, and insurance coverage.

A comparable school implementation manual covers similar territory and adds samples of the extensive materials that are introduced during the mentor/intern training session. Foremost among these are the work journal diagnostic report, the skill set development record sheets, and the automotive career passport.

For every vehicle they work on in the dealership, student interns use the work journal diagnostic report to record the "three C's"—the customer's concern, the identified cause, and corrective repair made. The student also notes the resources (e.g., service manuals and diagnostic equipment) that were used in making the diagnosis and repair. This exercise not only presses a student to be systematic in his or her thinking but it helps to build writing skills.

Each week, the student notes how many times a particular kind of repair was made and records this information on the skill set development record sheets. These sheets, which are based on the workplace skills defined by ASE, list the hundreds of different repair operations possible on a vehicle. Ultimately, the record sheets are reviewed by the dealership mentor and the school instructor to assess the student's technical skill; the results of this assessment are recorded in the student's pocket-sized automotive career passport, which becomes a permanent document in the student's portfolio.

Additionally, AYES has published a binder entitled Building Awareness for Automotive Careers, which is available upon request to dealerships that are *not* affiliated with AYES. (The information in this binder is included in the dealership implementation manual.) By using the ideas and strategies in the "awareness" binder, a dealer can make a strong local effort toward enhancing the image of dealership careers. For example, the binder provides different kinds of structured presentation

materials to be used in making presentations about auto
technology careers in the classroom, and in offering tours of
dealership facilities to students, educators, and parents.

Next Steps

Although AYES has made great strides in the short time
that it has been in operation, much remains to be done. The first
priority is developing a strong, up-to-the-minute automotive
curriculum that schools can incorporate into their programs. (At
this time, AYES schools use various curricula, though all pass
muster as ASE-approved programs.) The first component of the
AYES curriculum, soon to be pilot-tested, will address
electrical/electronic systems. This is a fundamental area of
today's automotive technology, and AYES students need to be
brought up to speed as early in their studies as possible.

In developing a model AYES curriculum for each of the
defined automotive service specialty areas, AYES developers
hope to infuse more academics, especially science and math,
than is available in most secondary automotive curricula today.
Discussions of Boyle's law and thermodynamics are as
appropriate and vital in the automotive classroom as they are in
the physics lab, and the auto technician with a strong foundation
in academics will certainly be better positioned for long-term
career success in automotive technology. Down the road, AYES
also anticipates developing automotive-technology-related
materials that can be incorporated into the academic classroom
in support of the ideals of contextual learning.

Another area currently being explored is that of taking
advantage of the possibilities for communication and training
offered by such new information-transfer technologies as the
Internet.

Key Elements of Success

As of spring 1998, seventy-four schools in fourteen states have been tapped to join AYES; about forty more have applied and are expected to join by the end of the year. What makes AYES so attractive? Why has this initiative succeeded where others have fallen short? At least five key elements can be cited:

1. *Top management buy-in.* AYES requires the commitment of the top school administrators and the dealerships' senior management before launching the initiative in any locale. Although AYES currently focuses on the role of service technician, it's not enough to secure the interest only of the school's automotive department and the dealership's service manager. Only when the top decision makers become champions of the initiative can there be an assurance that needed resources will be available over the long term.

2. *Local joint control.* The success of AYES in any given locale depends on the dedication and efforts of the local partners—the participating school representatives and dealership representatives. They rightfully consider themselves the "owners" of AYES, and, together, they establish the policies and procedures that provide maximum mutual benefit. They work together on an ongoing basis to assess achievements and make continuous improvements. In short, they make the initiative work for themselves.

3. *Solid, uniform structure.* The AYES agreement defines the specific commitments that must be made by the school and the dealership to ensure success. Then, AYES provides comprehensive materials, including a variety of forms, that can be readily used to make implementation a smooth process.

4. *Focus on real-world requirements.* AYES strives to make sure that what students learn in the classroom and

auto lab satisfies the needs of eager local employers. For
example, as automotive technology evolves to
incorporate electronic sensors and computers in nearly
every system, "electronics" must become a more
significant part of the school's automotive curriculum.
Additionally, AYES helps to create more opportunities
for the school's instructors to take technical coursework
at the participating manufacturers' training centers and
to confer frequently with dealership service managers.

5. *Emphasis on the Worksite Mentor.* As noted earlier,
   AYES has erased the distinction between "school" and
   "work"—lessons are to be learned and reinforced in both
   the classroom and the dealership. The technicians
   chosen to be mentors understand how crucial their role
   is, and they are provided with initial training and
   continuing support to ensure success.

As AYES builds on its successes, the organization looks at
more than just the growing number of participating schools and
dealerships. The personal stories of individual achievement are
especially satisfying.

Will Stevens, one of the first AYES graduates, is now
enrolled in GM ASEP at Oklahoma City Community College.
He acknowledges that he was close to dropping out of high
school until an instructor at Francis Tuttle VoTech in Oklahoma
City suggested he look into AYES. Initially, his parents, hoping
that he would opt, instead, for a college prep program, were not
enthusiastic. "My parents quickly changed their thinking after
they saw the technology I was working with," Will reports. "My
father was impressed with what I had learned."

Will's transformation from an almost-dropout to a hard-
working college student is not an isolated one. Of the AYES
students polled last year *before* their summer internship
experience, less than 20 percent anticipated going on to
postsecondary work. At the end of the summer, they were polled
again. Approximately 75 percent had elevated their academic

aspirations, and said they wanted to enroll in a manufacturer-supported college-level auto technology program after graduation. Now, that's an educational summer! They not only earned money while they learned the ropes of dealership service operations, they also learned that they're capable of doing the work and that there's a great deal more they need to master in order to be professional auto technicians.

Dealers, too, can tell success stories that go far beyond building a means of attracting new technicians. Henry Primeaux, the dealer principal of Crown Buick in Tulsa, Oklahoma, observed, "When I first agreed to take part in AYES, I didn't anticipate the positive effect it was going to have on my other employees. The technician-mentors, and all the people in the shop, have really taken pride in helping these young people. Even the service consultants are excited because of these kids. You worry about how the older people are going to accept these youngsters coming in, but I shouldn't have worried. Our service revenues are booming, and I believe a lot of that is due to a whole new attitude, a renewed enthusiasm for doing a good job that's evident here. That's what participation in AYES has done for us."

Renewed enthusiasm is evident in comments from educators, as well. As Robert Lees, director of Middle Bucks Institute of Technology, in Jamison, Pennsylvania, put it, "I believe our school was doing some very good things in vocational-technical education all along, and we enjoyed solid relationships with businesses and industry. But the model provided by the AYES initiative has helped us move to a whole new level of quality in preparing students and in assisting employers [the local dealerships] with their training and development needs."

Envisioning the Future

Although AYES has been launched in only a limited number of areas to date, it's not too extreme to say that the

AYES model is actually beginning to change the way education is designed and provided in this country. Participating educators have come to realize that making local businesses their partners results in increased financial support, a more up-to-date curriculum, and a shared responsibility for educating students. Businesses benefit, too, by having greater numbers of better prepared applicants! The ultimate winners, of course, are the participating students and the communities at large. The students typically become more goal directed, ambitious, and dedicated. The communities not only benefit by having productive, working young people prepared to take on responsibilities as tax-paying citizens, but also from ensuring that the automobile drivers in the community (a large part of the population) will have sufficient numbers of qualified, talented technicians available to work on their vehicles when the need arises.

Chapter 19

An Employer Participation Model

Margaret M. Leary

A cross the country, employers are being besieged by pressure from both within and without to participate in the development of a technically and academically skilled workforce. Externally, educators, workforce development agencies, and community organizations want employers to participate in Tech Prep and other school-to-career programs. Internally, companies need a pool of skilled and competent workers from which to recruit employees, and need to show a return on their investment in workforce preparation.

Because of this, the National Employer Leadership Council (NELC) has drawn up a model to help employers find ways to respond to education and workforce issues. The model is addressed to employers of all sizes, and can be customized to fit business capacity and community needs. The model describes fifty-six possible steps, which this chapter will summarize, for employer involvement in three areas:

> Employers working with students and teachers
>
> Employers strengthening company practice
>
> Employers building a system

1. Employers working with students and teachers

Providing information and experiences to prepare students for challenging careers, and partnering with teachers to improve student skills and academic performance are the challenges of the *first area*. A menu of activities in career awareness, career exploration, and career preparation enables employers to begin their education initiatives with fairly minimal involvement and work up from there as they gain confidence and realize benefits. Career awareness efforts are all self-explanatory. They include career talks requiring one to two hours' involvement; career days or career fairs, with from two to four hours' involvement; and workplace and industry tours requiring one to two hours' involvement. These activities are directed to students in kindergarten through postsecondary.

After career awareness comes career exploration, which can involve job shadowing, job rotation, internships, cooperative education, youth apprenticeship, registered apprenticeship, and mentoring programs.

In **job shadowing**, which addresses students from sixth grade through postsecondary school, a student follows an employee through the day to learn about his or her occupation. Such an experience helps the student explore a range of career objectives and select a career major. In the NELC model, the length of the shadowing experience varies from a day to two weeks. In other models, the shadowing experience can take only half a day. Each company must determine its capacity for offering job shadowing and other options.

In **job rotations**, students from ninth grade up move among a number of positions in the workplace that require different skills. This rotation enables them to see the steps that are needed to create a product or service. It also shows them how their effort affects the quality and efficiency of production and customer service, and how each part of the organization contributes to productivity. Rotation experiences vary in length.

In **internships**, students work for an employer for five to ten hours a week for a minimum of one semester, or full time for four to six weeks (usually during the summer). During their internships, students carry out special projects, a sample of tasks from different jobs, or tasks from a single occupation. Students participating in internships are usually in tenth grade or higher, and may or may not be paid for their work.

Cooperative education involves students (in tenth grade and above) in a workplace for at least three hours a week for one semester. During this time, students coordinate their studies with a job in a field related to their academic or occupational objectives. The students and businesses involved develop written training and evaluation plans to guide instruction, and students receive course credit for both classroom and work experiences.

Youth apprenticeships are multiyear programs combining school- and work-based learning in a specific occupational area or cluster. They involve students from tenth grade up in five to ten hours of work a week for a minimum of one semester. They are usually designed to lead directly to a related postsecondary program, an entry-level job, or a registered apprenticeship program. In youth apprenticeships, students are not paid for their work, although sometimes employers offer community college scholarships to students who successfully complete youth apprenticeships.

Registered apprenticeship programs meet specific federally approved standards. During a registered apprenticeship, the apprentice learns an occupation in a structured program sponsored jointly by employers and labor unions or employers and employee associations.

Mentoring programs require student participation of three to six hours a month for a minimum of ten months. An employee mentor who possesses the skills and knowledge the student wants to master instructs the student, critiques his or her performance, challenges him or her to do well, and consults with teachers and the employer.

Teacher opportunities. Working directly with teachers, employers can serve as mentors in project-based learning, collaborating with teachers and students on projects designed to find solutions to real problems and to develop new programs within the company. They can also provide expertise as consultants in school-based enterprise/entrepreneurial projects. Through these, they can help students assess, design, and start up businesses.

Employers can also offer teachers internships, externships, or sabbaticals in business. These are all opportunities for educators to explore a company or industry, and to develop their knowledge of workplace skill requirements. Such experiences enable educators to take back to their students what they have learned about the workplace.

Employers can also work with educators at the national and state levels to help link the curriculum to industry skill standards. This may mean that employers have to contact an industry association to help develop the standards, or the chief state school officer to offer to help write or review curricula for Tech Prep and other school-to-career programs. Employers can also find out from industry associations what materials are currently available for teachers. If none are available, developing compatible, inexpensive products, services, and software to help educators teach workplace and industry skills and knowledge is very helpful.

Employers can also provide a continuous flow of information and support to counselors and teachers on current industry practices, connecting them to projects that integrate skill standards, academic standards, and workplace assessment and credentials. Contacting local business organizations for information about programs that give teachers access to workplace resources enables employers to give educators information and increase their awareness of and skill in using technology.

2. Employers strengthening company practice

The second area of the NELC model is that of employers strengthening company practice. With the changes in business brought about by the introduction of continuous improvement practices, new technologies, and other factors, it may be time to reevaluate company practices in support of a new relationship with educators. With this in mind, NELC offers twenty-five possible steps under four headings. These are: Communicate Supplier Expectations, Enhance Employment Practices, Encourage Employee Development, and Extend Corporate Leadership.

Under the first heading, employers help develop skill-profile requirements and create an internal tracking system to follow workforce supplier (school, college, or other educational or training institution) graduates who are hired, retained, and promoted. This and other information can be given to the workforce suppliers.

Enhancing employment practices will probably require the participation of the CEO and senior management. They can implement hiring practices that will require applicants to demonstrate academic achievement and workplace experience with portfolios, transcripts, certificates of mastery, and industry skill standards certificates. Human resource departments can designate educational institutions as preferred suppliers, and identify the cost of hiring, training, and turnover for new entry-level hires. Human Resources can also introduce the use of skill standards as a framework for internal education, training, career development, and performance review for incumbent workers.

To encourage employee development, employers can partner with high schools, community colleges, adult schools, and universities to develop industry- and company-specific classroom and workplace learning services. They can also involve labor unions in defined work-based learning opportunities and prepare employees to supervise students in these. Company newsletters can be used to profile departments and employees who support education initiatives.

To extend corporate leadership, the CEO and senior management can conduct a high-visibility review of the company's existing involvement in education reform. A reprioritization of activities, a commitment of resources, and the attention of the CEO and senior management will set the example for employee involvement in education activities—as parents, community volunteers, and school board members.

Aligning company involvement in industry and business associations that strengthen the connection between earning and learning reinforces company commitment, as will creating senior management briefings on company commitment to high standards, workforce development, quality assessment, and accountability. Writing CEO editorials in industry/business magazines about the need for workforce/career preparation to support economic success is another way to strengthen company practice in support of education.

With community and volunteer programs, employers can focus on education partnerships and career preparation initiatives in the community, and recognize their efforts. Employer participation on school, parent, and partnership boards helps send out the message that education and workforce preparation are a concern of the business and industry sector.

3. Employers building the system

In the third area of the NELC model, business and industry are encouraged to work to narrow the focus and bring practical experience to policymakers looking at workforce development systems. At the local level, businesses can offer leadership in the provision of work-based learning opportunities. They can do this in partnership with other employers and employees, and with local education agencies, schools, educators, elected officials, labor organizations, students, parents, community-based organizations, rehabilitation agencies, vocational education agencies, and other local entities. Through an employer-led organization, they can work to create a process to provide a constant stream of skill standards information to all education institutions in the area.

Where possible, they can create or enhance a regional economic development plan so that education, labor market needs, and public and private resources are aligned to support workforce development programs.

At a state, multistate, multicounty, or multidistrict level, employers can provide leadership to Tech Prep directors and workforce development regulation boards. They can work with stakeholders to create a system of industry-recognized workplace assessments and credentials that can be used in schools and in workplaces. They can also provide marketing and employer recruitment support, and influence government to develop tax credits and other business incentives for employer involvement.

At the national level, employers can join NELC and work with other business organizations and employers to ensure a consistent workforce development focus in and across business organizations. They can also promote workforce development efforts in national industry-specific associations and participate in developing curricula and instructional materials driven by skill standards, but with special emphasis on high academic standards and work-based learning.

In addition to these efforts, employers can help in a national effort to identify and benchmark best practices in an array of program components. These may include employee recruitment practices, selection and assessment of work-based learning activities, and teacher internships, and can be used to continuously improve school-to-work, Tech Prep, and other workforce development programs. In addition, gathering, translating if necessary, and disseminating—through NELC and other business organizations—information on core skill requirements for industries in other countries can raise awareness of the standards and competencies expected of our competitors.

Finally, employers can help develop international benchmarks for academic and workplace requirements. This can be done through NELC and with national business organizations such as the National Skill Standards Board.

Employers participate at the level they can afford

Employers considering the NELC model[1] should realize that the level of their involvement in education and workforce preparation depends on their resources, their workplaces, and their capacity for change. Small companies can participate on a small scale, involving perhaps one employee in career talks. Participation in career days is minimal, but may reach more students per employee involved. Any other efforts can be scaled to meet company needs. However, all the signs point to the fact that participation in workforce development is the concern of any business that wants to remain competitive.

---

[1] For more information on the model, contact NELC at 800-360-NELC or check http://www.nelc.org/ or nelc@nelc.org.

Chapter 20

Business Practices for Partnering

Björn Olsson

Harmon Industries is a technological leader in signaling and train control for railroads and transit systems worldwide. Quality is very important to us, and our products reflect that. We make railroad signal and train control equipment, train inspection systems, rail and highway grade crossing hardware, and related packaging, and we provide design, installation, and maintenance services. We employ about 1,800 people at twelve locations in the United States, one in Canada, and one in England.

There was a time when I felt that there should be a wall between the academic and commercial worlds to protect the free-thinking style and long-term research arm of education from the short-term thinking of the commercial environment. However, I no longer think this. I think the time for big discoveries and inventions is over. What we're going to discover now is how to use technology to do things we couldn't do before, and to perform familiar tasks more efficiently. Consequently, I think there is a need to tie the academic world more closely to the commercial world.

One example of this closer relationship between education and business/industry is the research center set up by the telecommunication group Ericsson just outside the campus of my alma mater in Sweden. That is where the original research into wireless telecommunication took place. Ericsson now has a 30 percent share of the world market in telecommunication.

This background made it easy for Harmon Industries to support the concept of building partnerships with schools. So, when we were asked to build the model that would allow our company to become a laboratory for students, we agreed.

Benefits

Before I discuss the effort that is involved in building such partnerships—and there is considerable effort—I'd like to list some of the reasons you might want to try to do so.

1.   Harmon Industries has benefited significantly from working closely with schools and universities. Let me give you some examples. For a year and a half, Harmon and the University of Missouri at Rolla have collaborated in a joint research project to design new tools to automate a major portion of our application engineering process. One professor, two graduate students, and our engineers are working together on this project, and indications are that its end result will save us as much as 40 percent of the design time. Since we have 150 engineers, this represents a resource addition of the magnitude of sixty engineers—without our having to recruit one single person. With the great difficulty we have in recruiting qualified signal engineers, developing such a resource is very significant.

In a similar circumstance, we needed more welders for a contract we had just acquired. Through our relationship with the vocational technical schools in our area, we were able to obtain students who were trained in our welding processes. They contributed eighty hours to the project. By working together, all parties benefited. The students gained practical work experience, the school received financial support for a very expensive program, and we hired two of the students as soon as they graduated.

2. Local educators work in our facility during the summer, performing various functions. In doing so, they meet an immediate need of the company while learning skills they can share with their students during the school year.

3. Projects such as the two I mentioned above increase our company's visibility to highly skilled staff and students. Through other programs such as internships and job shadowing, students become acquainted with our projects, our culture, and our industry. We've found that this pays off. When we hired a large number of production operators recently, we found that 10 percent of the new hires had had their first experience with the company through a school-to-career/partnership activity.

4. Company employees take great pride in being involved in student learning. For many, it increases their interest in continuing their training and upgrading their skills.

The resources that can become available to us through such partnerships, and the benefits we can reap from them, are limited only by our imagination.

Tools for Building Partnerships

The two greatest tools Harmon offers a business-education partnership are 1) an operative structure and 2) commitment to a cost-effective quality product delivered in a timely fashion.

In our first partnership meeting, three of us from Harmon sat with fifteen top officials from a state university, two community colleges, and six school districts. We decided to go ahead with the partnership and established a working team to develop a plan of operation that included goals and strategies. The educators suggested a six-month timeline to accomplish this. We countered with six weeks, and that deadline was met. This was indicative of the manner in which we operate. All aspects of the partnership are addressed in a team fashion, but there is no question that it is industry driven.

As the president of our company, I serve on the partnership steering team, whose role is to set the mission and clear the way for its implementation. Others who serve with me include superintendents of the individual school districts, other CEOs, and the commissioner of education of the state of Missouri.

The role of a CEO

As a member of the team and the driver of the partnership, I have specific responsibilities.

1. **Attending all meetings**. I think this is important to show our support of the partnership. We have to "walk the talk." Also, I believe I can enhance the capabilities of my company and my employees substantially through this partnership, while playing an important role in the community.

2. **Providing company time for employee participation**. I have communicated to our employees that they are expected to be involved as they determine appropriate, and they are given company time to participate in partnership activities. Being busy is not an excuse for nonparticipation. Employees are encouraged to meet the challenge of a partnership request in the same way they would meet the request of a customer.

3.   **Ensuring accountability**. I hold my organization accountable for two things:

   a.   The mission of enhancing the learning of students

   b.   Committing company resources in line with agreed-upon plans and budgets

Through this process, we've had to develop our abilities in many areas:

- Giving effective tours.

- Preparing employees to be good mentors.

- Determining what projects we can share within the partnership to enhance learning.

- Defining which jobs can be given to students.

- Identifying what we can share.

- Determining what we can learn.

Student workers can contribute.

One of our plant managers was attempting to design a computer database to track orders and materials through the plant. Not far into the project, he realized he had reached the zenith of his computer skills. His first thought was to hire a consultant. His second thought was to offer the opportunity to a student training in computer skills at the local high school. The student delivered the finished project ahead of schedule and was able to assist the computer department throughout his internship. He has since graduated and is now one of our employees, working for the manager who gave him the database project.

This represents a whole new paradigm for us. We used to think that students graduating from school could not possibly be regarded as productive until we had trained them for about five years. Now, with the type of experience they gain through business-education partnerships, they can actually contribute on their first day. They are very familiar with computers and the latest software, and they quickly learn to apply new technologies to our problems.

Success Factors

I cannot state too strongly that the team process and a strong driving force are the two vital components of a successful partnership. However, a few other factors definitely contribute to success. I suggest anyone desiring to form a business-education partnership give these careful thought:

1.   Appoint one person to coordinate the partnership and related activities. Even though other employees are involved, this person's sole responsibility is to drive and coordinate the partnership activities until a working process is reached. Be sure to allocate sufficient resources to support the development of systems and processes.

2.   Give employees permission and recognition for participating in the partnership.

3.   Allow different employees to participate at the level with which they feel comfortable, then encourage them to grow from there. Our different plant locations and employees participate at levels that are appropriate for them. In the first three years of partnership, our employees worked with about 4,000 students and educators in various activities that support the mission of preparing a competitive workforce.

4.   Be flexible and willing to learn. The process may have to be changed to meet everyone's expectations, but don't be afraid to recommend those changes.

5.   Have patience. If partnerships were easy, they would be more plentiful. Much thinking and acting "out of the

box" is required. And you will meet defensive thinking, typified by statements such as: "Industries shouldn't come telling us how to run education," and "Education shouldn't be telling us how to run our business." Encourage open communication and help people move away from discussing a problem toward fixing it.

Despite the challenges of business-education partnerships, they are well worthwhile. They give a good return on investment for the company, and open the way for remarks like one I recently heard. I belong to a Lion's club, and one of our club members, who is the mother of two, was sitting next to me at our Wednesday meeting. She said, "Björn, you work for Harmon, don't you?" I said, "Yes." "Well, I'm not sure what you are doing with the school system, but whatever program you have going, I can tell you it works. Our thirteen-year-old son has never shown any interest in school or education. Yesterday, he came home and, for the first time ever, made a comment about school and talked about future opportunities. We just looked at him and finally asked, 'Son, what happened?' Well, he had been at the school-to-career program and visited Harmon and participated in job shadowing. All of a sudden, he sees a meaning and a goal for his education."

I feel pretty good about that comment.

Business Practices for Partnering

Before you begin your partnering activities, there are several points to consider:

1. Safety

    a. Clarify safety regulations and company policies with instructors as part of the planning process.

    b. Instruct students in safety regulations before they enter the facility.

    c. Reinforce safety regulations when they enter the facility.

    d. Strictly enforce safety practices.

2. Know your mission: School-to-work can be defined in many ways, with many types of opportunities. Select those that are consistent with your company's mission. Modify your mission as you become more experienced.

3. Be comfortable; control the experience. Plan the event with consideration of both student and employee. Determine how you will prepare each for a successful experience.

    a. Have adequate supervision.
Limit tours to small groups of five to ten when possible. Assign an employee and an instructor to be responsible for each group. Plan stopping points where students know what they can touch. Provide safety glasses and hearing protection if required. For job shadowing/internships, assign one employee to be responsible for one student when at the facility. Allow only one student per department. Be sure to have the phone or pager numbers of instructors or administrators on hand in case of an emergency.

    b. Consider the company's capacity.
At Harmon, we give priority to activities that last from four hours to one week. Plan in teams of two when possible, to build on employee strength and provide backup in the event that business requires one of the members to be absent. Document the process to reduce preparation time for the next event. This also allows you to involve more employees, and takes into consideration continuous process improvement. Realize that a class of twenty-five will tax a department of thirty employees. Explain the situation to the education partner and offer an alternative. Be aware of the fact

that the company's capacity changes at different times of the month or year. Be aware of heavy production schedules, a large number of employees on vacation, or a complex project under way. Be honest with your partners, and offer alternatives.

c. Be considerate of employees. Announce activities ahead of time so they are aware of what's happening. Clearly announce arrival and departure times of student groups so employees can plan activities accordingly.

4. Clarify the customer's needs.
   Ask for the event's objective. Does it have academic relevancy? Which career is being considered? What career opportunities should be addressed? Ask for planning time with the instructor before the students come to the plant. Be sure the school partner has directions to the facility, knows where to park a bus, and has the name or number of a company employee who will be the main contact. Provide bathroom breaks when appropriate. Realize that, if students walk through a break area, they will expect to eat.

5. Provide adequate resources.
   Establish a company contact person. Assist managers in budgeting for activities by communicating expectations and involving them in planning. Consider the cost of internships, meals, release time, and give-away items like product brochures, pens, and key chains. Tell employees how to charge time and travel when they are involved in partnership activities.

6. Address human resource policies.
   Follow child labor laws; know what applies to students in education activities. Establish a fair temporary employment rate. At Harmon, pay is 90 percent of the equivalent entry-level position. If the position exceeds

six months, the employee must be reevaluated and paid according to standard practices.

7.   Address turnover issues.
      Partnership practices can reduce and/or increase turnover, and this may require management to take uncalculated risks. Determine and communicate parameters.

Harmon Industries did not join an education partnership because we wanted new and better employees. What we really wanted was to develop SCANS skills in all our employees. As we participated in the partnership, however, it became clear that this was good business practice. Employee morale rose, and we discovered new opportunities and resources. Company visibility improved, and we found we were making a difference in the lives of students in the community.

I feel pretty good about that.

SECTION 5

Family and Community

Involvement

Overview

Thirty-five years ago, when many baby boomers were choosing careers, the process was traditional and simple. If you were female, it was suggested that you become a nurse, a teacher, or a secretary. If you were male, you could choose almost any career your abilities and your pocketbook could support. If you wanted to go to college, there were, it seemed, few limitations on your career choices. If college didn't interest you, you could go to the local plant and earn high wages by being there every day and doing what you were told. You got good benefits, and your job was secure.

In 1998, such a scenario is almost inconceivable. The number of choices available to students is much greater, but the process of choosing—and being successful in the ensuing career—is more complex and riskier. Many of the plants that once provided secure, well-paid jobs are closed, and the ones that are not are vastly different from the ones of thirty-five years ago. Because of this, employers are looking for employees with skills beyond those formerly expected of new hires. Technology and all its end-products have changed the face of business and industry and effected societal change far beyond the scope of change a generation usually sees. Many of today's students have to learn, through school- and work-based experiences, behaviors that were once considered automatic and learned almost through osmosis—punctuality, consistency in attendance, politeness and respect in dealing with others, self-esteem, and pride in workmanship.

Family and community still have a strong influence on students' education and career choices, and today have better ideas on how to focus this influence. Through all the changes due to technology and the resultant "shrinking" of the globe, what has not changed is the spark within us that lights up when something interests us. That spark is so frail in young children that it can be easily extinguished by a thoughtless comment; yet it reveals something vital, something that should be listened to and known. Parents try to listen, but they're not with their children all the time. Teachers try to encourage, but sometimes their preoccupation with other students or tasks prevents them from seeing it. Sometimes a park ranger, a postal employee, or a police officer will see that spark; but, unless they recognize it for what it is, it will go unacknowledged and may die. Sometimes a grandmother, aunt, or friend will see that spark and fan it into a flame with gentle words of encouragement.

That spark is a tiny glimpse of who we really are, before the prejudices and misconceptions of the world cloud our thinking and obscure our view. It's something that should be treasured; but, to be treasured, it has to be noticed. For it to be noticed, someone must be looking. For someone to be looking, a community must be involved in helping to raise and educate a child.

That's the focus of this section, which can be summed up by the adage, "It takes a village (read: community) to raise a child."[1] Before you scoff, read the next few chapters. These give you glimpses of communities working together to listen to the children in their midst, to help them find their interests, and to guide them toward career objectives that will enable them to pursue these interests. These are communities that believe that a key element in students' success is helping them match their talents to their career interests.

It seems a simple concept, matching talents and interests, but, to allow it to happen, a community's members must have made a commitment to involve themselves actively in the education of their children—in schools, at work, in community-based organizations, and anywhere else those children can be educated.

---

[1] African proverb.

And then—when a child has chosen a career interest, had it nurtured by an involved community, and pursued it through high school and work experiences—then, what happens? Does the local community college or university have the same interest in providing and ability to provide a contextual learning environment that continues the work of the village? That matches learning styles to teaching methods, and fosters student talents and interests in collaborative settings led by professors vitally involved with their students? Well . . . sometimes. Community colleges, particularly those involved in Tech Prep and other school-to-career partnerships, have made strides in this area. But chapter 24 will give you a glimpse into academia and what it will take to affect the mind-set and teaching practices of higher education, particularly of four-year colleges and universities.

To effect change at the university level will take time and a willingness among faculty and administration to reexamine teaching methodologies, curriculum processes, the culture of the university, and its position within the community. Old habits and ways of thinking die hard, but a community can be of great help. After all, higher education must have customers if it is to survive. And those customers can wield influence in demanding a more accountable system of teaching, with greater access to professors, and an environment that supports contextual teaching and learning and includes work-based (worksite) experiences. Once again, it will be through education-employer-community partnerships and through thoughtful, vocal consumers of higher education that such influence will be wielded and change initiated.

But where you read "community" in this context, realize that it includes you. Community is all *of us, not only parents and grandparents, but also those who have no children but who realize that the fate of this nation depends on our ability to compete in a global context. If we want our standard of living to continue or improve, we must be able to go head-to-head with our global competitors. We must have a skilled, competent workforce with a strong work ethic and the soft skills needed to work successfully in teams. We must also have university graduates who have not only the head skills but also the hand and people skills needed in today's high-performance workplaces.*

And this can happen . . . but only if an entire community is involved. In chapter 23, The Anita School Community demonstrates how this can be done, and be done well. This section may challenge your thinking and beliefs. Your first response may be, "Oh, that just wouldn't work here, in this community." But keep reading. You may find not only inspiration, but also techniques that will help you light a fire under your community—and make a difference in the way young people are able to identify their interests and talents, and then put those interests to work in careers that provide a good living and great satisfaction.

Chapter 21

Helping Students Discover Talents and Career Interests

Sandy Sarvis Brossard

One of the greatest challenges facing parents today is understanding their children's struggles to determine what they want to do when they grow up. Based on the comments of students, it seems that many parents have forgotten what it was like to be an adolescent, a senior in high school, or a college student still trying to find him/herself and decide on a career path. In some instances, this lack of understanding is due to the fact that the parents simply followed the path their parents predetermined for them through either direct or subtle messages. Consequently, they now want their children to do the same.

Almost everyone knows a parent who has told his or her child from the time the child was very young what the child wants to be when he grows up. Almost any adult can recall a Parent Teacher Organization meeting at an elementary school when one father could be overheard saying of his first-grade child, "When Susie grows up, she's going to be a doctor. Aren't you, Susie?" If Susie has expressed that desire and the father is reinforcing it, that's okay. However, in many situations, parents simply impose their wishes on their children—usually with the best of intentions, of course. Parents want their children to have better lives than they did.

The challenge teachers face—helping students recognize their interests while not imposing their own beliefs about what constitutes a "good" career and what does not—is equally formidable. Teachers have so much influence that one comment can literally change the course of a life. For example, a first grader named Holly had told her parents for months that, when she grew up, she wanted to drive an eighteen wheeler. Both her parents were well educated, her father an attorney and her mother a district-level administrator. They reinforced Holly's interests in the trucking industry, saying things like, "Yes, Holly. You could see all parts of the country in an eighteen wheeler."

One day in the car, after Holly had just used the appropriate gestures to have yet another eighteen-wheeler driver honk his horn, the family passed by the Overnite Transportation Company. The father casually called Holly's attention to the lot full of big trucks, and her eyes lit up! She was so excited that her father said, "Who knows? Maybe you'll have lots of eighteen wheelers like that one day, too, Holly." With that conversation, the child immediately decided that she would own a freight company so she could have lots of trucks. However, a few days later, Holly told her class and her teacher that, when she grew up, she wanted to have an "eighteen-wheeler company." To her amazement, the teacher said, "Oh, Holly!

You can't do that! You're too smart! You're so smart, you should be a doctor, or a lawyer, or a teacher."

When Holly returned home that afternoon, she was in despair. She told her mother what the teacher had said, and announced that she no longer wanted to own an eighteen-wheeler company. The child's ambition had been changed.

While the teacher had had the best intentions, she had ignored Holly's career interests because of her own perception of what constitutes a "good" career and what does not. Her message was powerful. "Holly, you're too smart to do what you want to do." The teacher did not see that an interest in eighteen wheelers did not limit the child but, rather, could have resulted in her becoming the CEO or CFO for a freight line or even mechanical engineer for a trucking firm. The teacher surely recognized that Holly had academic talents, but she failed to acknowledge or show respect for the child's interests.

A key element in helping students achieve success is helping them find the match between their talents—artistic, academic, skilled, and/or interpersonal—and their career interests. It is essential that both parents and teachers understand the importance of this match in helping children determine what they want to be when they grow up. If parents and teachers are to be successful in helping students become aware of their skills and career interests, they must recognize the importance of career exploration and the value of career information in helping students discover their futures.

Parents and Teachers Working Together

Career counselors, community leaders, guidance counselors, career exploration teachers, and school administrators all have roles in shaping a child's career aspirations. But the critical issue is how parents and teachers support each other in helping students become aware of their

skills and career interests. While some parents will come to the
school and seek assistance, the vast majority will not. Therefore,
it becomes the responsibility of the school or district to develop
a system to ensure that teachers and parents understand how and
why they should help students to make their own career
decisions. Using the resources of Tech Prep consortia enables
teachers and parents to access information needed in this role.

Teaching "to do's"

1. Help parents develop a strong foundation of
    understanding when their children are young so they can
    provide long-term career guidance. In particular, help
    them to understand that children:

    - develop at varying rates intellectually, socially,
      emotionally, and physically;

    - have individual interests that may be different from
      their own; and

    - have different learning styles that help them
      acquire knowledge and support career
      development.

2. Help parents understand how and why the world of work
    is changing. The job market is vastly different from
    when parents began to think about careers, and it is
    changing at a rapid pace—so rapid, in fact, that many of
    the careers of the future have not even been
    conceptualized!

3. Acquaint parents with sources of information regarding
    skills and career interests as well as job market trends.

4. Realize that it is difficult for some parents to understand
    the value of continuing education and the place of
    technology in the world when they have little education
    themselves and little exposure to or understanding of
    technology.

The effects of career counseling and Tech Prep in Lexington School District Four in Swansea, South Carolina, include a tremendous increase in adult education enrollment, adult graduation rates, participation in parent education classes for parents of children through age five, and a reduced dropout rate. When parents do not have career goals for themselves, it is difficult for them to support their children's career development.

5.   Recognize the power that teachers have over students and their parents, particularly at the elementary level. Remember the story of Holly? It is absolutely vital that elementary teachers, in particular, realize their power to influence through the subtle and direct messages they send to children and their parents.

6.   Use the expertise of the "experts." Make career connections to curriculum content whenever possible. Don't simply integrate academic and vocational content, but use input from "experts" in various occupations as often as you can to enhance the curriculum.

Parenting "to do's"

As their children's first and most important teachers, parents must realize the awesome responsibility they have for their children's futures. With that in mind, parents must

1.   Seek information from appropriate resources to enable them to guide their children in finding what is right for them.

2.   Pay close attention to every aspect of their children's development.

3.   Expect the school system to use appropriate information to guide their children in making choices. School systems that practice career guidance without using appropriate career assessment devices and do not stay

abreast of current trends in the workplace could actually lead students in inappropriate directions. In some professions, such actions would be deemed malpractice.

4.   Pay close attention to what your children say about their interests. Explore those interests with them. Even if you do not think the interest is worthy of a career, keep an open mind. Do you really think the parents of the developer of "pet rocks" thought an interest in rocks would lead to a business?

5.   Expose your children to a variety of careers. Career exploration should not be simply something done at school. Make career-exploration adventures of visits to zoos, the grocery store, the theater, automotive dealerships, the hospital, and anywhere else.

Practical Ways to Support the Development of Skills and Career Interests

Parents and schools can be involved in students' skills and career interest development in several practical ways without actually making choices for them. It is important that the teacher and parent roles be clearly defined and that each understands that "guidance" does not mean making choices for someone else. Providing guidance means that those guiding are enablers and facilitators of growth. Those who guide have a responsibility to teach children/students problem-solving skills, open-mindedness, skill and information acquisition, and decision-making skills so that the students can make the best choices for themselves. The level of skills taught by both parents and teachers should be appropriate to the developmental readiness of the students involved.

Some obvious strategies used by parents and schools to help students become informed about careers include career fairs, career days, Junior Achievement, job shadowing of parents and others, mentoring, internships, apprenticeships, and cooperative learning experiences. Many schools use "transition nights" to help students and their parents become aware not only of the requirements of the next level of schooling but also of various careers and what it will take for students to be prepared for those careers. Transitioning occurs from elementary school to middle school, from middle school to high school, and from high school to college. In many instances, career planners are completed at the eighth-grade level by students with their parents' approval. (Many of these strategies will be outlined in the discussion of the exemplary program at Dorchester School District Two.)

Some less obvious strategies for involving parents and teachers in helping their students explore careers may, however, be some of the most powerful. Typically, meetings of parents, teachers, students, and counselors to discuss careers, career interests, and career planning are very large. In fact, some meetings have several hundred parents and teachers sitting in the same room with their children to discuss such topics. While this may be an expedient means of providing information, it may not be the most effective means of creating an opportunity for real dialogue among stakeholders.

Did you ever go to a Tupperware, makeup, or dinnerware party? What typically occurs at such small gatherings is that the participants have the opportunity to ask questions and absorb answers in a way that is not provided at large-group sessions. A simple strategy based on the same principles as the Tupperware party is to find a parent who will agree to host three or four other families in his or her home for an evening. A trained group of two or three teachers, counselors, or business leaders then goes into the home and talks with parents about changes in the workplace and ways to assist their children in making decisions based on career interests and skills. For parents who are reluctant to have visitors in their homes (as some are), "shade-tree chats" have been very effectively used in Lexington

School District Four. For these, parents invite a small group of neighboring parents over to sit under a shade tree in lounge chairs: It's even acceptable to ask visitors to bring their own chairs! The value of "shade-tree chats" extends far beyond their ability to provide a forum for the dissemination of important information about careers and career planning. What parents, administrators, and teachers who have participated in such activities say is that such meetings provide an environment in which a sense of trust and mutual responsibility develops. It is absolutely vital that the stakeholders who are guiding students to discover their own talents and career interests trust each other!

Did you ever have a group golf or tennis lesson and then have an individualized one? Most people will agree that the individualized lesson better met their needs than the group lesson. The same is true of talking with parents about career guidance. That is why every teacher and administrator at all levels in the school system must fully understand the value of career exploration and helping students become more responsible in career decision making. Without such understanding, subtle, incorrect messages (like the one communicated to Holly) will continue to be sent. Sometimes, spontaneous conversations between parents and teachers at the grocery store have a greater effect than any planned conference. Therefore, the teacher must be fully equipped with understanding about career guidance. Teachers must understand career assessments and use the information gained from them to help parents help their children.

Another strategy that can be very effective is the use of media. School newsletters, the community newspaper, radio, and television are powerful forms of communication. Schools should use such to expose parents, students, and the community at large to information about career planning.

Many schools today are using the Internet to communicate with parents about career planning. As more and more schools and Tech Prep consortia develop web sites, these become effective means of providing information to parents to help them guide their children. Besides this, many parents use the discussion groups afforded by the web sites to ask questions about career planning. When responses are not easily generated in writing, teachers and counselors can set up follow-up conferences.

A major role for business, industry, and parents in supporting skills and career interest development is keeping legislators informed of what is needed in schools to help students discover their talents and career interests. Legislators are much more inclined to listen to parents than to educators talk about the lack of funding for school initiatives. Career assessment instruments are not cheap, and providing experiences for career exploration has a price tag as well. While funding is not the primary issue, it is a consideration, and well-informed parents and business/industry leaders play a vital role in communicating educational needs to those in control of funding at national and state levels.

Dorchester School District Two: An Exemplary Program[1]

Dorchester School District Two in Summerville, South Carolina, received the first Planning for Life Award in 1993. This national model offers a career guidance program that meets the career development needs of students through career awareness, career exploration, and career preparation. The district provides students with counseling, instruction,

---

[1] For additional information regarding Dorchester School District Two's nationally recognized program, contact Janice Jolly, School-to-Work/Career Exploration Coordinator, Summerville High School, 1101 Boone Hill Road, Summerville, SC 29483. Much of the information regarding this program was taken from the Planning for Life applicant information form.

experiences, and strategies that result in an ongoing, developmental, and nondiscriminatory program in career guidance. It involves parents and other appropriate stakeholders at every level.

The Dorchester School District Two community has over 80,000 residents with approximately 8,000 students at the middle school and high school levels alone. The community is both rural and suburban, and business activity has increased significantly over the past ten years.

Research tells us that a sound career awareness program at the elementary level promotes students' knowledge of self and others; an awareness of careers; and an awareness of collaboration among school, home, the community, and business and industry. Career awareness opportunities are provided in Dorchester School District Two for students in kindergarten through fifth grade. The efforts of the elementary program are communicated through school newsletters and the local newspaper. Career Day, D.A.R.E., Helping Hands, and Teacher Cadets are all programs that integrate the efforts of school, parents, community, and business to increase students' career awareness.

Career exploration activities begin at the sixth-grade level, when students take a one-semester exploratory class. During this class, students complete Career Targets, a self-scored, self-administered inventory linking their interests to fourteen career clusters. Teachers use the results of the inventory to help students explore career clusters as they develop decision-making skills related to careers.

Exploratory classes in industrial technology and keyboarding focus not only on technology, but also on the South Carolina Occupational Information System (SCOIS). SCOIS helps students explore careers and postsecondary schools.

When students reach the eighth grade, they are given the CAPS, COPS, and COPES assessments in an effort to gather information about their abilities, interests, and values. Letters informing parents of the assessments are sent home. After the assessments are analyzed, classroom guidance, small-group counseling, and individual counseling schedules for career-counseling activities are developed to help students make plans for their high school courses, which support a particular career cluster. At every stage of the process, parents are well informed and involved.

Career preparation at the secondary level involves matching the assessments of students' interests, abilities, and values to their plans for a program of study at the secondary and postsecondary levels. Other assessments,[2] such as the Boy Scouts of America Explorer Program, Armed Services Vocational Battery (ASVAB), the Holland Self-Directed Search, the Occu-Find Booklet, and various state achievement tests, are used in grades nine through twelve. An extensive school-to-work program and an outstanding guidance program serve as tools to help students make good decisions about their futures. Extensive documentation of all career-guidance and school-to-work experiences is maintained from grades six through twelve. At the completion of high school, each student has an extensive portfolio to share with postsecondary educators or employers.

One of the reasons Dorchester School District Two has been so successful in its efforts to help students discover their talents and interests is its realization that a comprehensive career guidance program depends on all the stakeholders understanding their roles and responsibilities. Teachers, counselors, and administrators are provided extensive training through two graduate courses—career life planning and applied

---

[2] Jerome T. Kapes and Tammi Vacha-Haase, *A Counselor's Guide User's Matrix: An Alphabetical Listing of Career Assessment Instruments by Category and Type of Use* (College Station, Texas: Department of Educational Psychology, Texas A&M University).

career counseling—offered to all certified personnel. Business leaders are helped to understand their responsibilities to students through specific training provided by the school-to-work/career exploration coordinator for the district. Parents are kept informed of the results of various assessments and the rationale for such assessments throughout the process, which is a K-16 and beyond effort. While the school system serves students only through grade twelve, it has developed clearly articulated programs of study with postsecondary education and the workplace with the help of the local consortium.

Strategies for Success

To help students discover their talents and career interests, stakeholders must work together. This requires two-way or multiple-way conversation—not one-way conversation, with schools doing all the talking. The dialogue must be rich and meaningful and have as much specificity about the students and careers involved as possible. The old assumptions upon which students were guided about career and continuing education choices are no longer acceptable. Numerous resources about career interests, abilities, and values are readily available to assist parents, teachers, counselors, and administrators in guiding students. But they will do no good unless they are used and their results shared with all those who have an influence on guiding students to make choices for themselves. Indeed, the conversations among parents, teachers, and other stakeholders who care about students' futures must reflect an understanding of the changing workplace and its implications for education.

Benefits, Outcomes, and Measurements

The benefits of helping students become aware of their individual skills and career interests are multifaceted. Not only will we develop a more prepared workforce in the future, we will develop a happier workforce. Many employees today suffer from stress related specifically to the fact that they are unhappy in their career choices. Had someone guided them to make decisions based more appropriately on their skills and career interests, employee burnout would not be so rampant and employer dissatisfaction would not be so great.

Moreover, if students felt that parents and teachers really listened to them and respected their interests, schools across our country would be more positive learning environments. While the administration of a career assessment might not please students, taking the time to respectfully explain the results to them communicates a sense of valuing their interests, abilities, and skills. Training students to make informed decisions for themselves is a strategy everyone can respect.

Additionally, when parents and school employees work together and talk specifically about the student and his or her individual interests, analyze data and work habits together, and agree to do what benefits the student, a sense of trust develops. This cannot necessarily be measured quantitatively. What will be apparent is that collaboration among parents, teachers, and other school officials results in a stronger sense of community and a determination to put students first.

Chapter 22

Exploring the Workplace in Communities

Fred Rau

Imagine that, one week out of the year, the community becomes the school. Students could ask questions of the board of a Fortune 500 corporation . . . lead a marketing team meeting for a new product line . . . suggest solutions to the city waste management agency . . . or probe into a crime laboratory. If the students could interact with medical researchers, corporate executives, policymakers, technicians, and creative advertising teams, they would find out why it is important to understand DNA and geometric equations as well as learn about negotiations, team building, and cooperation. Teams of students could work on problem-based projects with interdisciplinary learning objectives. They could interact with people in the workplace to complete their projects and demonstrate their knowledge to members of the community, who would evaluate the results. In addition, students could meet and interact with employees of cultures, races, and genders that may be similar to their own. More importantly, the realities of employment opportunities and the various types of careers would be more evident to students. The community environment could become a place for students to develop their goals and plans for future education and work.

Understanding the Environment of Work

Too often the four walls of a classroom teach students to ignore reality without realizing a vision for their future. According to the U.S. Bureau of Labor Statistics, the majority of high school students expect to become highly paid professionals such as doctors or lawyers, even though fewer than one in sixty of these students could earn placement in a graduate school for these professions, much less find employment.[1] This does not take into account the overwhelming majority of ninth-grade boys who still dream of becoming the next Michael Jordan or some other professional athlete.

Unfortunately, most students are not exposed to careers outside their familial experiences. And the days of "following in dad's or mom's footsteps" have diminished significantly since the economic shift to an information age. In other words, jobs are not just jobs anymore. Keeping pace with technology means that human skills and human organization must be continuously upgraded. Advancing communication systems have eliminated, created, reorganized, and combined jobs based on demands of the individual industry or company. Many companies have fewer than five job titles, and job descriptions are ambiguous at

[1] Lynn Olson, *The School-to-Work Revolution: How Employers and Educators Are Joining Forces to Prepare Tomorrow's Skilled Workforce* (Reading, Massachusetts: Addison-Wesley, 1997), p. 115.

best. The latest in high-performance management strategies, like matrix management or flat level organizations, define little more than job categories but emphasize work teams. Employees' skill sets and broad career aspirations may guide them into and out of four or five different divisions of a corporation within a week, month, or year. According to Ray Marshall, Secretary of Labor during the Carter administration, "This combination of rethinking the nature of work, decentralizing decisions, and setting up a participatory system is the only way we're likely to be competitive on terms that maintain and improve our incomes."[2] School systems are challenged to consider this new environment of work as a model for teaching and curriculum; otherwise, the result leaves students with little idea of or preparation for what they will do when they grow up.

The Challenge of Worksite Learning

Tech Prep was one of the first education reform efforts to consider these shifts in workplaces as a determining factor in what and how we teach students to prepare them for the workforce. Those Tech Prep consortia that listened to the business community and moved from narrow vocational skills training into broader, more comprehensive curricular structures have laid the groundwork for evolving work organizations. However, some Tech Prep consortia learned quickly that changes in curriculum were not enough to prepare students for the environment of work. By the early 1990s, efforts within and outside of Tech Prep began to develop mentoring programs, career academies, and even some junior apprenticeship programs. These programs quickly became recognized as

---

[2] Hedrick Smith, *Rethinking America* (New York: Random House Inc., 1995), p. 407.

worksite learning experiences, also referred to as work-based learning.

Even before the initiation of the 1994 School-to-Work Opportunities Act (and certainly ever since) policymakers, educators, and employers collectively agreed that it is critical for students to have some exposure to and experience in the workplace while in school. The intended purpose of the act is to provide federal seed money to states and schools for a period of five years so they can construct systems that will smooth the transition from school to the workplace.

National attention to the act has opened many eyes to the potential of worksite learning experiences (a required component of the school-to-work system) while also opening the debate on the need for all students to participate in some form of workforce preparation. The challenge of exposing every student to the workplace has been daunting. Issues about the logistics of worksite learning, including safety, cost, transportation, time, and access, have left the education community asking a series of questions:

- Can a high school provide all students with twenty-five- to thirty-hour interactive worksite learning experiences?

- Can a wide variety of local businesses and agencies provide time, facilities, and personnel for these types of worksite learning experiences?

- Can all faculty members in a high school step out of their subject matter areas to teach and counsel students on career exploration, preemployment training skills, and workplace basics?

A Model Program at Centennial High School

Beginning in 1991, Centennial High School in Gresham, Oregon, developed and piloted a program called Experiential

School, which has been answering yes to the above questions. Gresham, a suburb of Portland, is a mainly residential development with small businesses. The population of the high school has been about 1,500 students for the past few years; a mild growth trend is expected in the near future. Ethnic background as of March 1998 was 88 percent white, 6.8 percent Asian, 3 percent Hispanic, 1.7 percent African American, and 3 percent American Indian or Alaskan Native. Tech Prep at Centennial includes manufacturing (metals), production (wood), drafting, marketing, food service, and a business and management block that offers accounting and office systems. Worksite learning experiences such as cooperative work programs, job shadows, and internships are offered. The vision has been to provide every student with a meaningful worksite learning experience.

In the spring of 1992, Centennial hosted a school-to-work conference. Parents, teachers, students, and representatives of businesses from the greater Gresham and Portland area attended. The goal was to collectively determine the best course of action for expanding community involvement with our school and providing a worksite learning experience for all students. The topics for the conference included mentorships, apprenticeships, teacher job shadows or exchanges, the relevance of school to the workplace, values and job ethics, laws that impact juvenile workers, career flexibility, and service learning. The conference did a great deal to establish the beginning of a relationship among the four groups of participants. A number of recommendations came out of the conference. For instance, mentorships, teacher job shadows, and service learning have been incorporated over the past six years, as has a week-long worksite learning project called Experiential School.

Experiential School was conceived as a forest retreat. The idea was to incorporate into the core high school curriculum practical applications that illustrate how the school curriculum relates to life. Environmental studies and observations would apply mathematics and science concepts to water testing and population studies. Land use and development issues would apply to social studies and English/language arts. Ropes courses and group problem solving were intended to incorporate employability skills such as teamwork and communication.

A school counselor who served on the Experiential School planning committee recruited the involvement of Bonneville Power Administration (BPA). BPA is a large government agency involved in hydroelectric power generation. Representatives of BPA expressed a strong interest in becoming more proactively involved with education, and so started a partnership with Centennial to jointly develop Experiential School. *This experience illustrates two important points. First, businesses are often looking for an opportunity to become involved with schools but do not know how to make the first step. Second, it is important to nurture connections and networking opportunities among school employees, parents, and the business community.* Because of that connection, the focus of Experiential School evolved from a forest retreat format to a project-based business partnership activity that addressed the same goals.

As all schools work toward making their curricula relevant, providing practical application of skills and knowledge learned, and allowing students to explore potential careers, Centennial decided to set the following goals for Experiential School:

1. Students will realize that what they are learning in school is important in the workplace and will be of value later in life.

2. Students will apply skills such as teamwork, critical thinking, problem solving, and communication throughout the week's activities.

3. Students will learn how specific occupations are performed and become aware of the aptitudes,

education, and training required to be successful in those occupations.

For the first year's pilot, twenty students in their junior year were selected based on their interest in participating in a new program and their willingness to make up the work they would miss during their week at BPA. The first activities of the week were an orientation to BPA, a tour of its facility, and the completion of an application and a mock interview. Then students were presented with a focus problem for the week. BPA had been addressing the problem of balancing hydroelectric generation with the loss of fish habitat due to dams. The problem they posed to the student group was this: "Are fish worth saving?" Students worked in groups of five to gather information from the engineering, legal, public relations, and fish and wildlife departments at BPA. They job shadowed, attended meetings, and witnessed business operations. On Friday, the culminating activity for Experiential School was a presentation by the students to representatives of the agency. During the presentation, students proposed solutions based on their findings during the week.

The students evaluated the week on a positive scale. When they were asked if Experiential School was a better way of learning than in the classroom, the main response was "yes." The response of BPA was so positive that Centennial made arrangements with Boeing of Portland to participate as the second pilot site for the Experiential School in 1992.

Boeing of Portland manufactures large and small parts for commercial aircraft. Boeing has been an active business partner with Centennial since 1984 through job shadows, student and teacher internships, and advisory committee work with the manufacturing class. The Experiential School committee wanted to see if the format of the program would work with a manufacturing company as well as with a large government agency. With a second year's team attending Experiential School at BPA, a team of twenty students was also sent to

Boeing in the spring of 1992 to study the following problem: "How can Boeing remain competitive in a world economy?" While this may seem an overwhelming topic for high school students to tackle, they focused on manufacturing procedures, quality control, and communication, developing recommendations to Boeing. With favorable evaluations from students and host businesses participating in the three pilot programs, Centennial needed only the catalyst of the school-to-work conference recommendation to take Experiential School to scale.

Important Issues to Consider

It was proposed at the conference that Experiential School involve all students at the junior level. Several issues had to be resolved before partners could agree on the next phase of the project. Partners had to consider the following concerns and questions before allowing the entire junior class to be out of the school building for a full week.

Since many classes contain a mixture of freshmen, sophomores, and juniors, how will the curriculum progress during the week?

The previous pilot projects focused on only junior-level students; however, members of the consortium raised important issues about the need for freshman and sophomore students to have some career orientation.

How will make-up work be addressed?

During the pilot, students volunteered for Experiential School and agreed to make up all assignments missed. But, in this case, the faculty would be dealing with all the juniors, some of whom would find it difficult to make up work.

Should this week allow seniors time for projects and research papers?

Prior to the Experiential School, the senior class had been involved in a senior quest project for the preceding three years. The quest project is a graduation requirement at Centennial that allows graduating students to demonstrate skills they have learned throughout their high school years. It involves a research paper, a fifteen-hour related project done outside of school time, and an oral presentation to a board of faculty members, parents, and community representatives.

Will a career component be necessary for freshmen and sophomores?

The Experiential School committee proposed a freshman (level 1) and a sophomore (level 2) curriculum that would, with the junior Experiential School component, replace a required semester's career class. The proposal was presented to the faculty in a fall in-service meeting and was accepted by a majority vote.

The decision to move forward with the next phase of the project had two major impacts on classroom teachers. They would give up a full week of teaching time and thus would need to compress and restructure the curriculum; and they would be responsible for developing the curriculum and activities for the freshmen's and sophomores' career week. An expanded career week committee developed the outcomes for the freshman and sophomore levels. Resource materials were collected for teachers and time was provided for them to develop their plans for the week.

Preparation time was arranged by designating one meeting per month of the weekly morning academic seminar for career-week planning and by providing the teacher teams one day of release time through a school-improvement grant. It is important to note that the innovative nature of the school improvement grant allowed Centennial the freedom to develop a program that may have been unconventional but that focused on student achievement. A more restrictive grant would not have allowed the flexibility to develop the programs that have meshed well with state school-reform initiatives.

A Curriculum and a Plan for Each Grade Level

The intended objectives for the freshman (level-1) career week are career research, goal setting, team building, and written and oral communication. A career fair is held on one of the days; forty to fifty guest speakers present information on occupations within their business areas. Field trips to local businesses and group projects are also components of the week's activities.

The sophomore (level-2) career week places students in one of six occupational strands: arts and communication, business management and technology, health services, human resources, industrial and engineering technology, and natural resources. At the end of the freshman week, after the career research is completed, students choose which strand to focus on. The curriculum for the sophomore level includes workplace readiness skills, résumé writing, interview practice, and continued work on teamwork and oral and written communication skills. The Oregon Association of Temporary Staffing Services (OATSS) has sent a team of forty members to Centennial for each of the past five years to give the entire sophomore class practice interviews. OATSS has also developed a more student-relevant practice application for the activity and a curriculum to assist teachers in preparing the students. Associations such as OATSS are very valuable to the program in providing consistency and continuity. Career-week interviews have become an annual OATSS activity for their education program, called Preparing Youth for Industry.

Recruiting Business Sites

When the freshman, sophomore, and junior components were developed, it remained only to develop enough Experiential School business sites to serve the juniors. To test the program on a large scale, we set a goal of placing 200 juniors in the first year. In addition to Bonneville Power Administration and Boeing of Portland, thirty-one businesses and agencies were recruited to be Experiential School sites. One group of sixty-five juniors would remain at the high school during the upcoming career week. This was planned because it was not certain that enough sites could be recruited for the entire class the first year, and because the school group could serve as a control for evaluation purposes. The junior group at the high school addressed some of the same goals as the worksite teams, but had community service as its focus. They planned school improvement programs and worked with the Gresham Parks Department on a tree-planting project. The teachers who planned the school-based junior group tried to compensate for what students were missing by adding a number of recreational activities and even a pizza lunch or two. Throughout the week, the students placed at business and agency sites worked in their groups to job shadow, solve problems, participate in projects, and make up their presentations. When the week was over and one of the students placed on a job site had a chance to discuss the week with a friend who had stayed at school, he learned of the recreational activities and the pizza lunches. His comment to me was, "It wasn't fair, Mr. Rau; you made us think." I realized at that moment that we had developed a program that *all* Centennial students needed to experience.

Experiential School has served all junior students at Centennial for the past five years. Over 160 businesses and government agencies have hosted almost 1,800 students during that time. Some businesses, like Boeing, have participated every year. The format has remained the same since the initial two pilot sites for Experiential School. Preparation for the week, establishing student expectations, and monitoring progress at the host sites are the responsibilities given to site supervisors. The site supervisors, who are selected from among Centennial teachers, leave the school building for a week and see with the students what the "real world" is like. To ensure that all teachers have an opportunity for the experience, a new group of site supervisors is selected each year. To provide for the diverse interests of students and to ensure that all of our state-identified occupational strands are represented, we have recruited sites ranging from advertising to zoology. This year, ninety businesses and agencies are participating in the program. Because of the diverse nature of the sites, the original plan of presenting a problem to solve has been revised to presenting a focus project. The project may be anything from a problem-solving activity such as "How can our car dealership improve its customer service satisfaction?" to a project such as developing a fire-prevention presentation directed at elementary school children for a local fire department. Over the past five years, students have evaluated cashier-training programs for a large retailer, developed a disaster-preparedness program with the Gresham Fire Department for our own high school, designed a swimsuit for a sportswear company, and, through our local cable access company, produced a video about Experiential School to explain the program to freshman and sophomore groups.

The aspect of Experiential School I consider one of its major contributing factors for success is the grouping process for the student teams. After previously participating sites and newly recruited sites are confirmed for the year, a selection list is presented to junior students in their English classes. Students select their top three choices of occupational interests (e.g., hotel/restaurant management, elementary education, or graphic design). That information is entered in a database along with essential composite ratings on students by their first-semester teachers. Teachers are asked to rate the students on how they think the students will perform on the worksite, based on their academic performance and attitude. Each student receives a one (high rating), two (middle rating), or three (low rating) based on class performance during the first semester. The students' occupational interests and ratings are used to place them in the teams for each of the Experiential School sites. The number of students at a site ranges from three to twelve depending on the size of the organization, its facilities, and the number of employees committed to the program.

Benefits and Lessons Learned

The purpose of the first two pilot projects was to identify both successes and failures. A clearly defined list of benefits and lessons learned is outlined below. Both students and participating businesses must become winners in this project for it to continue year after year.

Important lessons learned

1. *Students are motivated to raise their level of achievement through cooperative learning.*
    The theory of cooperative learning definitely applies to this project. Students with lower motivation and academic skills rise to the levels of higher-achieving group members. In some cases, students who were identified as needing extra help with the activity have even taken on leadership roles.

2. *Students gain firsthand experience in team building.*
    Grouping students with similar occupational interests gives them a jump-start on bonding and team building. The social benefit is that they are frequently teamed with students they may never have known or worked with in high school.

3.   *A common focus on a project or problem-solving
     activity reduces conflicts.*
     Issues of diversity that may have caused problems in
     school are reduced because of the need to achieve
     similar goals.

4.   *Coordinated student groupings create more effective
     teams.*
     Each business or agency is provided with a mix of
     student performance levels (a combination of one-rated,
     two-rated, and three-rated students). A coordinated mix
     of students rather than random placement increases the
     likelihood of creating balanced teams that have
     leadership and are motivated to perform.

5.   *Diverse workplaces are a positive reinforcement.*
     The week-long activity is an opportunity for students to
     appreciate how employees of diverse backgrounds work
     together to accomplish common goals.

6.   *Businesses should witness student performance
     firsthand.*
     Local businesses have become more aware of the diverse
     population the public school system serves and have a
     better understanding of the challenge this presents. In
     addition, throughout the course of this project, many
     businesses have been impressed with the students'
     accomplishments. The participation of business
     representatives in this project has given new meaning to
     the school-business relationship because both parties
     have a better appreciation of each other's environment
     and the goals that drive each organization.

7.   *Businesses gain a new perspective.*
     A number of business and agency participants have
     mentioned that their employees have had the opportunity
     to improve their communication skills and have gained a
     different perspective of their jobs by working with the
     students.

Student benefits

1. The project causes students to become familiar with the way a company is organized and how different jobs and people contribute their skills to reaching a goal.

2. Students can begin to form their own opinions of what they like and don't like about certain careers and industries.

3. Students develop a network of people who become helpful resources in the future.

4. Students establish contacts for immediate and future employment opportunities.

5. The experience gives students an idea of how to map out plans for what they will do after high school.

6. The business exposure gives students an appreciation of the roles participating companies play in their lives.

Evaluation of the Experiential School

Experiential School has worked successfully for Centennial High School and the 1,800 students who have gone through the program. Evaluations done by students and businesses have maintained 87 to 97 percent approval on all evaluation criteria, and, for the past two years, graduating seniors have given the experience an average 94 percent rating of positive to highly valuable.

An active advisory committee has been an essential part of the development and success of Experiential School. The committee comprises six business representatives and four senior students who went through Experiential School the previous year. A new group of students is added each year, but businesses remain on the committee as long as they wish, some for five years. Each fall, the advisory committee reviews student and business evaluations of the program and makes recommendations for change based on those evaluations. It also updates the student notebook each year, and plans and presents an orientation meeting for new businesses each February. This meeting, which presents information on Experiential School from both a business and a student perspective, has been very popular with new business partners.

Standards for Career-Related Learning

Part of the school reform initiative in Oregon is the Certificate of Initial Mastery (CIM) and the Certificate of Advanced Mastery (CAM), a set of standards in which all students must demonstrate mastery to graduate from high school. Part of the CIM and CAM includes content standards for career-related learning. The following is an illustration of how Experiential School allows students to demonstrate the career-related learning standards:

Personal management

Demonstrate appropriate workplace behaviors.

Students are expected to be on time each day at the workplace. They are responsible for planning, organizing, and completing their projects in a timely fashion. Because of the short time involved, they need to budget their time and resources effectively.

Problem solving

Apply decision-making and problem-solving techniques in workplace situations.

The focus project established by the host Experiential School site is a realistic, practical experience for students. They must identify cause-and-effect relationships, select alternatives for a given situation, and use problem-solving strategies to reach solutions or complete projects.

Teamwork

Demonstrate effective teamwork.

Because of the team format of Experiential School, students are able to identify their roles in the team and practice behaviors that contribute to team effectiveness, contribute positively to the success of the team project, recognize how differences in culture and individual differences affect interaction with others, and observe effective teamwork practices through job shadowing.

Communication

Apply the principles of effective communication to give and receive information (speaking, writing, reading, listening).

Throughout Experiential School week, students receive information through print, video (training films), discussion, and oral presentation. They also take notes, answer daily questions, conduct informal interviews, and have daily meetings with their team members to discuss their projects.

Acquire, use, and transfer information.

The information gathered during the week is organized, developed into a presentation, and presented by students to representatives of the host site at the end of the week.

Career development

Assess the relationship of educational achievement to career goals.

Through job shadowing and informal interviewing, and by participating in project work, students learn what aptitudes, education, training, and experience are required for successful careers in their fields of interest.

Assess characteristics related to personal, educational, and career goals.

Through the weeklong experience, students can determine if their career goals are in line with the routines, challenges, and demands of the workplace.

Employment foundations

Demonstrate the academic knowledge and technical skills required for successful employment with a career-endorsement area.

Students are given the opportunity to apply academic knowledge and basic technical skills related to an endorsement area (e.g., drafting in the arts and communication endorsement area).

Strategies for Success

Before a program like Experiential School is established, some groundwork must be laid. First, the value of career education must be understood and accepted by the district administrators, the school principal, and the faculty. The following are additional steps that would enhance the prospect for success of a program like Experiential School:

1. Hold a summit or conference involving all players.

2. Establish a full- or part-time position to develop and coordinate programs.

3. Nurture networks among school employees, parents, and business/agency partners.

4. Align program goals with local and state school-reform initiatives.

5. Develop a broad base of business and agency partners to provide for a variety of occupational interests among students.

6. Assist business partners in developing interactive, hands-on, project-based experiences for students.

7. Establish and empower an advisory committee of business partners and students.

8. Include faculty participation in site supervision to foster "ownership" in the program and to allow teachers to have an extended experience with business partners.

9. Evaluate programs from the student and business partner perspectives, and use those evaluations for program improvement.

10. Provide adequate recognition for business and agency partners.

Whether the entire program is used or a variation of the interactive, project-based format, all school districts should consider the benefit of an extended worksite experience for all students.

Chapter 23

The Role of Family and Community

Donna Swim

The community partnership in which the Anita School is involved works with all youth, in school and out of school. Our mission statement is: "The Anita School's Community shall provide optimum educational opportunities and challenges for all students." With this mission in mind, we must look at the issues involved.

1. We consider our parents/guardians, families, and community to be very important participants.

2. We feel it is paramount that they understand the role played by the learning style of each individual student in designing a career plan.

3. We realize we must examine the fears and the realities of family members, business representatives,

parents/guardians, and education personnel. When will everyone have time? What will each one's role be? How can we help the life of each student, including those with special needs? Why should we approach educating our youth as a community partnership?

The statement "It takes a whole community to raise a child" is the motto for our initiative. The school administration decided that, if we were to prepare the youth of this community to be productive citizens in the twenty-first century, everyone would have to work as a team. "Everyone" includes all those whose lives touch the lives of the children.

Research shows that students whose parents are actively involved in their education do better in school than students whose parents are not. When we conducted surveys, we found many families whose only involvement in their children's education was attending parent-teacher conferences. Consequently, as a school partner, we decided to form focus groups to discuss why this was happening.

After meeting with the more than twenty identified population entities in our area, we discovered that many of the parents' parents hadn't been involved in their schooling. This created one barrier. An additional barrier was the idea that parents must be invited by the school before they could take part. To improve parent and family participation, we began designing strategies.

The first step we took was to form a committee called "home/school partnership." This was made up of teachers and parents of children from a range of grade levels (prekindergarten, early education, middle school, and high school). The school principal and school-to-work coordinator rounded out the committee. The task of this group was and is to bring others—parents, guardians, and grandparents—into the school system.

The second step the school initiated was the training of parents and their children in self-determination. In this training, families go through eight hours of sessions together. They examine ways to build self-concepts and create understanding between them, and discuss how to build successful career skills for themselves and their children.

Unexpected Benefit

This training turned out to be very worthwhile for reasons we didn't expect. Our original goal was to give students the skills necessary to compete in careers as adults and to inform the parents about the skills, also. But the greatest success of the first training was the impact our parents made as they identified what they saw to be necessary for educating young people today, and the relationship this built between parents and the school. At this point, the parents became partners, ready to help design their children's education system.

With many of our parents now becoming our future business partners, we were one step closer to involving the entire community. In a sense, each person there taught someone else. With the school-to-work coordinator serving as the central facilitator for all partners, the entire community became empowered to be teachers of our youth.

This concept is very important. Today's youth need to see and experience what they need to know. This cannot be done in an abstract setting within the four walls of a school building. Without parent, family, and community involvement, we cannot offer our students an educational experience that prepares them for life in the twenty-first century.

Training

After establishing the importance of our entire community's involvement, we began to train school staff, parents, family members, and community businesses in learning styles. The parents were offered early-morning, late-afternoon, and evening sessions to learn about strategies to be used with different learning styles. All education personnel and students were given learning-style evaluations. This gave parents and faculty an understanding of how our youth learn best. In-service training was offered to anyone interested in understanding multiple intelligences.

One of our greatest challenges was creating a learning system that was responsive to the many groups in our community. We discovered that you must make everyone comfortable with the teaching and learning that are taking place. For example, when we first began to change our class offerings, our employer partners were hesitant to do some of the hands-on skill training. We found it very important to be conscious of how each employer, parent, and student felt. If we were to have applied learning classes in a school-based setting to match our work-based learning outside the school building, everyone needed to understand what we were doing.

To connect everyone, we began to hold training sessions during the summer months. These sessions are open to students, parents, businesses, adult service providers, and anyone who wants to attend. The sessions begin with large-group participation, but the final session is individualized for those who have not reached the level of efficiency we expect in the job skills being learned. This is true for all student, parent, and business participants. We believe that applied learning must be integrated and that all personnel must be involved, or a gap occurs either for the student trying to learn or for the person trying to teach.

Career Planning

Another important part of every student's life in our system is career planning. Our school-to-work system's first priority is to help children in our community realize the importance of growing up ready to be productive citizens. To accomplish this, we begin looking at broad career categories, like medicine or agriculture, in the early childhood years. The education staff at the lower levels brings business representatives to the school and visits businesses where children can role-play what they would do if that were the career they would choose as adults. For example, our first graders went to our hospital and took on the roles required to conduct a tonsillectomy.

We believe it is very important for children to begin to look at the world of work early in life. Children should be taught to think of work as positive, rather than as something negative or a part of life that they dread. Therefore, all students, starting with our kindergartners, are integrated into experiences outside the classroom. They progress to more advanced levels of experience as they move through their educational learning. They begin to job shadow their parents or community members, and parents and community members come to the school setting to share their work lives with the students. During our follow-up interviews, one business manager stated, "I thought this would be an obligation role, but it has created energy, motivation, and excitement in my employees that we couldn't create as business management."

Transitioning

Transition times are very important. As students enter their junior high years, career planning intensifies. Our youth have now reached one of the turning points in their lives; they will develop life skills that will continue into adulthood. Research completed by schools in Iowa shows that the skill patterns children have in seventh grade follow them through their secondary and postsecondary years. For example, a student who doesn't complete classroom assignments at this grade level often drops out or fails to complete requirements at a higher level. Those of this group who *do* graduate often fail at postsecondary experiences. For this reason, all students at the seventh- and eighth-grade levels participate in project success classes.

At our school, this involves classes in job skills (organization, responsibility, time on task, teamwork, self-discipline, and lifelong learning techniques) and service learning projects. The families and community give a lot of volunteer time to the students at this stage. Also, an extensive career exploration unit is integrated into their English classes at the eighth-grade level. In this unit, students choose careers they think they would enjoy as adults. They collect information from Choices, do interest inventories, write résumés, interview someone in that career field, and write reports covering all the information they have gathered from the Internet and other sources. As a climax to the unit, students make oral presentations with visuals and details on the selected careers. This process gives them broad exposure to many career areas from the viewpoints of adults actually involved in the careers.

After eighth grade, we are ready to develop a more intensified experience with career planning. This becomes a very important time for parents/guardians and community. Parents need to know and understand the processes and opportunities. They need to help their child and our student move into his or her young adult years with excitement and motivation in preparing for an adult career. Through the school-to-work coordinator, we have conducted interviews with the parents from the kindergarten level on for each grade level. We know the goals and priorities each parent has for his or her children. At this point we do transition planning and begin to examine career areas we offer with classes beginning in the freshman year. The parents, students, school-to-work coordinator, counselor, and principal talk about and visit with the team in each student's life; by registration time, each has chosen one career cluster area to begin exploring, taking introductory classroom classes. It is very important to have all team members, especially family, involved in this process. If the family doesn't believe in striving for goals, the child's dream is often lost.

Life-Changing Process

This transition period is one of the most important cultural changes for a family. At this time, their child begins to move into a period of independence. Therefore, all team members must be consistent in dealing with the plans for the lives of their students. This becomes very true for parents and guardians of our "at risk" population of youth. A parent of an at-risk student exclaimed, "If only I'd had someone helping me put my life together, I would not have ended up in the welfare system." The good news is that this parent and his child are both successful now. The parent completed his GED and moved from a life of not knowing how to be a working citizen into a life of work. This all took place four years ago and he is still employed. His child is involved in work-based computer experiences and no one in the family is being supported by public assistance.

We believe in our school-to-career system change because we see it changing the lives of entire families.

Senior High Years

We have looked at what transpires in our partnership system through the freshman year of school. We are now ready to look at the senior high years of our students' learning experience. At this point, businesses in the community and extended community become involved. Parents start looking more closely at the futures of their young adults. Students begin developing goals with skills they have learned in project success classes with the help of the school-to-work coordinator and counselor. Great care is taken to interview all the students (in school, out of school) in our community. Their goals and aspirations are discussed with team members at the middle of the second semester of the sophomore year. All youth in every setting in our community are entered into job-shadowing experiences for three full days. These experiences center around career plans the students have designed for themselves in the preceding years. They choose and contact businesses, arrange to be interviewed, and write résumés before they actually spend any time shadowing. It is their responsibility to accomplish these tasks.

During the second semester, all juniors and sophomores begin extensive planning sessions with the school-to-work coordinator. Goals are revisited and the steps needed to meet those goals are established. Hand in hand, so to speak, we begin planning for work-based class time in a business setting that correlates with the student's chosen career. We try to gain enough information from students and parents to arrive at the business partnership that fits the students' desires. During their senior year (and occasionally their junior year), students are put in work settings. Once again, they must prepare for their work-based classes during the summer before school starts in the fall. They must complete all steps independently. If we find that a student is unable to do so, a transition specialist is assigned to him or her. Adult service providers join the team with job coaches at the site. Our top priority is the success of the student, and all decisions center around that focal point. For our students with special needs, this process has increased the success level almost 100 percent. For example, one student who had a special education plan is having his training paid for by a local business, and he has been promised a job when he is finished that will pay him more than $30,000 annually. Our students with high academic grades are receiving scholarships because they have been in work-based experiences. Colleges have told our students they like giving scholarships to them because they have a high likelihood of completing four-year degrees. With this systems change, our student success level has been above 98 percent.

We believe a community's involvement in teaching a child develops a productive citizen for society. It truly takes a team effort to achieve such a high level of success. Keeping parents involved in our training sessions and inviting them in to do at least two hours of volunteer time in the school-based classroom has created a real-world learning cycle for our youth as they grow up.

Addressing Fears

One very important aspect of creating systemic change is to recognize and address the fears of every participant. The two greatest fears of the business and community partners are liability and their lack of understanding of our youth. We overcome these by first introducing them to the Fair Labor Act for the school-to-work initiative. This allays their biggest fear. Then we have our business and community partners come to the school to spend time with and gain an understanding of our youth.

The greatest fears of the education staff are the amount of time these systemic changes will take and how staff members will have to change their educational instruction time. To alleviate these fears, we increased our class periods to ninety minutes and the counselor changed some of his responsibilities. We also train staff members in contextual learning and multiple intelligences. This is done continually so new staff members can move into the systems change for our school improvement process.

Another very important challenge is learning to be team players. Teachers team teach classes. Parents and retired citizens help while projects are developing. Retired citizens, who give countless hours of time in the school-based classroom, have given inspiration and knowledge to our students. In the work-based setting, they have often inspired our at-risk population to reach for new heights. These retirees have the fewest fears of all.

Parents' fears revolve more around the idea that not everyone will be able to participate. After we assure them that all students can participate, we don't have to deal with other fears. One reason for this is that we spend a lot of time with parents, so there are no hidden gaps in the school-to-careers effort in our community.

Members of our school partnership are very flexible in working with volunteers, families, community members, and education personnel; this is another key element in increasing parent/community/business involvement. For too long, school communities have failed to adjust their schedules and activities to accommodate parents and community partners. We have discovered that families and businesses need to plan in the early-morning hours, before scheduled school hours, or in the evenings. We make these accommodations by having a school-to-work coordinator arrange a schedule that helps rather than hinders the team members. The home-school partnership committee, which is also under the direction of volunteer parents, takes time at town festivals, school activities, and any other opportune occasion to insert people into a flowchart according to the times they say they can volunteer. This is developed into a calendar for each month, which is posted in the work areas in the school system so teachers know when they will have volunteers.

Before any volunteer participates, he or she takes part in training conducted by the principal and/or school-to-work coordinator. From focus groups, surveys, and interviews, we know what the expectations are in both the school-based and work-based classrooms. We are a team working toward the development of our youth for their adult lives. The YORP youth organization has a quote with which we agree very strongly: "It is easier to mold a child than it is to repair an adult."

The benefits of working as a team rather than separately can best be expressed by those who have experienced the activities and practices of the Anita School system. Appended to this chapter are four letters. The first is from a volunteer retired citizen and grandparent of a former student. The next letters are from students who are now seniors and a volunteer retired citizen.

I will close with the motto we post at all service sessions:

School and Community

Together

We Create Dreams

and

Build Careers.

Empower your team members and move ahead!

*　　*　　*

From a volunteer . . .

Dear Mrs. Swim,

I want to thank you and the school administration for giving me the opportunity to work on the school/home partnership team (for the development of the volunteer program at the Anita schools). It has been an interesting year!

Benefits from this program were realized from the beginning. Parents, teachers, and administration met to devise a plan of action for implementing this program. We were not divided according to our specific roles, but were there for one common purpose . . . to enhance the education of our children through a volunteer program. All ideas were treated equally, and we freely shared our thoughts. I feel that a communication barrier was broken and an attitude of cooperation was developed in this initial stage.

It has been exciting to see that from this core group of people a volunteer program involving many people has developed.

Thanks to the support and cooperation of the teachers and administration, the program was made possible and will be able to continue. Without their sense of community and dedication to our children, this program could not exist.

With the teachers to support us, we were able to reach out and ask for community involvement. It was exciting to learn that over 130 people are willing to give their time and talents to the students. These people range in age from college-aged to senior citizens. It must make our youth feel pretty important to see so many people take an active interest in their education. (As you know, a significant number of these people have already volunteered this year in various activities, including sports events, listening to elementary students read, and judging speech contests.)

I feel that both the students and the volunteers derive benefits from this program. By getting involved, the volunteers can see the students in a positive light—as people with growing minds and ideas to share. The kids see the adults as caring and concerned people, with their own ideas to share. I think this nurtures an environment of understanding, communication, and respect between people of different age groups and possibly different socioeconomic standing.

Another benefit I can see as a result of this program is the example the adults set by being responsible and caring members of a community.

I have been happy to discover that the kids are also encouraged to volunteer. For example, isn't it great that our youth have had a hand in developing the trail from the town to the lake? They have helped to clear the path, pick up trash, and even helped to write a grant! What a great way to feel a sense of belonging and a pride in their community!

I hope this program will continue to grow for both the students and the adults so that the community of Anita and Anita Community Schools can work together for the benefit of all.

Thanks again,

LeAnn Josephsen

From a student who is now a senior . . .

Dear Anita Community School,

I have been involved in the School-to-work (STW) program during my senior year. With the STW program, I have been able to work in four internships as well as the entrepreneurship business. In my internships, I worked with students in the special education area and in the regular classroom setting. My internships have been one of the most rewarding classes that I have taken throughout my high school career. I found that I enjoy working with students with special needs just as much as I do in the regular classroom. When I started my senior year, I was still somewhat unsure of what I wanted my career to be. While in my internships, I was lucky to have teachers who actually got me involved in the teaching of the classes. Because of my internships, I have decided to go into the education field, teaching in the social science and special education areas. I also served as the president of the student-owned business (entrepreneurship). As I served in this position, I found that management of a business is not an easy task. I also found that I enjoyed the excitement and frustrations and all other aspects of running a business. This has led me to look into the administrative side of teaching. With both of these areas interesting me, I plan on pursuing both areas in college. I feel that the whole STW program is the best classroom for those who are in all stages of their high school career. Everyone needs the basic classes, but the STW program teaches you something no teacher lecturing could ever do.

Sincerely,

Amber Pringnitz

From a retired citizen . . .

My experience with the "school-to-work" program has been very satisfying.

In one part of the program we were involved in estimating the materials cost of repair, or even renovation, of a residential property. In another area two business properties were involved.

Those students involved were very interested in the number of skills which would be required. They were also very interested in the financial aspects, such as:

- The priority of the various projects as they would affect rental income.

- The effect on a property appraisal and the resulting salability.

- The effect of an appraisal in a loan application.

However, my primary interest was in the volunteer program. In addition to the exposure to some of the skills required to complete a project, it was very evident there was a feeling of accomplishment and a sense of pride in their contribution.

Without a question the efforts and accomplishments of others involved in community service were recognized, as was the importance of a community working together to accomplish goals.

Al (Jr.) Karns

4/15/98

From another student now a senior . . .

Adam Nelsen
809 Chestnut Street
Anita, Iowa 50020

Anita Community Schools,

Hello, my name is Adam Nelsen and I have attended Anita Community School K-12 and I am currently finishing my senior year in high school here in Anita. This letter is addressing the school-to-work program that was offered to me this year (1997-98). I think that the program is a huge success and should be available for students to participate in because it offers them a hands-on view of the working environment.

Upon graduating I plan to attend Iowa State University where my major will be graphic design. I had a small understanding of my field of study but I didn't realize the endless opportunities until my first day on the "job." I have served with two companies while interning, Atlantic Signs and Clarinda Company. Atlantic Signs showed the smaller business aspects, while Clarinda Company was a much larger firm with several deadlines to make at once.

Through the school-to-work program I have an advantage on other students coming out of high school. An experience advantage that could mean the difference on a résumé. I also realized that this was the career that I would like to continue to study for. Not many students around the state of Iowa or even the country are able to attend work with wonderful people like I have, and they end up spending thousands of dollars on wasted education trying to find a career they enjoy.

I also must commend Donna Swim on her hard work and dedication to making this program work. She motivates students that are willing to do the work and helps them out any way possible. Donna Swim and the administration have made this program work for the better of the students.

Adam Nelsen
Anita High School Senior and Intern

Chapter 24

University Schools of Education As Partners

Charles D. Schmitz

Imagine: What if we, as passengers on "spaceship earth," made a habit of finding ways to connect with the world around us? What if we lived in a world where people combined their limited resources in creative ways to learn, produce, and live better lives? What if we continuously sought methods to break down barriers, accept each other, care for each other, and praise each other? What if we as a nation came together to collectively educate and "raise" our most valuable resource— our children, our citizens? Imagine what a future we could create.

A Vision Starts with Opportunity

In the next ten years, two million new teachers will be hired. According to the National Commission on Teaching and America's Future, this reflects an enormous turnover among the more than three million teachers currently in our nation's elementary and secondary schools.[1] The result will be a radical shift in the education system as well as a challenge and an opportunity to sustain and accelerate school improvement efforts. Reform efforts like Tech Prep that rely on innovations in teaching and learning could be greatly aided by changes in the teacher workforce. Those who are committed to the goals of Tech Prep—improving contextual learning, increasing linkages between the school and the workplace, and infusing new methods of educational technology in the classroom—must recognize that teacher in-service by itself cannot continue to supply adequate professional development. And university schools of education can no longer build lifelong careers for their graduates if they operate in a vacuum. University schools of education must meet with school districts, businesses, and their communities at large. All must have open minds and be ready to work toward realizing the vision of twenty-first-century schools.

A Vital Need for Collaboration

School administrators and teachers are eager to address school improvement, but opportunities to do this have been limited. For decades, teachers have had to develop innovative pedagogy and learn new technologies while maintaining their everyday workloads. Designing new teaching methodologies requires extensive research and evaluation, and teachers, like

---

[1] National Commission on Teaching and America's Future, *What Matters Most: Teaching for America's Future, 1996*, p. 8.

their students, benefit from a broad spectrum of activities as they discover, make connections to the real world, and reflect upon first-hand experiences. It is unrealistic to expect teachers to "figure it out" in isolation or at one-shot in-service training workshops. Unfortunately, school districts are limited by the costs of and time needed for professional development. It is estimated that in the United States only 1 to 3 percent of school district expenditures is devoted to teacher development, far less than is spent by most corporations and by school systems in other countries.[2]

Similarly, professional education students need relevant continuous learning experiences that build upon practice. Unfortunately, many undergraduate and graduate programs are isolated and irrelevant. Thus, teachers currently in the classroom and students seeking education credentials often find themselves part of a cyclical process of traditional education. They teach their classes as they were taught—with lecture and chalkboard—looking out on students aligned in neat rows of chairs. Though we live in the so-called information age, we have factory-era schools. Education secretary Richard Riley describes this state of affairs in this way: "Knowledge is exploding all around us. We live in a new golden age of discovery. Astronomers probe the unfolding majesty of the universe, even as scientists race to map the genetic makeup of humanity. Yet we struggle to put the old industrial model of education behind us."

Most educators have never been a part of the world of business and industry, and have little or no exposure to the innovations taking place outside the classroom. Consequently, they become married to pencil and paper. But the digital age is upon us, and no educational reform movement can progress

---

[2] Thomas B. Corcoran, "Helping Teachers Teach Well: Transforming Professional Development," *CPRE Policy Brief #RB-16* (Brunswick, New Jersey: Consortium for Policy Research in Education, June 1995).

without a strong reliance on technology. As Nicholas Negroponte says, "Computing is not about computers any more. It is about living."[3] The importance of technology to school and teacher-education reform cannot be overemphasized. Schools and teacher-education programs must be among the first places in which innovative technology is implemented. Thus far, this has typically not been the case.

It is understandable, then, that one-third of all new teachers leave the profession within the first three years.[4] Traditional methods have proven ineffective with the new generation of students, who are more responsive to a laptop than a textbook. It is unrealistic to expect most teachers to have studied cognitive science, to understand the latest developments in teaching and learning, and to have had any introduction to the effective uses of educational technology. Also, the number of underprepared teachers entering the workforce is staggering. More than 12 percent of all newly hired teachers enter the profession with no training, and another 15 percent enter without having fully met state standards. How can we, as a community, assume that short-term training programs or outdated models of teacher preparation can equip teachers for the next century?

The National Commission on Teaching and America's Future suggests that the future of education rests upon three simple premises:

1. What teachers know and can do is the most important influence on what students learn.

2. Recruiting, preparing, and retaining good teachers is the central strategy for improving our schools.

---

[3] Nicholas Negroponte, *Being Digital* (New York: Alfred A. Knopf, 1995), p. 6.
[4] National Commission on Teaching and America's Future, p. 34.

3.   School reform cannot succeed unless it focuses on creating the conditions in which teachers can teach, and teach well.

All educators and community leaders should embrace these premises as common grounds for collaboration among school districts, universities, teacher-education schools, businesses, policymakers, and community organizations. As partners, we should leave behind the old blueprint for education and collectively create a new infrastructure for teacher recruitment, professional development, research, and perpetual learning.

The preparation of our teachers and young people is too important to leave in the hands of colleges and schools of education alone. Only through collaborative efforts can the teacher-education reform movement be effective in preparing educators to build bridges between the worlds of school and work.

A New Culture and a New Mind-Set

Anyone wanting to transform the culture of teacher education must first consider all aspects of learning organizations. After three decades of research in the cognitive sciences, a deeper understanding of how people learn has prompted a reappraisal of teaching practices. For instance, research indicates that knowledge is not passively received, but actively constructed on the basis of previous knowledge, attitudes, and values. Therefore, single sources of information, like textbooks, are less effective learning tools than the multiple sources that can be accessed through contextual or work-based experiences and technology.

Additionally, educational research supports the notion that teaching and learning in the information age should be aligned with new boundaries of place and time. Traditionally, emphasis has been placed on the lecture-centered, time-structured classroom. However, experts in telecommunication technology and distance learning predict that time-based learning will be replaced by a system that fuses learning and work. (See chapter 7.) The Society for College and University Planning (SCUP) considers this new phenomenon with respect to colleges and universities in the report *Transforming Higher Education: A Vision for Learning in the 21st Century*. In this report, SCUP states that there will be a realignment and redesign of learning organizations from the Industrial Age to the Information Age around the following metaphors:[5]

From the Industrial Age	To the Information Age
Classrooms, libraries, and laboratories	Network
Teaching	Learning
Seat-time-based learning	Achievement-based learning
Classroom-centered instruction	Network learning
Information acquisition	Knowledge navigation
Distance education	Distance-free learning
Continuing education	Perpetual learning
Time out for learning	Fusion of learning and work
Separation of learners and learning systems	Fusion of learning systems

Essential to creating this new infrastructure is a changing mind-set in people and learning organizations. Choices made by teachers, researchers, practitioners, and learners will set the course for new learning environments.

---

[5] Society for College and University Planning, *Transforming Higher Education: A Vision for Learning in the 21st Century* (Ann Arbor, Michigan, 1995), p. 58.

New roles and forms of professional development

Collaborations within the community—not only within K-12 systems or teacher-education colleges—can create a powerful infrastructure for increased accountability and resources. Businesses, unions, government agencies, and community-based organizations can all contribute. Since preservice and in-service teachers need to learn about the worksite, the simultaneous renewal of schools and educator-preparation programs[6] can be effective only if they are actively connected to the world of work. As society places more demands on those entering the workplace, it is imperative that both educators and students have firsthand knowledge of employer expectations.

Educational technology and telecommunication

The changes technology has brought to the workplace have enormous implications for teacher education. New telecommunication technology can break down the walls of isolation and introduce future education professionals not only to the local school and business community, but also to a world-based economy. Imagine the possibilities for Tech Prep if videoconferencing technology brought the world of work to schools and teacher-education colleges. Teacher-education students could, for the first time, begin to make personal connections between their teaching subjects and the real world. Technology like this could open minds to the way concepts are used in various workplaces—a method of pedagogy that should be modeled in schools of education for future practice in classrooms.

---

[6] John I. Goodlad, *Educational Renewal: Better Teachers, Better Schools* (San Francisco: Jossey-Bass Inc., Publishers, 1994).

Equally exciting is the idea of college faculty comfortably E-mailing students, using listservs for projects and instruction, and introducing future teachers to software that will enhance instruction. These teaching tools could generate new teacher/student relationships, while mastery of this type of technology would introduce teachers to the tools of the typical office environment and mimic workplace communication.

In the past few years, leadership groups have pushed innovative issues such as educational technology to the forefront of discussion in teacher education. Consequently, national attention has begun to focus on technology in teacher preparation, and change is taking place. For instance, the National Council for Accreditation of Teacher Education (NCATE) has made three broad recommendations regarding technology in the accreditation of teacher-education programs:

1. Stimulate more effective uses of technology in teacher-education programs.

2. Use technology to improve the existing accreditation process to reconceptualize accreditation for the twenty-first century.

3. Improve and expand NCATE's own operations through greater uses of technology.

Coming from an organization with a national constituency, statements like these are evidence that schools of education are beginning to seek changes in their traditional programs. As new attitudes, ideas, and methodologies continue to emerge, Tech Prep practitioners should also express their ideas for transforming teacher education.

The professional development school

Professional education students, like their future students, need to take cues from the innovations and developing practices of their future workplace. According to the National Education

Association, most university education programs do not require more than one or two semesters of student teaching. These student-teaching experiences are limited by exposure to the practicing schools, which rarely reflect the latest innovations in school improvement. If professional education students are introduced to new concepts in teaching and learning in their college programs but do not observe these practices in schools, they are unlikely to use them in their own teaching.

A growing new concept and venue for developing future teachers is called the professional development school (PDS). Modeled after the teaching hospital, the PDS is designed for undergraduates to explore the practicalities and applications of the latest research and teaching in the education profession. Because PDS school sites are selected for best practices, teacher-education students are exposed to a variety of excellent practitioners. The experience has been very effective for future teachers, education professors, and current school administrators and teachers. The National Association of Secondary School Principals applauds the PDS concept in its recent report, *Breaking Ranks: Changing an American Institution,* and includes the concept in its list of recommendations: "Teacher education programs can best measure the needs of the schools by having their professors work closely with the schools. . . . From such collaboration will emerge ideas and opportunities to enhance the education, performance, and evaluation of educators."[7]

Tech Prep practitioners should note the growing interest in and success of the PDS, since there is great opportunity for collaboration between Tech Prep consortia and teacher-education students. The PDS experience could introduce Tech Prep concepts to teacher-education students and help Tech Prep

---

[7] National Association of Secondary School Principals (NASSP), *Breaking Ranks: Changing an American Institution* (Reston, Virginia: NASSP, 1996), p. 85.

consortia find methods of integrating the latest in education
research into evolving Tech Prep programs.

New relationships within the university setting

The responsibility of preparing future teachers should not
fall entirely on the school of education, but also on other
departments or colleges in the university. Typically,
undergraduates take more general courses and courses in their
academic majors than courses in the school of education. Thus,
all aspects of the undergraduate's professional education
experience must be considered. Yet the schools of education
and departments of mathematics and science today work
independently of each other in most respects. They concentrate
separately on the *art of teaching* and the *mastery of content*. But
the process fails to provide entering new teachers with
knowledge of *connectivity*, the bedrock of motivation for all
students. There should be a common purpose among these
departments to jointly use their talents to educate future
teachers. The common goal should be to turn out elementary
and secondary school teachers who know the *what* (subject
matter content), the *how* (the art of teaching), and the *why* (the
importance of the subject to the student—the connection to the
real world).

Imagine the student response in an algebra or geometry
class where teachers are prepared to discuss the inside diameter
of automotive cylinders and involve students in mathematics
laboratories with Vernier calipers—where diameters and depths
of cylinders (cans) are measured and "piston-displacement"
volume is calculated. Or where mathematics teachers use ratio
and proportion to determine the mechanical advantage of a
robot arm or the concentration of an etching solution in
semiconductor manufacturing. Or where science teachers use
exponential decay to determine the level of nuclear waste.
Imagine the excitement when science teachers introduce their
students to digital meters, dual-trace oscilloscopes, function

generators, sensors, computer interfaces, piezoelectric transducers, fiber optics, and lasers—and show them how to use these instruments to solve the real-world problems found at General Motors, Texas Instruments, and AT&T.

To provide our future teachers with mastery of subject matter and delivery, there must be a system for cooperation among the schools of education and the university departments of mathematics, science, technology, and other disciplines. Collectively, future teachers must also master how concepts relate to practice. If the connectivity between theory and practice continues to be ignored, there will be more uninterested students and fewer motivated learners.

> The future is not a result of choices among alternative paths offered by the present, but a place that is created—created first in the mind and will, created next in activity. The future is not some place we are going to, but one we are creating. The paths to it are not found but made, and the activity of making them changes both the maker and the destination.
>
> —John Schaar

University of Missouri-Saint Louis School of Education: The Future of Education

As the largest preparer of new teachers in Missouri, the University of Missouri-Saint Louis School of Education (UMSL-SOE) takes seriously the special duty and privilege of helping prepare tomorrow's education professionals. With the support of community leaders in St. Louis, a metropolitan area of nearly 2.6 million people, UMSL-SOE has developed a long-term partnership with businesses, K-12 school systems, and community organizations.

Despite its fragmented government and inner-city decline, the St. Louis region holds 52 percent of the business payroll for all Missouri. The area accounts for $5.4 billion per year in exports, penetrating 178 markets around the world. Now, various parts of the community are recognizing economic interdependence: If one part of the region suffers, the disease will spread and government will never have enough money to care for the casualties. Consequently, new economic strategies are (1) forging alliances to attract and grow industry clusters involving dozens (if not hundreds) of related companies, (2) upgrading workforce skills to attract world-class industries; (3) developing quality rail and port facilities and roads; and (4) building a strong telecommunication capability.

As a result, instead of looking at college as the only ticket to prosperity, the focus is now on lifelong learning and career training and retraining for every economic class. Instead of rigidly separated social services for dependent clients, the focus is on integrated services for families and communities. The culmination of these local economic initiatives and the growing global need for change in education have caused the administration and faculty to realize a new vision for UMSL-SOE. Through this change, we seek to

1.   Respond to the communities in which we serve,

2.   Retool with new learning technologies, and

3.   Rethink our approaches to teaching and learning.

With partners, we are creating a responsive, field-based, collaboration for preparing new—and helping already practicing—educators. This model is based on the belief that education counselors, teachers, students, parents, schools, universities, and community resources like the corporate and business community, cultural institutions, youth service organizations, and other health and welfare organizations, must all join in raising our children.

Four components to realizing our vision

During the next three to five years, we will institute changes that will make us a very different organization. While developing new understandings, approaches, roles, and attitudes, we are also developing specific characteristics that balance vision with reality. Four main components of the preparation program have been identified:

1. ***Relevance.*** *The formal preparation and continuing education of classroom teachers is a collaborative effort involving many committed partners.*

Students spend less time in lecture halls and more learning time in K-12 schools, working with practicing professionals and collaborating with the community in ways that are relevant to the future workplace. As part of the St. Louis Professional Development Schools Collaborative, which includes eighteen PDSs affiliated with seven universities, UMSL-SOE is developing fifteen to twenty more PDSs to give teacher-education students wider experience. The schools incorporate contextual learning experiences, using field work and internship programs.

Creating experiences that enable students to see the relationship between what they teach in the classroom and the demands of the workplace is critical. Some students are now doing field work in the St. Louis Career Education District—a breakthrough for the UMSL-SOE.

2. ***Technology.*** *Teacher-education programs adapt to methods that redefine the way teachers are prepared.*

Technology will be the glue that connects our SOE with community partners and the rest of the world. Our goal is to use technology to reach—not further alienate—children at risk. Videoconferencing technology is a planned component of PDSs that is intended to create stronger links between UMSL-SOE faculty and practicing professionals. Also, several new approaches to the use of educational technology, from software to the Internet, will be used in the E. Desmond Lee Technology and Learning Center designed to provide professional development to both preservice and in-service teachers.

*3. **Perpetual Learning**. We support career-long professional development for teachers.*

The old premise that a teacher can be prepared for a lifetime in a four- or five-year preservice program is no longer educationally sound. Combining preservice and in-service professional development will strengthen school-improvement goals. With the use of technology links and interactive communication, more efforts are being made between the SOE and community partners to get professional development to all teachers. One recent example is a partnership with the Rankin Technical College in St. Louis; jointly, we are seeking resources for videoconferencing links to develop opportunities for educating faculty and students.

*4. **Community**. The UMSL-SOE is an active part of the St. Louis community.*

We are enlisting the help of community resources and building partnerships and collaborations to be responsive to the needs of this region—the future workforce needs, the education needs, the social needs, and the career-preparation needs of our children. *What is taught in the classroom, the way teachers are prepared, and the demands of the workplace must have a high correlation if we are to become and remain a dynamic and economically stable region.*

First things first—building collaboration

The UMSL-SOE addresses all four of the listed components by proactive leadership and relationships within the community. After two years of setting up an infrastructure and building these new relationships, we have redefined our organization and developed a new culture and mind-set, and we are ready to redesign our curriculum and teaching methods. The efforts are guided by one important lesson expressed with a quotation: "Insanity is expecting different results while continuing to do the same thing." It was absolutely critical to change structures before changing anything else.

Changing our internal culture was difficult, but partnering and collaboration are even more difficult. As faculty and administration came to grips with the need for and purpose of new partnerships, it became apparent that we must send a strong and positive message to our potential partners. Top-level leadership of the SOE was required to meet one-on-one with representatives of businesses, civic groups, human service agencies, cultural institutions, scientific institutions, and school districts. Our message was clear: "We will not have a good workforce without a good education system, and we won't have a good education system without good teachers. The entire community must be involved. The University of Missouri-St. Louis wants to be your partner."

We learned that it is important to get people together physically, not just virtually. It took several attempts with each partner before we finally did so, but then the magic started to happen. People talked to each other. Trust began to develop, and each partner felt empowered.

St. Louis Regional Center for Education and Work

The emerging St. Louis Regional Center for Education and Work represents one of the first attempts at a broad collaborative partnership that joins business, labor, industry, local government leaders, human service agencies, community members, educators, and university personnel. This partnership will provide broad-based support for education and work initiatives in the region.

**The St. Louis Regional
Institute for
Science Education
(UMSL-SOE)**

**St. Louis Regional
Professional Development
Center**

**WorkABLE St. Louis
(A school-to-work
consortium)**

**State Initiatives
of the Missouri
Department
of Elementary
and Secondary
Education**

**St. Louis
Regional
Center for
Education
and Work**

**St. Louis
Labor Council,
AFL-CIO**

**University of
Missouri-St. Louis
School of Education**

**The Regional
Commerce and
Growth Association
of Greater St. Louis**

**University
Extension**

**The Cooperating
School Districts of
Greater St. Louis Staff
Development Division**

**The St. Louis
Professional Development
Schools Collaborative**

The goals of the partnership are as follows:

1.   To provide professional development for teachers,
     counselors, and education leaders in the design and
     implementation of school-to-work reforms.

2.   To study, research, and report best practices in
     collaborative school-to-work initiatives developed
     through the Regional Center for Education and Work.

3.   To become an educational resources center for
     workplace skills assessment, training, and guidance.

4.   To create action-oriented programs among the
     collaborations and networks that effectively address
     workplace skills preparation.

Technology and learning center

Plans for developing the next collaboration are under way. By creating a rich environment of resources, best practices, and hands-on experiences, the E. Desmond Lee Technology and Learning Center will be reaching diverse school districts, from inner-city to rural. The center will serve both preservice and in-service professional educators with new approaches to education that incorporate technology, lifelong learning and professional development, and career preparation for students and adults. The key goals of the center are these:

- Establishing a model classroom environment for hands-on practice in managing new methods of teaching through technology.

- Researching and developing new technology-enhanced teaching methods and approaches to engage students from disadvantaged backgrounds.

- Creating programs that connect school classrooms with the workplace, show theoretical concepts applied in the workplace, and encourage students to communicate with on-the-job professionals and labor-force employees.

- Developing with education and school administration professionals innovative ways to create attractive, modern, well-equipped, and technologically advanced learning environments.

Recommendations

Tech Prep, school-to-work, and other community initiatives share many strategies. My viewpoint is that of the dean of a university school of education who seeks change in education and values the importance of preparing people for the world of work. This viewpoint was important in bringing about the changes needed to develop the collaborations mentioned earlier. There are many deans of schools of education who share similar views and want new opportunities to work with Tech Prep consortia and communities in preparing teachers for the next century. In working with such organizations, it is important to remember some key issues.

1. Help each partner understand that partnering enhances rather than diminishes our opportunities.

2. Teach people how to facilitate, not control. Meet regularly at mutually agreeable locations.

3. Start your relationship with easy-to-accomplish projects. Partnering requires baby steps.

4. Develop trust by making a commitment and sticking with it.

5. Find ways to give up something to make the partnership work.

6. Combine resources to hire a single director for professional and staff development.

All collaborations seek out resources. While most partners have limited funds, collectively they can be strong. Schools of education need resources but can contribute influence, reputation, and stability. The ten endowed professorships UMSL-SOE has established are critical to the collaboration because they connect the SOE with important scientific, cultural, and human service agencies in the greater St. Louis community. The relationships with these organizations provide consortia not only with a pool of resources but also with many opportunities for contextual learning and workplace exploration. These will have a lasting impact on the SOE and its partners.

SECTION 6

Putting the Vision

into Practice

The Winning Edge—Tech Prep

Elaine Sullivan, Ed.D., 1998 NASSP/Met Life
Principal of the Year; Principal—Hernando High
School, Brooksville, Florida

*As the 1998 NASSP/Met Life Principal of the Year, I am
often asked what I believe gave me the edge over other
principals. My response is Tech Prep. Tech Prep dovetails with
my beliefs about education and is the core for creating change
at my school.*

*About eight years ago, Hernando High School's staff began
a journey, learning new strategies to reach today's students.
Most teachers believed that they had done everything the right
way and that the students were the problem. In conversations
with staff members about unsuccessful students, I noted that, as
teachers, they might be competent in their approach, but our
students were not succeeding. We are judged and rated on our
students' success—or lack thereof. Additionally, our business
community had been telling us that students were not ready for
work. At the same time, some of the staff and I had come to the
conclusion that students were unmotivated, which we believe
impacted their learning. So the journey began—to motivate kids
and become more effective teachers in the hope that students
would become involved in the learning process.*

*Tech Prep has been the nucleus for our approach to whole
school reform and serves as the vehicle in our quest to become
better teachers and motivate more students. Additionally, Tech
Prep transformed my staff into a community of leaders and
learners. Teachers started collaborating. School improvement
interdisciplinary communication teams became the backbone
for communication and for creating committees to take action.
Staff members emerged as formal and informal leaders. As a
school, we are now more focused on the student and on the need
for a career focus.*

We established higher expectations for all students, not just the middle majority. Our curriculum is now more rigorous and relevant. The applied teaching philosophy and courses have become the guiding premises for reworking the curriculum and our beliefs about how to teach. This work continues today. We changed to block scheduling six years ago. Opportunities for parallel teaching units or integrated units were created. This next year, the staff will be planning for the next step of our restructuring into career clusters.

Now we have started learning how to incorporate "brain-based" research and the "multiple intelligences" into our teaching. This is the next piece to be added into our teaching in a contextual setting. The world of work and the career context have become major underpinnings for guiding our school. Tech Prep changed a very conservative, traditional school of more than one hundred years of pride, tradition, and "we have always done it this way" to a leader in education reform.

Chapter 25

The Next Generation

Julie Hull Grevelle

*I*t is no failure to fall short of realizing a vision. The failure is
to fall short of visioning what we might realize (Don Clifton,
CEO, The Gallup Organization). It is clear from the ideas
described in the preceding pages that we have yet to realize the
full vision of Tech Prep. But, as Elaine Sullivan predicts, Tech
Prep can be the winning edge we need for total school reform.
The potential of Tech Prep starts with the ideas offered by the
authors who contributed to this book. When the concepts for
curriculum, teaching, and learning are accepted as the core for
creating change in any school, the possibilities are limitless.

The test for the future of Tech Prep lies in the hands of the
local leadership. The Tech Prep coordinators, principals, college
presidents, and employers who steer the activities of their *local*
consortia will set the path for Tech Prep in the next five to ten
years. Will they—by allowing partnerships to stagnate and
narrow, old-fashioned concepts of articulation and vocational

education to persist—allow Tech Prep to become just another program. Or will they use the original goals of Tech Prep as a springboard for bold new plans, exciting new curricula, and innovative teaching methods? If you are a local leader of Tech Prep, take a moment to honestly answer these questions before closing this book. If you have said to yourself, "We are already doing this," reread some of the chapters and make a true assessment of your local initiatives. The window of opportunity for directing a new Tech Prep path is open now. Enter it before state and federal leadership and resources direct the path for you.

A Leap of Faith

There is always plenty of room for improvement in Tech Prep programs. The Tech Prep director of a national award-winning program recently said, "It is a little scary to know that we are ranked among the best Tech Prep programs in the country when I notice the tremendous amount of work we still have ahead of us." However, this is exactly the sort of forward thinking that will continue to foster a nationally recognized model.

Meanwhile, the tendency for most of us is to be retrospective. Who can blame us for being proud of our accomplishments or ashamed of our mistakes? Many of us are hanging onto the original problems or barriers of implementation as excuses for failed attempts at innovation. But by shedding some old standards and original means, we are capable of achieving much more.

As a matter of fact, the ideas set forth in this book represent a giant leap of faith into new and uncharted territories for many consortia, which is exactly the kind of gutsy risk-taking chance that most of us took almost ten years ago with the start of Tech Prep. As a former Tech Prep coordinator, I remember walking into my first meeting with five college presidents. I was faced with the task of convincing them that Tech Prep was worth the investment of staff time and resources and making curricular changes. These distinguished individuals looked at me as a crazy, young, idealistic person. But I walked away from that meeting successful in arguing for change because the concepts of Tech Prep were practical and met a real need for a population of students these educators knew all too well. These were students who did not have a chance for fulfilling careers after high school for a variety of reasons, but mostly because they were not taught in a way they could learn. So the risk of failure in Tech Prep has been worth the investment of faith, time, and lots of resources. Most consortia need to reassess this risk before moving forward with a new vision.

Leadership with Vision

My experience is not unlike those of many Tech Prep coordinators. We are each what Stephen Covey refers to as a "transition person," someone who links the past with the future, an idealist who has a fresh perspective and is ready to take on many battles for the mission of Tech Prep. Reform efforts like Tech Prep need transition persons to keep the motivation level high and to help envision the future for others. But, as soon as Tech Prep becomes entrenched in the status quo, a transition person typically moves on or loses his or her identity in the past, leaving the efforts for change lacking in motivation or stamina. Whether a new person is required or just a new outlook, a transition person is needed to keep Tech Prep evolving in a fluid form. Any consortium that is developing a new vision for Tech Prep should consider the value of a transition person who is not scarred by many battles or tied to the past. While most of us think of a Tech Prep coordinator as playing this role, others in a consortium may be able to serve as equally effective transition persons.

A transition person is not the only one who should lead a visioning process for Tech Prep. Each stakeholder of the consortium can bring new life into Tech Prep. Many local Tech Prep consortia still operate with the original steering committees and chairpersons. As with any organization or institution, this committee should rotate members regularly to generate new perspectives, fresh ideas, and enthusiasm. The leadership of a steering committee can play a pivotal role in setting a vision for Tech Prep, but members who may have difficulty letting go of old baggage will hamper the progress of Tech Prep as a whole.

Leaders at the state and federal levels have a unique influence on the future of reforms like Tech Prep. Unfortunately, if inconsistent messages are sent and there is little continuity from one reform effort to the next, this influence may confuse local educators more than it helps. Clearly, Tech Prep has been affected by changing presidential administrations, governors, budget-cutting congresspeople, and leaders among education and workforce training organizations. However, the perseverance of local Tech Prep practitioners has reinforced the importance of Tech Prep in the national education community. As workforce education fads lose steam, Tech Prep is going strong. The discussion among national leaders centers around the need for a clear and consistent message about the future of Tech Prep that will support the important work that local Tech Prep and school-to-work consortia already have in place.

A Time of Renewal

Time is often what we want most and use worst. We should consider 1999 and the new millennium as an opportunity for renewal. This means we begin again the process of planning, designing, and implementing new ideas that will enhance, improve, and revive Tech Prep for the next generation of students. Concepts presented in this book, such as the deeper involvement of families, communities, and higher education, and the importance of educational technology and telecommunication, will open doors for a connection to total school reform.

Renewal of Tech Prep also means ridding ourselves of practices that are no longer effective. The first step in developing a Tech Prep vision should be an opportunity for stakeholders to unload the white elephants that have been dragging down the progress of Tech Prep for some time. This means that we should swallow our pride, roll up our sleeves, and think about the bureaucracies we have created in the past few years and the bad ideas that just won't go away. Following are some steps with which to begin:

1. *Do away with committees that no longer serve a purpose.* A committee usually keeps minutes but often wastes hours that could be better spent on other activities. Reconsider why the committee was organized and whether its purpose could be served in another way.

2. *Eliminate paperwork and processes that take time but contribute nothing useful.* If the reports and surveys being used are not providing new information, do away with them. Streamline processes for initiating change based on your past experience. The best way to do this is to ask the opinions of those most affected by the processes—usually teachers.

3. *Cut meetings that generate discussion with no results.* Some meetings may have been organized to establish trust and communication. If these have been established, find another means for these people to keep in contact. This is the perfect opportunity to introduce E-mail and listservs.

4. *Eliminate workshops that don't work.* Some professional development programs just aren't effective, or they have outlived their purpose. Look into chapter 14 and begin thinking about more comprehensive methods of

professional development, rather than a one-shot workshop.

5.   *Remove new courses that represent old ideas.* As new ideas from SCANS and other aspects of career exploration were introduced, many schools generated new courses in isolation without considering these concepts in the total curriculum and pedagogy. Reconsider the purpose of these courses, and remove the ones that waste time.

6.   *Get rid of cynicism and introduce idealism.* Personalities, time, and many battles fought can leave scars of cynicism. These can be difficult barriers to overcome. By introducing new leadership or new personalities, a consortium can clean the slate for new ideas and energy.

7.   *Involve new players in the school system.* As you consider educational technology, family involvement, and other broad education issues, involve key experts within your school systems. Often individuals at the state and local levels are looking for means to work within the system and also can bring resources to bear.

Taking Tech Prep to Scale

Recent studies of Tech Prep questioned the actual numbers of students involved in Tech Prep at schools. While schools and colleges in a Tech Prep consortium report high percentages of participation as institutions, there has been some difficulty in determining how many students are "enrolled" in Tech Prep. The national evaluation of Tech Prep conducted by Mathematica Policy Research indicated in its 1997 report[1] that

---

[1] *Heading Students Toward Career Horizons: Tech-Prep Implementation Progress* (Princeton, New Jersey: Mathematica Policy Research, 1997).

numbers of participating students were low in proportion to the numbers of schools involved in Tech Prep. As mentioned in the report, it has been difficult to collect these data in a reliable fashion because of the differences in the way schools define Tech Prep and a Tech Prep student. Nevertheless, the potential numbers of students who are exposed to the concepts of Tech Prep exceed 80 percent of the student population. This provides the opportunity for Tech Prep to impact total school reforms.

While Tech Prep is not intended to be the magic bullet for education reform, there is, nonetheless, a purpose that this concept can serve in any schoolwide agenda. How can a new vision for Tech Prep bring enrollment to scale? If Tech Prep has been at a pilot stage or limited to small experimental populations, it may be time to expand the successful efforts to more students and more teachers. Increasing professional development programs should not only improve practice for a few teachers, but also train those teachers to prepare others. Question whether Tech Prep has become a pet program for a select number of teachers and has not been opened up to other teachers and educators in schools and colleges. Has Tech Prep been limited in its numbers of students because options in the curriculum have been limiting students' opportunities following high school graduation? Addressing issues like these will help lay the groundwork for revealing the way to reach more students.

The ideas suggested in this book are intended to provoke serious discussions within Tech Prep consortia about the future of Tech Prep. The contributing authors can only suggest models that have worked for them. It will be the task of each individual consortium to determine the fate of Tech Prep and its next generation of students.

Index

A

advanced skills, 21, 28, 35, 36, 86, 153, 155, 171
America's Choice: high skills or low wages!, 24
American Mathematical Association of Two-Year Colleges (AMATYC), 154, 158
Anita School System, 345, 381, 390, 391, 392, 393, 395
Appalachian Regional Commission (ARC), 232
applied academics, 6, 23, 28, 83, 106, 151, 169, 172, 195, 241, 245, 253, 254, 283
apprenticeships, 8, 10, 26, 35, 69, 93, 106, 114, 140, 160, 161, 166, 273, 282, 283, 295, 298, 300, 301, 309, 310, 324, 325, 353, 363, 365
articulation (2+2), 23, 83, 84, 106, 300
articulation (4+2), 23, 25, 84, 85, 86, 94, 153
assessment, xix, 39, 41, 42, 51, 55, 56, 58, 59, 62, 66, 70, 72, 79, 105, 108, 116, 140, 142, 144, 145, 147, 148, 164, 168, 173, 174, 179, 190, 195, 196, 219, 231, 240, 265, 269, 327, 328, 329, 330, 351, 354, 355, 356, 357, 358, 359, 412, 420

Automotive Youth Educational System (AYES), 138, 310, 311, 312, 313, 314, 315, 316, 317, 318, 319, 320, 321

B

Batavia (New York) High School, 8
Baughn, Juan R., ix, 279
Ben Baruch, Ephraim, *Conceptions of Time*, 132
Bloom, Benjamin S., *Taxonomy of Educational Objectives Handbook*, 132, 133
Boeing, 23, 25, 48, 124, 138, 246, 367, 371
Bollier, David, 17
Bottoms, Gene, x, 41, 46, 64, 65, 69, 241
Bowling Green State University, 157, 164
Boyer, Ernest, *Scholarship Reconsidered*, 257, 258, 259
Breaking Ranks, 11, 248, 405
Brooklyn Tech, 76
business practices for partnering, 331

C

Cahill, Sue Magee, x, 279
Caine, Renate Nummela, and Caine, Geoffrey, *Education on the Edge of Possibility*, 242, 245

career (term defined), 88
career camps, 282, 286
career education, 89, 107, 109, 111, 378
career interest development, 352, 355
career major (term defined), 90
career major core curriculum (term defined), 92
career pathway (term defined), 90
career pathway portfolio, 107
career pathways, 105
career-related learning, 376
Carnegie Foundation for the Advancement of Teaching, 257, 258
Catlin (Illinois) High School, 8
Centennial High School, 364, 366, 367, 368, 369, 370, 371, 372, 375
Center for Occupational Research and Development (CORD), vi, 23, 46, 207, 245, 246
Chaska High School, 127
cluster (term defined), 90
cluster core curriculum (term defined), 92
cluster curriculum structure, 96
coherent contextual program, 259
common core curriculum (term defined), 92
community colleges, 151, 156, 158, 161
contextual connection, 189
contextual learning, 11, 28, 29, 156, 157, 158, 169, 178, 179, 180, 183, 184, 188, 189, 191, 192, 193, 194, 195, 196, 236, 240, 242, 248, 250, 280, 287, 318, 344, 389, 398, 409, 414
contextual teaching, vi, 10, 28, 120, 157, 158, 172, 240, 244, 249, 252, 259, 260, 262, 263, 267, 268, 269, 344

Cooley, Richard, *Computers and Classrooms*, 232
co-op, 282, 283, 285
cooperative education, 197, 309, 324
cooperative learning, 54, 55, 156, 172, 193, 353, 373
Corcoran, Thomas B., *Helping Teachers Teach Well*, 399
course projects, criteria for selecting, 76
course syllabus, 49, 80, 81, 99, 100, 214, 260, 261
curriculum integration, 64
Curriculum Integrator, 46, 50, 51, 54, 56, 58, 59, 62, 65, 101
curriculum redundancy, 85
Cuyahoga Community College (CCC), 157, 164, 165

D

Davis, Bob, and Wessel, David, *Prosperity*, 18
Designing Challenging Vocational Courses, 82
Devro-Teepak, 8, 273
Dorchester School District, 353, 355, 356, 357

E

Edgar, Elaine D., x, 163
Edling, Walter, x, 35, 39, 56, 83
education reform, v, vi, 11, 13, 28, 39, 40, 43, 45, 47, 63, 87, 119, 120, 123, 130, 135, 152, 175, 192, 195, 240, 276, 287, 288, 328, 363, 399, 400, 401, 418, 425
educators in the workplace, 283
Electronics Technician Advanced Program (ETAP), 297, 298
employer as educator, 305

Experiential School, 365, 366,
367, 368, 369, 371, 372, 375,
376, 377, 378
extending the school year, 124

F

faculty development, 212
flexible time policies, 129
Francis Tuttle Technology
Center, 160, 320

G

Gallup, 12, 419
Gardner, Howard, 141, 184, 245
Gardner, John, v
Genessee Community College, 8
Goals 2000, 39, 40
Goodlad, John I., *Educational
Renewal*, 403
Gray, Don, xi, 305
Grevelle, Julie Hull, v, ix, 180,
239, 419

H

hands-on learning, 189
Harmon Industries, 331, 332,
334, 337, 338, 339, 340
High Schools That Work
(HSTW), 11, 13, 41, 46, 69,
241
higher expectations, 11
Holmes, Karen R., xi, 279
Hull, Dan, v, vi, ix, 3, 15, 21, 24,
83, 151, 158
Hull, Dan, *Opening Minds,
Opening Doors*, 23, 24, 84,
162, 188, 195

I

Integrated Curriculum Standards
(ICS), 46
Integrated System for Workforce
Education Curricula (ISWEC),
101
interdisciplinary projects, 282,
287
Intermediate School 218 (New
York City), 129

J

Jennings, John F., *Why National
Standards and Tests?*, 40
job (term defined), 88

K

Kincaid, Sharyl, xi, 180, 239
Kolb, David, 185, 186

L

Lakeland Tech Prep Consortium,
169, 170, 172
leadership with vision, 421
Leander (Texas) High School,
106, 107, 110
Leary, Margaret, xii, 323
Libbey High School (Toledo,
Ohio), 77
lifetime credentials, 160
Loring, Ruth M., 56

M

Mason City (Iowa) High School,
9
Mathematica Policy Research
(MPR), 241, 424
McLean (Virginia) High School,
77

mentoring, 10, 114, 124, 129,
191, 219, 222, 282, 284, 285,
295, 315, 324, 353, 363
Miami Valley Tech Prep
Consortium (Dayton, Ohio), 22
model partnership program, 289

N

Nation At Risk, A, 5
National Assessment of
Educational Progress (NAEP),
41
National Association of
Secondary School Principals
(NASSP), 248, 405
National Commission on
Teaching and America's
Future, xvii, 398, 400
National Council for
Accreditation of Teacher
Education (NCATE), 404
National Council of Teachers of
Mathematics (NCTM), 192,
215
National Employer Leadership
Council, 273, 294, 323
National Evaluation of Tech Prep,
241
National Skill Standards Act, 24
National Tech Prep Network
(NTPN), ix, x, 27, 29, 246
Negroponte, Nicholas, *Being
Digital*, 400
Neighborhood Academic
Initiative, 131
new vision, xix, xx, 11, 13, 27,
31, 63, 64, 71, 74, 77, 80, 239,
408, 421, 425
North Iowa Area Community
College, 9

O

occupation (term defined), 89
occupational specialty (term
defined), 90
Ohio Board of Regents, 165
Ohio Department of Education, x,
165
Ohio Tech Prep plan, 166, 167
Oklahoma City Community
College, 160, 320
Olson, Lynn, *The School-to-Work
Revolution*, 362
Olsson, Björn, xii, 331

P

Packer, Arnold, xii, 160, 179,
185, 199, 229
parenting *to do's*, 351
parents and teachers working
together, 349
Parnell, Dale, vi, xii, 21, 119
Parnell, Dale, *The Neglected
Majority*, 21
Peters, Roy Jr., xiii, 139
Pierce, David, xiii, 151
Pool, Carolyn R.,
*Perspectives/Centuries of
Learning*, 217
portfolios, 56, 139, 140, 142,
144, 146, 147, 148, 149, 196
Prescott, Carolyn, xiii, 179, 217
Principles of Technology, 48, 85,
100, 106, 195, 245, 246
professional development, xvii,
28, 116, 157, 158, 165, 172,
173, 174, 180, 219, 232, 239,
240, 241, 242, 244, 247, 248,
251, 252, 280, 289, 398, 399,
401, 403, 404, 405, 409, 410,
412, 413, 423, 425
professional development school
(PDS), 405

Project ABLE, 298, 299
project-based learning, 55, 158, 189, 199, 207, 208, 218
Providence (Rhode Island) Metropolitan Center, 127

R

Rau, Fred, xiv, 361
recruiting business sites, 371
related technical curriculum (term defined), 93
requirements for the technical core, 93
Reynolds High School (Troutdale, Oregon), 128
role of a CEO, 334
Rouse, Charles, xiv, 103

S

Sarvis Brossard, Sandy, xiv, 347
SCANS, 5, 10, 24, 25, 35, 43, 44, 51, 65, 66, 86, 98, 110, 159, 161, 186, 202, 204, 206, 208, 209, 210, 212, 213, 229, 254, 293, 297, 300, 340, 424
Schmitz, Charles D., xv, 397
Seminole Community College, 301
shadowing, 10, 80, 124, 145, 254, 255, 282, 285, 289, 290, 304, 313, 314, 317, 324, 333, 337, 338, 353, 377, 388
shared facilities, 172
Siemens, 273, 294, 297, 298, 299, 300, 301, 302, 303
Sinclair Community College, 8, 22, 277
Smith, Hedrick, *Rethinking America*, 363
Society for College and University Planning (SCUP), 402

Souders, John C. Jr., xv, 158, 179, 181, 247
Southern Regional Education Board (SREB), x, 41, 46, 69, 82
steps in curriculum design, 64
steps to forming partnerships, 282
student workers, 301
students in the workplace, 282, 283
Sullivan, Elaine, xv, 417, 419
Swim, Donna, xvi, 381, 395

T

teacher internships, 288
teacher training, 241, 250
teaching *to do's*, 350
teamwork, 43, 51, 52, 53, 54, 55, 58, 59, 73, 76, 78, 124, 141, 144, 145, 193, 210, 213, 275, 280, 366, 370, 377, 386
Tech Prep Associate Degree (TPAD), v, 6
Tech Prep curriculum model, 94, 95
Tech Prep Vision, 20, 63, 415
Tech Prep/School-to-Work Index, 12
technical competency profile, 166, 168
technical core curriculum (term defined), 92
technical specialty curriculum (term defined), 92
technology in the classroom, 29, 217, 398
Thurow, Lester, *Head to Head*, 182
Tobin, John P., xvi, 293
tools for building partnerships, 333
Topeka (Kansas) West High School, 77

TQM (total quality management), 173, 183

U

University of Missouri-Saint Louis School of Education (UMSL-SOE), 407, 408, 409, 410, 414

V

videoconferencing, 191, 220, 221, 223, 230, 231, 232, 251, 252

W

West End Tech Prep Consortium (Claremont, California), 253

Wilson, Kenneth G., and Daviss, Bennett, *Redesigning Education*, 19, 20, 64
workplace tours, 288
worksite learning, 10, 25, 53, 291, 309, 364, 365
WORKTECH, 224

Y

Youngstown State University, 173
youth apprenticeships, 159

Z

Zimpher, Nancy L., xvi, 180, 257